GRAMGEETA
- TUKADOJI

TRANSLATION

RATNAKAR D. BHELKAR

ATLANTIC

PUBLISHERS & DISTRIBUTORS (P) LTD

ATLANTIC
PUBLISHERS & DISTRIBUTORS (P) LTD
7/22, Ansari Road, Darya Ganj, New Delhi
Tel.: +91-11-4077 5252, 2327 3880
E-mail: orders@atlanticbooks.com
Web: www.atlanticbooks.com

Published by Atlantic Publishers & Distributors (P) Ltd 2023

Reprinted in 2025

Printed & bound in India by Atlantic Print Services

Contents

Ideal Life Quinate

Introduction

Venturing to Translation: Visibility and Invisibility

In the age of globalisation, translation is a mode to link multi-linguistic and multi-cultural societies which have their own identities. It is the means for cultural transmission, and used to communicate within the literatures of different languages—indigenous and foreign languages. In Europe, Bible was translated from Hebrew into different European languages to propagate Christian values; Buddhist texts in Pali were translated into Japanese, Chinese, Tibetan, and Korean languages to spread Buddhism; and the Koran was translated from Arabic into various languages to project Islam. In the 7th–8th centuries AD, Gunadhya's *Brihatkatha* was written in Paisachi lnaguage, but it was not accepted by the Sanskrit Scholars; and he took the extreme step of burning it. However, Somadeva translated its 2400 *slokas* into Sanskrit and compiled them as *Kathasaritsagara*. Thus, translation is an act of freedom from the linguistic and cultural hegemony, for example, *Jnaneshwari* is the discourse in Marathi on *Bhagavadgeeta*, written in Sanskrit, the language of elites. *Jnaneshwari* is a *suta* text (to be sung in another language) than a *mantra* text (Sanskrit verse). Since Sanskrit was the language of canonical status, other Indian languages were looked with contempt.

Translations of *Ramayana* exist in various versions. Tulsidas' *Ramayana*, written in *braj* dialect, is the renarration of Valmiki's

Ramayana, Kambar's *Ramayana*, Padmavati's *Ramayana*, and Cambodian version of *Ramayana*, and all these versions exhibit intertextuality, which provokes to think of other texts. In India, translation means transcreation rather than faithful rendering of meaning, for example, *Ramayana* and *Mahabharata* were reproduced in various Indian languages, which were essentially in oral tradition. In the process of creating a new version, adaptation, renarration, condensation, or expansion operate. Deviation from the source text, sometimes, leads to distortion as can be found in *Ravanayana*, 19th-century counter text in Bengali, by Michael Madhusudan Dutt, and parody of the *Mahabharata*, *The Great Indian Novel* by Shashi Tharoor.

During the colonial rule of East India Company, before handing over the power to the British Empire in 1858, the writings on Indian society in English or the translations of Indian texts, especially from Sanskrit into English, was the facet of cultural politics, triggered by William Jones, to know Indian geography, society, religions, cultures, laws, agriculture, manufacture and trade, science, philology, arts, and literature to formulate a tactics for political, economic, and cultural dominance. William Jones translated Kalidasa's *Shakuntala*; Nathaniel Brassey Halhed, the anthology of Hindu laws, drawn from *Manusmriti*; and Charles Wilkins, *Bhagavadgeeta*, the first translation into English, published as *Bhagavadgeeta or Dialogues of Kreeshna and Arjoon* by the East India Company with an introduction by Warren Hastings. British Education Policy, conceptualised and declared by Thomas Babington Macaulay in 1835, was the calculative drive to suppress whatever was Indian, and the texts included in the curricula were imperial voices. Edward Said has deciphered, unmasking the face in *Orientalism*, "The relationship between Occident and Orient is a relationship of power, of domination, of varying degrees of a complex hegemony"[1], and it is obviously true of Richard Burton, Edward Lane, Charles Doughty, Gustave Flaubert, William Jones, and Macaulay.

Besides these, Max Muller translated the Indian texts into English, such as *Rig-Veda Sanhita*, and edited the translations of the Asian religious texts, such as *The Sacred Books of East*. He also translated the texts in Persian into English, from the

West Asia and the Middle East. After handing over the company governance to the British Crown in 1876, the imperial power operated in the garb of 'civilizing force', through political, economical, and cultural hegemony. In the revival phase (1876–1950), the Indian writers, such as Rabindranath Tagore and Aurobindo, being conscious of native cultural roots, translated the Indian texts like Kabir's verses and Upanishads into English. In the post-colonial discourse, the translations from indigenous languages are cultural voices, the projections of identities, and spaces for subalterns to breath free air, which were suppressed and marginalised in cultural politics. At the backdrop of these scenarios in the terrain of translation, it is pertinent and logical to venture to reassess the Indian approaches, the Western Purviews, and Translation Studies with external current and under current, visibility and invisibility.

I

European literary historiography is, in fact, steeped in a tradition that has always been suspicious of 'the other', and the Europeans feared foreign culture, entering in their lives through translation. On the other hand, India possesses an amazing capacity to assimilate alien cultures. Its acceptance of Vedantic oneness, enumerated by Upanishads, has always paved the way for obliterating between *swa* and *para*, the self and the other.[2] In European and Indian literary historiographies, linguistic dominance, cultural hegemony, and translated versions of the source texts reveal that versions of the source texts' translation are to be viewed from historical and cultural perspectives.

The Indian Approaches

Ayyappa Paniker introduced the concepts prevalent in the medieval Indian translations of Sanskrit classics—*anukruti* which is an imitation of the original, *arthakriya* which emphasises on the manifold ways in which meanings are enacted in different texts, *Vyaktivivekam* which denotes the rendering of meaning by the reader, and *ullurai* which primarily means inner speech, not the heard but the one unheard. These concepts validate the distinctive theory of translation that points at creative freedom, with the absence of anxiety relating to fidelity.

The whole medieval *Bhakti* (devotional) movement of poetry in India ventured to translate the content of spirituality from Sanskrit into indigenous languages, such as Marathi, Hindi, Bengali, Tamil, Kannada, Telugu, Gujarati, Rajasthani, and Kashmiri, and tried to liberate the scriptures from the dominance of elite strata. Those translations were liberating endeavours from linguistic as well as cultural hegemony, and became the mass communicative means to reorganise society. The medieval India did not believe in literal translation even though Indian writers were familiar with the concept of a verbatim translation, known as *chhaya* (shadow) of Pakrit text into Sanskrit, often found in Sanskrit drama. Indians preferred adaptation to verbatim tradition.

Rabindranath Tagore began his discussion on translation, back in 1913, focusing on the central issues. Unlike J.S. Holmes or Andre Lefevere, Tagore didn't write any treatise or manifesto, but to him, translation was a creative process rather than a mechanical practice.He treated translation as rewriting as enumerated in his letter to Rothenstein on 31st December, 1915. By rewriting he meant the creative translation, and it was applied by him for translating *Gitanjali* (1912); and was later on adopted by Nabokov and Samuel Beckett. In his letter to Indira Devi, on 6th May, 1913, he writes about, what he attempted to practice in the poems of *Gitanjali*, "I simply felt an urge to recapture through the medium of another language, the feelings and sentiments which had created such a feast of joy within me in the days gone by."[3] Translation needs to be essentially creative and at the same time an independent work in its own right. Tagore implies that freshness of the original writing is considerably lost in its translation, and inevitable loss is to be compensated by the translator's creative freedom. To face the problem of untranslatability, he asserts to recreate or rewrite the original importing content.

When Tagore speaks of the translation of his *Gitanjali*, he operates the words like 'reincarnation', 'rebirth', and 'transmigration' which connotes the creative nature of his translation. In transcreation or creative translation, the spirit of the original undergoes rebirth or reincarnation in the target language only through the transmission of essential spirit or soul. By nurturing this standpoint, Tagore has added Indian dimension to translation process, predefining the nature of ensuing Translation Studies.

To Aurobindo, who translated Upanishads and *Bhagavadgeeta* into English, translation is a cognitive process, and behind this cognitive process there are three levels *nama* (name), *rupa* (form of meaning), and *swarupa* (essential figure of truth). Gopinathan explores that these three levels are analogous to the three levels of language mentioned by Bhartrihari in his *Vakyapadiyam*, and they are—*vaikhari* (spoken level of language), *madhyama* (immediate level between articulation and conception), and *pasyanti* (the highest level where a thought is at its nebulous stage). Aurobindo developed his concept from these levels and "gives a further psycho-spiritual division of the levels of consciousness at the physical, mental, and supra mental levels."[4] He opined that translation becomes more communicative when the higher meaning of the text is comprehended.

A.K. Ramanujan, a translator and theorist, was instrumental to perceive the beauty of the Indian texts other than in Sanskrit, such as classical and *bhakti* poetry in Tamil, the Virashaiva's *Vachanas* in Kannada, *bhakti* and court literature in Telugu, folktales and women' oral narratives in nineteenth century, and U.R. Ananthamurthy's *Sanskara*. He attempted to distinguish between 'inner poetic core' and 'other poetic core', for the optimum approximation to source language text. Representing exterior and interior worlds in the *sangam* tradition in Tamil literature, he made distinction between *'akam'* and *'puram'* poetries. Vinay Dharwadker thought that Ramanujan developed his ideas of outer and inner poetic forms from two different sources—Noam Chomsky's concept of 'deep structure' and 'surface structure', Roman Jakobson's distinction between 'verse instance' and 'verse design', and similarities between Julia Kristeva's distinction between 'phonetext' (the manifest text) and 'genotext' (the innate signifying structure). Ramanujan argued that a translator carried over a particular text from one culture to another, and has to translate the reader from the second culture in the first one.[5] This can be feasible through notes and prefaces written by a translator.

The Western Purviews

The earlier translation dates back to 3000 BC in the bilingual Egyptian inscription. In the western literary historiography, Cicero, Jerome, and Horace stressed on sense to sense translation, and not on word to word translation or literal translation, relying on the judgement of translations from Greek to Latin. Etienne Dolet formulated the principals[6] for the translators to avoid word for word renderings and choose and order words appropriate to produce correct tone. In tune with Dolet, George Chapman, the translator of Homer's *Iliad* and *Odyssey*, opined that a translator should recognise the spirit of text, and not transfer word for word. John Dryden in *The Preface to Ovid's Epistles* (1680) demarcated three types of translations[7]—metaphrase, paraphrase, and limitation. Alexander Fraser Tytler in *Essay* on *the Principles of Translation* (1791) outlined three basic principles[8] to enable translation—to have the idea of the original work, the style and manner of the original, and the ease of the original composition. During the romantic age, there were two views about translation—it is in creative nature and is mechanical process. In the post-romantic period, Thomas Carlyle, William Morris, and Matthew Arnold pleaded for a close fidelity of the source language (SL) text. H.W. Longfellow was of the same opinion and while speaking of his translation of Dante's *Divine Commedia,* he explained that the translator's purview is what an author says, and not what s/he means. In Frank Kermode's view, a translation has to be exotic, and in order to do so, a translator takes liberties with an original to create new text.

Translation Studies in the twentieth century received impetus from the Russian Formalist Circle in 1920s and subsequently by Prague Linguistic Circle and its disciples. Voloshinov's work on Marxism and Philosophy; Mukarovsky's on the semiotics of art; and Jacobson, Prochazka, and Levy on translation have provided a new criteria for a theory on translation. Translation involving more than a working acquaintance with two languages is aptly pointed by Levy, when he asserted that translation is not a monistic composition, but an interpenetration and conglomerate of two structures. On the one hand, there are the semantic content and the formal contour of the original, and on the other hand, the entire system of aesthetic features bound up with the language of the translation.

The stress on linguistics and the early experiments with machine translation in the 1950s led to the rapid development of Translation Studies in Eastern Europe first and then in the English speaking world. In the early 1960's, the significant changes have taken place in the area of Translation Studies, with the acceptance of the study of linguistics and stylistics within literary criticism that has led to the development in critical methodology with the rediscovery of the Russian Formalist Circle.

In 1960's, the pioneering works of two scholars, namely J.C. Catford (1965) and Eugene A. Nida (1969), resulted into the development of the theory of the linguistic process of translation or testing of translated texts. Susan Bassnett in *Translation Studies* while acknowledging the contribution of translators also adds:

> Nor should we forget the enormous importance of such figures as J.C. Catford, Michael Halliday, Peter Newmark and Eugene Nida whose research into translation before Translation Studies started to evolve as a discipline in its own right laid the foundations for what was to follow.[9]

Thus, the onus of the study was whether there could be exact procedures for the analysis, transfer, and restructuring of the message of the original text to the translated one.

Catford's theory is within the framework of the theory of language structure proposed by M.A.K. Halliday in '*Categories of the Theory of Grammar*' (Vol. 17, No. 3, 1961). Catford has propounded his theory in *Language Theory and Translation Practice* and defined translation from the linguistic point of view, as the replacement of textual material in one language (source language) by equivalent material in another language (target language), and he further alleged:

> Translation is an operation performed on languages, a process of substituting a text in one language for a text

> in another. Clearly, then, any theory of translation must draw upon a theory of language—a general linguistic theory.[10]
>
> Translation is transference of meaning in another language. There are not much difficulties in non-literary translation but the difficulty arises when we have to translate creative in literature. It is not easy to find equivalent textual and literary material of the source language in the target language and so the central problem of translation practice is that of finding TL translation equivalents.[11]

It is easier perhaps to find structural equivalence in comparison to semantic ones. But, there cannot be textual equivalence at all levels—phonological, graphological, grammatical, lexical, and semantics. Hence, textural equivalence should be related to contextual equivalence as far as possible keeping in view the grammatical and lexical equivalence, and along with contextual, cultural meaning should also be given prominence. In translation, meaning is not transferred but substituted, rather 'translation is neither transference nor transporting of meaning but a substitution of meaning'.[12]

During translation, language varieties like dialect, idiolect, temporal dialect (contemporary versus archaic), class dialect (upper class versus lower class speech), and style have to be taken into consideration. However, in spite of them, all translations face difficulties owing to linguistic, cultural, and untranslatability. He exhorted:

> There is no way in which we can replace SL 'contextual units' by equivalent TL 'contextual units' without simultaneously replacing SL grammatical/lexical units by equivalent TL grammatical/lexical units. It is only by virtue of their encapsulation, 'contextual units' exists. Both surface and deep structures are to be taken into cognizance. Cultural and contextual meaning should be given prominences.[13]

His translation techniques are based on social function, class shifts, intra system shifts, structure shifts, unit shifts, level shifts, and the types of translation from SL to TL. Catford provides us a scientifically viable theory of translation as well as the right procedures towards judgement of the translation of a text. Thus, he allows us to choose the best of translation that is one which is nearest in semantics and style.

Eugene Nida's approach to translation leans on transformational generative grammar and componential semantics. It also relates to the use of case grammar of Fillmore and Langendoen and systemic grammar of Halliday. The test of validity of translation in Nida's theory is simplified as he thought if TL receptors understand the nearly equivalent meaning of the SL text, the purpose of translation is served. Identical equivalents are neither available nor expected. Two types of equivalence, dynamic and formal, have been traced and developed by the twentieth century linguists. Nida defines dynamic equivalence as 'the closest natural equivalent to the source language message' while transference of linguistic equivalents irrespective of content or meaning is called formal equivalence.

The three aspects—grammatical relationship between parts, referential meaning of semantic units, and connotative value of grammatical semantic structure—form the basis of a translated text. An addition to this, Nida's postulate on the transference of meaning is as follows:

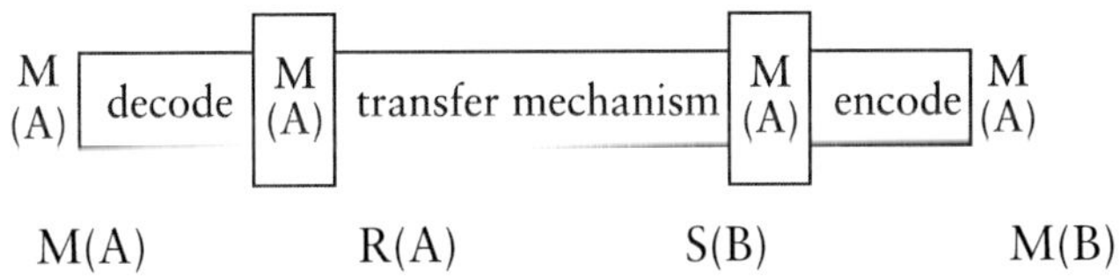

The translator is visualised as a member of two speech communities, M(A) and M(B), and in the source language, s/he acts as a listener or receiver, R(A), decoding the message, and in the target language, s/he acts as a speaker, S(B), encoding her/his message from the product of the transfer phase.

Nida's theory suggests that in translation it is not the words but their referential meanings or the componential features which are transported from SL to TL. The referential meanings and stylistic features are difficult to transfer. Moreover, receptors/readers in SL and TL have different approaches because of the difference in their cultures. Nida construes that translation is a complex procedure and journey deep into the 'core structure' where grammatical relations are expressed. The meaning to be transferred is divided into separate semantic and syntactic structures. Nida emphasises that translation would never allow a distortion of meaning but renders freedom for certain amount of restructuring on formal and functional grounds; and it is perhaps an inevitable dimension of a translation process.

Mika (1970) proposed to focus on what happens to the formal features of a text in translations, and Popovic (1970) recognised that some translations transform texts and the study of translation should focus on what is changed as much as what remains the same. During 1960's to 1970's, the pivotal concept in Translation Studies was of 'equivalence'. When this concept is applied to translation, it is viewed as the process of communicating SLT via creation, or relationship of identity with SLT.

Translation Studies after 1970s

After 1970s, Translation Studies had received momentum and there was visibility of translations and interpreters in society, besides the tilting of axis towards receptors, and translation as a new product.

Untill the end of 1980s, Translation Studies was dominated by systematic approach pioneered by Itamar Even-Zohar and Gideon Toury. Polysystem theory was a radical development because it shifted the focus of attention away from arid debates about faithfulness and equivalence towards an examination of the role of the translated text in its new context. In 1995, Toury reassessed the Polysystem approach which over emphasises on the target system. Toury pleaded that since a translation is designed primarily to fill a need in the target culture, it is logical to make the target system the object of study. Polysystem theory filled the gap that opened up in the 1970s between linguistics and literary studies, and provided the base upon which the new interdisciplinary Translation Studies could be built. Central to polysystem is an emphasis on the poetics of target culture.

Whereas previously the emphasis had been on comparing translation with the original, often with a view to establish what had been 'lost' or 'betrayed' in the translation process, the new approach took a resolutely different line, seeking not to evaluate but to understand the shifts of emphasis that had taken place during the transfer of texts from one literary system into another. Theo Hermans and Gideon Toury sought to establish theoretical and methodological parameters within which the subject might develop; and Andre Lefevere and Lawrence Venuti began to explore the implications of translation in a much broader cultural and historical frame. Lefevere developed his idea of translation as refraction rather than reflection. He doesn't treat translation as a mirror of original, but to him, translation as refraction is a denial of any linear notion of the translation process. Texts are complex signifying the systems, and the task of translator is to de-code and re-encode whichever of those systems is accessible. Theorising about translation is based on translation practice between European languages, and pointed out that the problem of accessibility of linguistic and cultural codes intensifies once we move out beyond western boundaries. Lefevere suggested, "Problems in translating are caused at least as much by discrepancies in conceptual and textual grids, as by discrepancies in languages".[14]

The cultural grids determine how reality is constructed in both source and target texts, and highlight the creativity of translator, because s/he is inevitably engaged in a complex creative process. The skill of translator determines the success of translation. Venuti insisted on the creativity of a translator and upon her/his visible presence in a translation. Translation, according to Venuti, with its allegiance both to source and target cultures, is a reminder that no act of interpretation can be definitive.[15]

In 1990, the figure of a subservient translator is replaced with the visible manipulative translator, a creative artist mediating between cultures and languages. This new emphasis on subjectivity derives from two distinct influences—the growing importance of research into the ethics of translation and a much attention to the philosophical issues that underpin translation.

Jacques Derrida's rereading of Walter Benjamin opened the flood-gates to a re-evaluation of the importance of translation not only as a form of communication but also as continuity. Translation, he pleaded, ensures the survival of a text, a new 'original' in another language. This constructive view of translation serves to reinforce the importance of translating as an act both of inter-lingual and inter-cultural communication.

Derrida construed that each new instance of reading the text is a different occasion to experience the absence of meaning. He, thus, granted the translation the status of literature, since the translator, like a creative artist, signifies meaning as an independent presence and develops a more dynamic theory between the relationship of meaning and language.[16] He explores that language structure has 'phonetic manifestation' and 'semantic realisation', which resemble *'nada'* and *'sphota'* in Bhartrhari's explanation of *sphota* theory and the reflection of the sun in water.[17] The reflection of the object acquires mutiplicity due to the movements of water waves. Meaning exists in language not only as direct presence but also as absence which reveals its independent presence.

From the perspective of readers, Roland Barthes saw the literary text as that of making the reader not so much a 'consumer' but as a 'producer' of the text. Translation being the act of inter-lingual and inter-cultural communication, it is logical to know how is the translated text received by the readers in the target language and the target culture? The receptors produce their texts on the basis of their comprehension and the ideological viewpoints.

The translation of the poetical works of forgotten women poets of ancient Greece by Josephine Balmer has opened the access to their works or the translation of Omar Khayyam's Rubaiyat by Fitzgerald has exposed Persian poetry to readers on wider scale.

Gayatri Chakravorty Spivak, Tejaswini Niranjana, and Eric Cheyfitz argue that translation was effectively used in the past as an instrument of colonial domination, a mean of depriving the colonised people of a voice. In the colonial model, one culture dominates and others are subservient, hence translation reinforces power hierarchy. As Anuradha Dingwaney Needham puts it, "The process of translation involved in making another culture comprehensible entails varying degrees of violence, especially when the culture being translated is constituted as that of the 'other'."[18]

In the 1990s, two contrasting images of the translator emerged. According to one of the readings on the translator's role, the translator is a force for good, a creative artist who ensures the survival of writing across time and space, an intercultural mediator and interpreter, and a figure whose importance to the continuity and diffusion of culture is immeasurable. In contrast, another interpretation sees translation as a highly suspect activity, one where an inequality of power relations (inequalities of economics, politics, gender, and geography) is reflected in the mechanics of textual production.

In the new, post-colonial perception of the relationship between source and target texts, inequality of status has been reviewed. Both original and translation are now deemed as equal products of the creativity of writer and translator. As Octavio Paz pointed out, it is up to the writer to fix words in an ideal, unchangeable form and it is the task of translator to liberate those words from the confines of their source language and allow them to live again in the language into which they are translated.[19]

Homi Bhabha used the term 'translation' not to describe a transition between texts and languages but in the etymological sense of being carried across from one place to another. He applied translation metaphorically to describe the condition of the contemporary world, a world in which millions of people migrate and change their location every day. We should remember that it is the 'inter', the cutting edge of translation and renegotiation, in between space—that carries the burden of the meaning of culture.[20]

The translator is seen as a liberator, someone who frees the text from the fixed signs of its original shape. As Vanamala Viswanatha and Sherry Simon argued, "translations provide an especially revealing entry point into the dynamics of cultural identity—formation in the colonial and post-colonial contexts".[21]

During the colonial time, colonisation seemed to be a civilizing mission, and on the other, translation was the instrument for the projection of colonisation, propagation of Christianity to dominate colonised, and to create the process of othering (on which Edward Said has focussed in *Orientalism*). Translation as a cultural encounter was the mode for cultural hegemony and considered as the political act. Mona Baker stresses the ethical facet of Translation Studies, and demonstrates that translators and interpreters participate in circulating as well as resisting the narratives that create the intellectual and moral environment for violent conflict.[22] A translator has an accountability for translation which may have its impact on others in the contexts of court's verdicts, minority groups, and historical and cultural conflicts. What to translate, what not to translate, and how to translate are the ideological choices of a translator. Emily Apter treats translation as the zone for new comparative literature. She has embarked to rethink critical paradigms in the humanities after 9/11, with special emphasis on language and war, the problem of creolisation and the mapping of languages "in-trans" shifts in the world canon and literary markets, and the impact of enhanced information technology on translation. She has ventured "to imagine a program for a new comparative literature using translation as a fulcrum",[23] and it reveals how comparative literature contributes to Translation Studies which was once exclusively considered as the branch of linguistics.

Envisaging translation as a creative process, Lawrence Venuti introduced in his book, *The Translator's Invisibility: A History of Translation,* the two terms in 1995—'domestication', the strategy of making text closely confirm to the culture of the language being translated to, which may involve the loss of information from the source text, and 'foreignisation', the strategy of retaining information from the source text, and involves deliberately breaking conventions of the target language to preserve its meaning. Venuti's innovation to the terrain was his standpoint that the dichotomy between 'domestication' and 'foreignisation' is an ideological one; and he views 'foreignisation' as an ethical choice for translation to make. Anthony Pym emphasises upon 'foreignisation' in translation in which source language is visible in the form of untranslatable words.[24] It is an addition to target language.

Indra Nath Choudhuri in his essay, 'Towards an Indian Theory of Translation', has alleged:

> In comparison to Faizy in the sixteenth century and Dow in the eighteenth century, our situation in the twenty-first century of translating Sanskrit or *bhasha* texts into English or another Indian *bhasha* is far less problematic and considerably more propitious. With the increase in translation activities, the development of Indian theory of translation now becomes plausible. Such a theory would not reject the pragmatic approach of sameness in translation, but would go a step further emotionally reconstructing a verbal art into a different language. In the process, if the text looked metaphorically like a golden chain but not the pendant but in its recreation in another language, if is lost its chain but not the pendant, and if the pendant looked attractive, then we should not hesitate to say the translator, 'Congratulations, you have nailed it'.[25]

This translation theory stresses the pragmatic approach of sameness, and treats translation as restructure, recreative act. On one side, it does not deviate from equivalence of SLT, but on another reiterates that translation is not an escape from the original. Whenever equivalence is not plausible, it results into restructuring, recreating, and transforming to create a new text.

Problems of Equivalence

Translation Studies bridges the gap between the vast area of stylistics, literary history, linguistics, semiotics, and aesthetics. But, it must not be forgotten that this is a discipline based on practical application. Translation Studies deal with stress on different levels:

Input		Output
Reactants orientation	Process orientation →	Product orientation

In orientation of reactants, emphasis is on components in SLT—semiotic and semantic aspects, and inclusiveness of historical and cultural contexts; process orientation involves actual analysis of components, turning reactants into products, which includes equivalence, untranslatability, transference, transcreation, adaption, renarration, and product; and orientation stresses upon translated text, new text creativity, absorption of SLT into TLT, and readers' acceptance in cultural encounter. Edward Sapir claims that language is a guide to social reality, a medium of expression in human society, and delineates the relation between language and society:

> No two languages are ever sufficiently similar to be considered as representing the same social reality. The worlds in which different societies live are distinct worlds, not merely the same world with different labels attached.[26]

Language exists in the context of culture, and interaction between language and culture is the seminal facet in Translation Studies. A translator has to process a text in historical and cultural contexts.

The central problem in all types is that there is no full equivalence through translation and so, Roman Jakobson declares that all poetic arts are, therefore, technically untranslatable. Only creative transposition is possible: either intralingual transposition—from one poetic shape into another, or interlingual transposition—from one language into another, or finally inter-semiotic transposition—from one system of signs into another, e.g. from verbal art into music, dance, cinema, or painting. Jakobson's view is supported by Georges Mounin, the French theorist, who perceives translation as a series of operations of which the starting point and the end product are significations and function within a given culture.

Equivalence in translation should not be approached as a search for sameness, since sameness cannot even exist between two TL versions of the same text. A translator has to take the question of interpretation into account in addition to the problem of selecting TL phrase and idiom which will have approximately similar meanings. As such, a translator has to be conscious about untranslatability in historical and cultural contexts.

Untranslatability

Untranslatability operates on linguistic and cultural levels. On the linguistic level, it occurs when there is no lexical or syntactical substitute in the TL for SL item. The problem of untranslatability creeps with region and culture specific words—the words like *'chandramadhaviche pradesh'* in Grace's poem, *'pushakala'* in P.S. Rege's poem, *'fugadi'* and *'wamangi'* in Arun Kolatkar's poems; phrases and idioms in dialects, such as bhojpuri and garhwali of Hindi; self narratives in Marathi, such as Daya Pawar's *Baluta*, Laxman Gaikwad's *Uchalaya* (translated in English as *Branded*), Sharankumar Limbale's *Akkarmashi*, and in other Indian regional languages; in African English, American English, Canadian English, Australian English, Carribean English, and Cockney, Wales, and Scottish in England, and Irish in Ireland. French, Spanish, German, Italian, Arabic, and Persian face the same problems of untranslatability.

Untranslatability also pertains to connotative level of words in source language and, therefore, it becomes difficult or sometime impossible to translate in target language. *'Araspani'* in Marathi connotes reflectivity of mirror as well as transparency of water. It is difficult to the extent of impossibility to capture the nuances of *'araspani'* in English. The translation of dialectical songs and folk songs faces the problem of untranslatability because of region, culture, and specific words, e.g. the translation of Bhojpuri songs, Goan songs, and Konkani songs, in English.

Loss and Gain

Once the principle is accepted that sameness cannot exist between two languages, it becomes possible to approach the question of loss and gain in Translation Studies. The problem of loss in translation creeps up about the difficulties encountered by a translator when s/he faces with terms or concepts in the SL that do not exist in the TL. TLT receives an addition when a word or a concept in SLT is added in TLT and when an added word or concept is explained with note. In the recent time, the approach is to free TLT from the dominance of SLT to provide freedom for a translator in creative process which results into a product, which tilts to adaption, renarration, and transcreation.

In India today, plurilingual authors, writing in the language of ex-coloniser or in various Indian *bhashas* are challenging and redefining the accepted notions of equivalence, loss or gain in translation theories. We can no longer confine ourselves to the conventional notions of linguistic equivalence, loss or gain. We can no longer practice this because of the extensive use of different *bhashas'* dialects by Indian writers, such as Kambar in Tamil; Meera, Surdas, and Krishna Sobti in Hindi; Mahasweta Devi in Bengali; G.A. Kulkarni, Uddhav Shelke, and Daya Pawar in Marathi; Pannalal Patel in Gujrati; and Ravindra Kelekar in Konkani. Complexity of equivalence, untranslatability, and loss or gain has increased in Indian languages with multi-linguistic and multi-cultural ramifications. I contend that to retain the flavour of original, 'foreignisation' is preferable which enriches products, the receptors of which comprehend cultural martix.

In the post-colonial time, translation is the projection of cultural voice, not subjugation of it, not to differentiate and create other to be dominated. In the twenty-first century, political, geographical, and cultural boundaries are perceived as fluid, and are expanding because of the dissoluble nuances between language, text, and culture. Cultural contexts are of seminar significance and as such, translated texts from various languages inclusive of texts in vernacular languages prepare the ground for comparative cultural studies.

II

Historical and Cultural Contexts

Born on 30th April, 1909, at Yawali, in the Central Province in the colonial India, now in Maharashtra, Manik was educated at Yawali and Warkhed. Assisting his father's tailoring work, he had learnt *khanjiri*[a] and *ektari*[b] to sing *bhajans*[c], initiated by Samarth Adkoji, his mentor, who addressed him as Tukadya while sharing a piece of morsel, and the title became popular to attribute his identity. He fulfilled the arduous task of penance at Kapurbawdi, Narayan hill, and in the forests of Ramtek, Gondola, and Tadoba. He was instrumental in organising *Salbuldi yagnya*[d] (1935) to ban animal sacrifice to instill the spirit of unity for mass enlightenment as done earlier by Buddha and Mahavira. For a month in 1936, he was at Bapu-Kuti at Sevagram on the invitation by Mahatma Gandhi, where he interacted with the Indian nationalists, such as Rajendra Prasad, Jawaharlal Nehru, Vallabhbhai Patel, Lal Bahadur Shashtri, and Maulana Abdul Kalam Azad. He composed and sang the patriotic songs with *khanjiri*, and with the accomplices of the activists of *Aarti Mandal*, ignited the masses to involve in Quit India Movement (1942) to topple down the colonial power. His *bhajan,* with the militant tone:

> Trees, brooms will be weapons; devotee army;
> Stones will be bombs; the boat will be the shore.[27]

was banned by the Britishers, recalls Subramania Bharati's verses in Tamil, and he was imprisoned in the Central Jails of Nagpur and Raipur.

The publication of *Sri Gurudeo* (1943), the monthly, and the foundation of *Sri Gurudeo Seva Mandal* (1943), known as *Aarti Mandal* earlier, at Gurukunj Mozari, were the practical parameters to propagate and implement Tukadoji's conceptual perceptions. The women's wing of the *Mandal* was steered by Vimala Thakar, and with the cohort of Prabhatai Deshmukh, Radhadevi Goyenka, Venutai Wankhede, Narmadabai Sapkal, Renukadevi Birle, Sarojabai Malgujar, Hiratai Boke, and Rukhminibai Goswami, she embarked on empowering women, making them conscious of rural reality and national upheavals. Tukadoji ventured to eradicate superstitions along with Gadgebaba in 1945 and to open access to untouchables at Pandharpur temple along with Sane Guruji in 1947 and at other places. He practiced collective meals in 1947, reminiscent of the *langar* tradition in Sikhism, irrespective of caste, creed, and religion.

After independence, in the post-colonial India, Tukadoji's insistence was on constructive governance, with self-reliance and secular approach, epitomising the constitutional values of India—freedom, unity, equality, and justice. He awakened masses on the border of Nizam province to resist *Razakars'* drive to uphold Islamic domination in Hyderabad state and support for its integration into domination of India. He addressed *Sarvodaya* meets at Sevagram, Banaras (North India), and Kanchipuram (South India). Rajendra Prasad, the first President of India, graced the first Gandhi Memorial Celebration in 1949 at Gurukunj and bestowed upon Tukadoji the honour of *Rashtrasant*, envisioning his humanitarian vision of national welfare, the confluence of conceptual approach, and programmatic stance.

Anticipating the call by Vinoba Bhave, Tukadoji involved in the Land Donation Movement in 1953 and donated 11,410 acres of land to landless tribals at Aheri and Bastar zones. For rural reform, he coordinated Ideal Villages Convention (inclusive of 100 villages) on 20th, 24th, and 30th January, 1953, at Amagaon, in which Lal Bahadur Shastri and Gulzarilal Nanda were also present.

World Religion Conference for World Peace was organised at Shimizu, Japan, from 23rd to 25th July, 1955, where the representatives from various nations, such as USA, England, Greece, Indonesia, and Malaysia were invited. It was inaugurated by *Rashtrasant* Tukadoji with his *bhajan*, "O! the Mover of world, render me the consciousness of the world,"[28] and he discoursed stressing on coordination, love, freedom, peace, unity, and equality. Tukaramdada Gitacharya, Appex Officer of *Sri Gurudeo Seva Mandal,* accompanied him as bilingual, besides Shivacharan Sinha Wirik, the representative from the Indian Embassy. Paying heed to his humanitarian spirit and coordinative endeavour for world peace, he was nominated on the Advisory Committee of World Religion Conference. Unifying energy, which brings together diversities, is enthused in the *bhajan,* composed in Tokyo, on 3rd August, 1955:

> You in every nation, You in every attire;
> Your names many, You are One;
> Filled this world, Your stage. ||[29]

In all sports, spirit of harmony is imminent in every attire. The world is a stage and though, 'You' exists in transformative forms, the beauty is I, 'You', and all are one. Though waves on surface seem different, water beneath is same. Panchsheel Resolution (Five Principles of Peaceful Coexistence) was accepted at the World Religion Conference, Tokyo, because of the leadership of Tukadoji. It was put earlier at the Asian-African Conference, Bandung, Indonesia, in April 1955.

At All India Vedanta Conference (1955) in Amritsar (Punjab), Tukadoji discoursed and, also, addressed the valedictory session of All Religions Meet (1956) at Srikshetra Nathdwara in Rajasthan. He motivated the natives to shun off the shackles of Portuguese in the Goa Freedom struggle; resolved to utilise one crore hours of 'donated time' for mass enlightenment on the completion of 2500 years of Buddha's *nirvana*; opened tribal school at Kamalapur; established Ayurvedic College at Gurukunj; and organised Indian Farmers' Rail Fair (1961) to visit dams, water storages, and projects for productions. At the time of Indo-China War (1962) and the aggression by Pakistan (1965), he motivated soldiers, with his spirited *bhajan*, to combat; and addressed National Security Conference in 1966. During the disaster phases, such as Koyna earthquake and Bengal famine, he involved in rehabilitation and consoled the sufferers with the performances, compassion, and empathy.

Being multifaceted, Tukadoji, a bilingual, who penned in Marathi and Hindi, and recalls 12th–13th centuries bilingual saint poet, Namdev, was a poet, writer, singer, *khanjiri* player, and reformer. His literary oeuvre comprises of the anthologies of *bhajans, powada*[f], *abhanga*[g], letters, essays, travelogue, autobiography, and *Gramgeeta*, magnum opus.

When we trace the location of his poetry in the ambit of Marathi poetry, it has nuances with saints' progressive thought in devotional poetry; the reformative fervours in the *abhanga; powada* of Jyotirao Phule who whipped on slavery, social stratification, orthodox religion, and insisted on the investigation of truth; his closeness with the lyrics and *abhanga* of Keshavasuta who resisted socio-economic inequality, oppression, superstitions, and appealed for awakening to combat against the counter forces; has kinship with Kusumagraj's lyrics which deal with peripheral, deprived, exploited, and highlight national spirit in Indian freedom struggle to revolt and joy, wish fulfillment in independence; and Bal Sitaram Mardhekar's poems, which are the derivatives of tradition and modernity, imbue *abhanga* as a traditional form in saint poetry, with modern import to stress bloodshed in communal riots, erosion of values paving road to new, clevages between rich and poor, inner impoverishment, and spiritual orientation. Tukadoji's Hindi poetry reveals the parallel with the tradition of *nirguna* devotion of Ramanand and Kabir; spiritual urge of Tulsidas, Raidas, and Meerabai; the unity between Hindu and Muslim in *sufi* poetry; and patriotic vein in the poetries of Maithilisharan Gupt and Ramdhari Singh 'Dinkar'.

At the backdrop of Indian cultural renaissance in 19th–20th centuries; the reformative measures by Jyotirao Phule, Gopal Ganesh Agarkar, Vivekananda, Ram Mohan Roy, Dayanand Saraswati, Rajashri Shahu Maharaj, Vittal Ramaji Shinde, Lokmanya Tilak, Periyar Swami, Narayana Guru, Mahatma Gandhi, Babasaheb Ambedkar, Karmaveer Bhaurao Patil, and Punjabrao Deshmukh; the crucial transformative events, such as the Second World War and its socio-economic-psychological-philosophical impacts; and the political freedom of India and decolonisation process in the world, *Gramgeeta* was published in 1955, the post-colonial zone, and further translated into English, Hindi, Sanskrit, Urdu, Gujarati, and Telugu.

We observe that during the global and national events on socio-economic fronts, the two world wars, and the crisis and migration during Indo-Pak partition, Indian English poetry had a lull period. It was rare that the poets attempted to look beyond personal experiences, at the larger Indian reality to hobnob with the spirit of soil, and develop with it. We perceive it happening in the poetical creations of Sarojini Naidu, Aurobindo, Rabindranath Tagore, A.K. Ramanujan, Jayant Mahapatra, Dilip Chitre, and Arun Kolatkar. Tukadoji created the poetry, beginning from individual to collective consciousness in terms of village, society, the world, and then to cosmic vision, rooted in indigenous culture and moving beyond its contours too.

In the post-colonial expanse, *Gramgeeta* has oriented Indian poetry from elitism to masses. Tukadoji was conscious and assured that:

> ...the *Mandal's* philosophy is aloof from the confines of caste-cult-party-religion-region-language, and beyond it. The ideal of humanity and human religion are dear

> and near to it. I observe, with my eyes, the world is slowly slowly orienting towards this.[30]

Seva Mandal's philosophy is relied on human essence and human religion, and in the phase of national and international turmoil and unrest, it is indispensable to orient towards it to live and search the values in life. Tukadoji discerned in his last performance at Pandharpur:

> Say Tukdya, to bring tempest; to live though demised;
> Intend to revolt some; to ebb the wave of this energy.[31]

These lines reveal his vision of life to operate potential energy to kinetise it to revolt and bring reformation and transformation. From Bombay Hospital, Tukadoji appealed fervently to readers, audiences, and activists "to be dutyful to propagate his literature to crores of tongues and ears."[32] The then Hon'ble President of India, Pratibha Patil, in the Birth Centenary lecture of Tukadoji on 6th January, 2010, reiterated the legacy of saint's poetry tradition, the indispensability of *Gramgeeta's* vision in the present time and its repercussions in future.[33] As, thus, it is of paramount significance to translate such literary text and treasury of literatures in indigenous languages to render wider canvas of receptors in India and abroad, envisaging linguistic and cultural diversities.

III

Translation Process of *Gramgeeta*

The present translation is the full length translation of *Gramgeeta*, the ninth version in Marathi, published on 15th January, 1988, by Director, Spiritual Center, *Sri Gurudeo Atmanusandhan Tekadi* (Adyal) and the founder member of *Akhil Bhartiya Gurudeo Seva Mandal*, and its rights are with the masses, as enumerated by Tukadoji in his last message from Bombay Hospital on 6th July, 1968. Tukadoji's *Gramgeeta* published in 1955, comprises 8 Quintets, 41 Cantos, 4674 *ovi*/couplets, and 9348 lines. In the complete translation of *Gramgeeta,* the efforts are directed to maintain the form of couplet. The original form in Marathi is *ovi*, the couplet form, with rhymes at three places and caesura at four places. The liberty is taken in translating *Gramgeeta* to provide elasticity to original form keeping pace with the contour of the content.

Semiotic Facets

Syntax

Syntaxes in the first line and the second line of the couplet are statement oriented, and sometimes the changes in the location of verb and object attribute to poetic effect.

> King ruled and left, their laws perished;
> Assembly of power devastated but saint rules. ||31||[34]
>
> (Canto VIII, 'Significance of Propagation')

The syntax in *Gramgeeta* has simplicity and fluidity, and helps to develop rapport with readers. Narration is in dialogue form between an audience and a narrator, and has colloquial and rhetoric tone. Narration in dialogue form can be seen between Krishna and Arjuna in *Bhagavadgeeta* and *Jnaneshwari*, a narrator and a disciple in Ramdas' *Dasbodh*, and a teacher and a disciple in Plato's *Republic*.

In *Gramgeeta*, an audience asks query sometime once as in Canto XV: 'Improvement of Cow Race' (Couplets 1 to 6), Canto XVI: 'Wealth of Garment' (Couplets 30 to 33), Canto XVII: 'Poverty-Richness' (Couplets 1 to 4), Canto XIX: 'Life-Education' (Couplets 1 to 3), Canto XXIII: 'Festival Celebration' (Couplets 1 to 3), Canto XXIV: 'Pilgrimage-Assembly' (Couplets 1 to 8), Canto XXVI: 'Idol Worship' (Couplets 1 to 4), Canto XXVII: 'Collective Prayer' (Couplets 11 to 12), Canto XXVIII: 'Prayer and World Religion' (Couplets 1 to 4), Canto XXX: 'Influence of *Bhajan*' (Couplets 1 to 2), Canto XXXII: 'Nature of Saint' (Couplets 1 to 2); sometime twice as in Canto XI: 'Village Security' (Couplets 2 to 8, 35), Canto XII: 'Village Purification' (Couplets 1 to 5, 76), Canto XXV: 'God-Temples' (Couplets 7 to 58), Canto XXIX: 'Service of Downtrodden' (Couplets 1, 2, and 40 to 44), Canto XXXI: 'Miracle of Saint' (Couplets 1 to 8, 51 to 53), and sometime thrice as in Canto 10: 'Power of Organisation' (Couplets 1 to 30, 46, 62) and Canto XIV: 'Village Hygiene' (Couplets 1 to 4, 72 to 73, 104).

Narrative style is not monotonous, but applies the varied modes to converse and develop intimacy with readers.

1. Appeal

Oh! Awake! Awake rich! Officers! Intellectuals!
Literates! Sages ! Call for revolution. ||114||

Enlight every village, diminish differences completely;
Light the lamp of village elevation, Tukadya says. ||115||
(Canto XVI, 'Poverty-Richness')

2. Alertness

Equality, not in words; wealth, respect, education in practice;
Those who divide, to be expelled, dividers in village. ||58||

Those who don't listen, have to teach lesson by law;
Then structure to base on equality, with honesty. ||59||
(Canto XVI, 'Poverty-Richness')

3. Insistence, request

Education of life elevation, the enrichment in village only. ||58||
(Canto XIX, 'Life Education')

This not to occur, all to improve mentally;
As thus my request to all earnestly. ||48||
(Canto XVIII, 'Labour Wealth')

4. Colloquial tone

Friend! Have seen you but virtual, unreal it is. ||54||
(Canto XXXI, 'Saint Miracle')

Friend! not to forget; we, all activators, destroyer. ||30||
(Canto XXXV, 'Effect Influence')

5. Irony

Made caste for work, caste remained forgetting work. ||12||

Deposit kept with one, enjoyed he without thought. ||15||

Worshipper assigned in temple, eclipsed he temple. ||16||

Exploited thousand lives to increase diseases in them;
Then opened charity dispensaries, treating oneself religious. ||24||

(Canto XVI, 'Poverty-Richness')

6. Paradox

Animal instincts of dogs give birth to beings;
Once born, puppies are left over by all means. ||22||

It, not of human beings; their living of responsibility;
Single offspring, of great work in time span. ||23||

(Canto XXI, 'Wedded Life')

Observe planets in the sky, here in nature different insistence. ||78||

(Canto XXI, 'Wedded Life')

7. Satire

After death, spirit wanders; goes to heaven after offering *pind;*
Otherwise falls in hell, meaningless such words are. ||67||

Do insects salvate when they die in the water of Ganga. ||86||

(Canto XXII, 'Funeral *Sanskar*')

For an idol of lord, fix gold, diamond in crown;
A cloth's strip not given to labourer, died in building temple. ||24||

What a worship of lord? Mockery of an idol worship?
What an ignorance percolated in our mind. ||25||

(Canto XXVI, 'An Idol Worship')

8. Humour

I spoke with him humorously, "How can achieve life beyond?"
For it analysis exhaustive to be of righteous books. ||60||

Pounding them in mortar, consume powder with milk in morning;
Or, drinking of water, not fresh, will suffice. ||61||

(Canto LX, 'The Study of Book')

9. Illustration

Fragrance in vicinity though threw dirt from drainage;
Taken out one crystal sugar from the closed palm. ||52||

Supplied food from small container, filled audiences' eye with joy;
Stopped watches all by one, in village entire. ||53||

Friend! Have seen you but virtual, unreal it is;
No signs of saints these, never, at any time. ||54||

(Canto XXXI, 'Saint Miracle')

Taking rope of chain to tie wooden pieces;
If breaks single ring, all disrupt. ||109||

(Canto XVII, 'Poverty Richness')

10. Epigrammatic terseness

One who links with truth, infuses with gravitational force. ||29||

One, mine competent worker, great than last speakers. ||107||

(Canto XVII, 'Significance of Behaviour')

Time this of mass strategy, energy in all;
Can bow down empire, the power of people determination. ||14||

(Canto XI, 'Village Security')

Real service is detached work. ||82||

Service of self, not of senses. ||96||

(Canto IX, 'Power of Service')

Village service as the service to God. ||39||

(Canto X, 'Organisation Unity')

Organisation, formula of village's energy to create village state. ||17||

Pity, the crux of religion. ||58||

(Canto XI, 'Village Security')

Being the ideal village, the foundation of nation. ||28||

(Canto XII, 'Village Purification')

Glamour of outside items, an expression of inside lacuna. ||26||

(Canto XVI, 'Raiment Wealth')

Not immersing nose in temple, better to pick up thorns on road;

To provide water to sufferer, the best pilgrim place. ||19||

To dig a land of hand length, worship better than others;

Effect its more than hundred lectures. ||20||

What makes food available labour, work is the best than *Yajna;*

Otherwise something else not to support by mentioning *Geeta.* ||21||

(Canto XVIII, 'Labour Wealth')

In tender buds, Jnaneshwar, Ravindra, Shivaji hidden;

Blossoming they, hundred great persons, will emerge. ||76||

(Canto XIX, 'Life Education')

Not to succumb to orthodoxy or dry intellect. ||47||

Less knowledgeable being moulded cosmic. ||97||

(Canto XXXI, 'Saint Miracle')

Differences in the world to cease; isms to be complimentary. ||11||

(Canto XXXVIII, 'Village Family')

Not to succumb to orthodoxy or dry intellect. ||47||

Self-realisation means divine vision, individual, collective and beyond. ||113||

(Canto XL, 'The Study of Book')

11. Proverbs

Vote is double sided sword. ||96||

(Canto X, 'Power of Organisation')

On tongue Rama, in hand work. ||65||

(Canto XIII, 'Art of Village Creation')

Eat in hotel, go to cemetery. ||11||
(Canto XIV, 'Village Hygiene')

Hand that rocks the cradle. ||3||

Offspring as father. ||5||
(Canto XX, 'Women Elevation')

Mighty is powerful. ||63||
(Canto XXVIII, 'Prayer and World Prayer')

Visualises in dream what is in mind. ||53||
(Canto XXXV, 'Effort Influence')

12. Reference

Taj Mahal, single in nation, determines it not nation's situation;
Bankrupt people in home to home, how can it be evaluated? ||77||
(Canto XVIII, 'Labour Wealth')

Selects devotee Kabir, the resident of Kashi, Magahar for *samadhi;*
Door to hell, people call it turned into holy land. ||87||
(Canto XXII, 'Funeral *Sanskar*')

To improve devotional ritual in Bengal, the stories of Krishna retold;
United different sects of trustees, pandits by Chaitanya Prabhu. ||24||

Witnessed period tense, changed the mean of worship;
Directed Tulsidas, Ramdas at Rama, the bow man. ||25||

The prayer of *Veda*, *Upanishad*, "happiness to all beings";
Proposition for elevation of all beings in the prayer of sages. ||88||

Prayed Jesus Christ for peace of all beings;
Blessed him the deity of tolerance. ||89||

Prayed Muhammad to make wise scattered Islam?
Organised he people his at that time. ||90||

Piousness taught by Zarathustra; control by Mahavira;
Developed Buddha non-violence sang by the prayer. ||91||

(Canto XXVII, 'Collective Prayer')

13. Allusions

Vanishes darkness as rises the Sun in the sky;
Manifest you in heart; becomes being cosmic. ||21||

(Canto I, 'Vision of God')

The allusion to Eknath's couplet which exhorts that the *Gurudeo* rises to enlight as the sunrise wakes up from slumber.

When an elephant visible complete, then no blind, one sided;
Will not deceive others saying different parts as an elephant. ||92||

(Canto XXIV, 'Pilgrimage Assembly')

Here is the allusion to the anecdote in *Lilacharitra* by Chakradhar Swami.

Saint's heart though kind, harsh than hard time. ||48||

(Canto XXXII, 'Saint Nature')

The allusion to Tukaram's line, "As self as wax, pierceable to hard *vajra*" is found here:

Downpour from cloud, no *guru*-disciple there;
Self spirited see all, saint, righteous one. ||100||

(Canto XXXII, 'Saint Nature')

The allusion to *Jnaneshwari* unfolds that downpour doesn't differentiate among beings and objects.

In *Gramgeeta*, the words like *upanayan, kirtana, dandhar, purushartha, dindi, khanjiri, Ramdhun, warkari, tamasha, dahikala,* and *kumbhamela* have the cultural, folk, and ritualistic connotations; and so, culture, folk, and ritual specific words have been explained with footnotes to render clarity to expressions for the readers in English. *Upanayan* is the word which relates to twice born ceremony in the elite Hindu culture in SL and does not exist in culture in TL. So, it is impossible to find linguistic and semantic equivalence in TL. Consequently, in such situation, the word '*upanayan*' is transported to TLT, which is an addition to it.

In *Gramgeeta,* the narration has cause and effect relationship which attributes scientific precision; and envisaging the nature of problems, remedies are posited.

Cause

An action to everyone, an action is body's religion;
There purposefully to work, this speech contradictory. ||2||

(Canto XVIII, 'Labour Wealth')

Effect

Only to work for belly, not pious labour;
An act of service in time left, religion it is. ||12||

This not to occur, all to improve mentally;
As thus my request to all earnestly. ||48||

(XVIII, 'Labour Wealth')

Remedy

In village business committee. ||87||

Single grain store to be to run village transaction. ||93||

Village bank will paralyse business man, money lender. ||96||

In village oil mill necessary, the sign of pure oil products. ||97||

(XVIII, 'Labour Wealth')

Remedies are real situation based and the measures suggested are practical and feasible.

The narration in the text is statement oriented and the statements are hypotheses and inferences. Hypotheses are tested with the means of validity and practical measures, and inferences are drawn from the valid hypotheses, which are elucidated.

Topic: Life Education (Canto XIX)

Hypotheses

Many will be service oriented, many skilled artists;
Village they will enrich with industries business. ||77||

Many will created machines, many will be historian;
Some will be skilled advisers in our village. ||78||

Many will be judges, many creator of poetic world;
Many will increase yields in farm by new research. ||79||

Many will be politicians, many philosophers;
Many will bring laurels in sports for village. ||80||

Many saint adviser, many brave protector;
Many expert in commerce, serviceman, in every work. ||81||

(Canto XIX, 'Life Education')

Inference

Village rules village state; no overindulgence of anyone. ||83||

(Canto XIX, 'Life Education')

Topic: Collective Prayer (Canto XXVII)

Hypothesis

There collective God to imagine, then to experience in work later;
The *Gurudeo* mine in cosmic form to be seen. ||47||

(Canto XXVII, 'Collective Prayer')

Inference

Prayer, the school of humanities; the core feel of rural culture;
In the mould of prayer, ends conception of difference. ||96||

(Canto XXVII, 'Collective Prayer')

The narrative structure in *Gramgeeta* constitutes of topic selected, hypothesis, and inference.

Diction

The diction in *Gramgeeta* is familiar and known. The aquatics/animals/birds/reptiles mentioned are: fish (XXIX: 9), snake-mongoose (XXI: 41), elephant (XXIV: 92), tiger, lion, and wild dogs (XI: 15), swan, blue pigeon, and parrot (XIII: 27), *chakor* (I: 22), firefly (I: 17), deer (I: 31), and black kite (I:

36). The water reservoirs/plants/materials and others mentioned are: weeds, acanthus, bunions, and cassia tora (XII: 70), sandle (XXXII: 56), lotus (I: 24), star (I: 18), sunray (I: 20), the Sun (I: 21), the Moon (I: 22), water and milk (I: 25), lightening (I: 26), oasis (I: 31), salt (I: 34), sea (I: 34), glass ball (XXI: 41), diamond (XXIV: 90), touchstone, gold, and iron (XXXI: 14), cloud pouring (XXXII: 100), the Ganga (XXX: 79, 80), and atom, molecule, and mountain (XXXVII: 53).

Besides these, culture specific, religion specific, and myth and legend specific images are operable to form the matrix of the text.

Culture Specific

Shankrapat (V: 54), *lavani* (V: 62), *tamasha* (V: 63), *kirtan* and *bhajan* (V: 68), *dandhar* (V: 80), *rakshabandhan* and *makarsankranti* (XXIII: 29), *pola* (XXIII: 32), *vijayadashami* (XXIII: 39), *diwali* (XXIII: 45), *holi* (XXIII: 66), and *upanay* (XI: 48).

Religion Specific

Ganesh and Sharada (I: 4), Krishna (I: 60), Hanumant (XV: 75), Laxmi (XVII: 92), the birth anniversaries of Dutta, Hanuman, Krishna, Shivratri, and Ashadi (XXIII: 28), the worship of Gauri, Mhasoba, and Khandoba (XXXIII: 42).

Myth and Legend Specific

Kausalya, Devki, and Pralhad's mother Kayadhu (XX: 9), vatsavitri (XXIII: 29), Pralhad and Dhruva (XXXVII: 22).

These culture specific, religion specific, and myth and legend specific images have no equivalent in TLT and so, the transfer of these words to TLT is the gain to TLT as it enriches the diction of TLT by foreignisation.

Dialects

Bolbhand, mudadefaras, and *kajjedalal* (XI: 7), *buwa* (XI: 53), *godari* (XII: 20), *khandara* (XII: 22), *daware* and *wakhar* (XIII: 39), *berdya* and *muske* (XIII: 40), *hude* (XIII: 78), *fadi* (XIII: 38), *pandan*, and *borang* are Marathi dialects. Varhadi dialects are native in SLT. These dialects have no equivalent in TL and they are not comprehensible to TL readers. So, to facilitate the rapport with TL readers, the parallel meaning of dialects are incorporated in TLT and as thus, untranslatability of dialects in SLT is lost in the translation process of SLT to TLT. Attempts are made to explain dialects and native words with footnotes, whenever necessary.

Images, simile, and metaphors are functional in *Gramgeeta* with individuality and varied pointers.

Simile

Regales *chakor* when shines the moonlight;
As thou embrace, then relieves our pain. ||22||

Blossoms and smiles lotus in the life giving sunlight;
Like it, your vision blesses beings. ||23||

Water and milk separate by swan's bill;
Realises virtue, flaw as mind grasps Thy knowledge. ||25||

Flashes lightening in inky darkness, sees one at distance;
Prevails peace as Thy presence experienced. ||26||

Nourishes a black bee worm, makes like oneself;
Likewise embraces God devotees spreading a web of means. ||27||

(Canto I, 'Vision of God')

As leukoderma on body, apparels it misfit;
The ideal, systematic village to be our art. ||64||

(Canto XIII, 'Art of Village Creation')

The best land for the best seed, rapidly tree grows;
Offering to be like this as Balbhim strong. ||27||

(Canto XXI, 'Wedded Life')

As river merges into sea leaving all differences;
So the work to perform to meet with the sea. ||5||

But, the importance of sea to her, likewise man is;
Breaking bondages of attachment turns to self-nature. ||7||

(Canto XXII, 'Funeral *Sanskar*')

As rivers merges in sea, experience holiness;
Make village holy unifying all sects. ||98||

(Canto XXIV, 'Pilgrimage Assembly')

The elaborate simile in Canto X compares nature, images, creepers, fruits, storm, and cleavages in villages, and then emphasises upon organisation and unity.

> Planted in courtyard beautiful creepers, watering with labour;
> Blossomed with fruits, kissing the sky. ||9||
>
> As storm roared, dropped fruits, flowers, yellow leaves;
> In no time, creepers too squashed to ground. ||10||
>
> Why one will not dishearten, who nourished them?
> All of sudden a beauty of home is lost? ||11||
>
> Likewise village cared with strategy, nourished children;
> Love flourished each other with service qualities sportively. ||12||
>
> But intruded a village divider to fulfill selfish motives;
> Misdirecting illusioned mind, formed cleavage. ||13||
>
> Erected decorum of service, intruded flatterers;
> Blamed serviceman whenever a wrong takes place. ||14||
>
> Valiant they are to trigger off arrow pin pointedly;
> But village was crushed creating rift. ||15||
>
> Numerous differences, upheaval by different parties;
> Sometimes hidden, sometime openly started they work. ||16||
>
> Confused the masses; love power, topsy-turvy;
> Pervades everywhere the attitude of fragmentation. ||17||
>
> Some righteous people built village; some village bully spoiled it;
> Various ludicrous shows performed in our village. ||18||
>
> Selfishness surged, every one projected as king;
> Entangled entire society in various inducements. ||19||
>
> Hook sheathed under allurement but a fish sees only allurement;
> Likewise people illusioned due to seduction. ||20||
>
> (Canto X, 'Organisation Unity')

Metaphors

> What is appreciated to swim in dry tank?
> Essence lies in the swimming resisting the waves of flood. ||37||
> (Canto X, 'Organisation Unity')

> Grass rope controls an elephant, ants injure a serpent;
> Tore tiger, lion when skilled wild dogs united. ||15||
> (Canto XI, 'Village Security')

> Though ours is blue pigeon, good other's swan;
> But parrot of art, self reliant to call by everyone. ||27||
> (Canto XIII, 'Art of Village Creation')

> One has more glass balls, belonged to him, says he;
> Then ceased other's game due to one's greed. ||10||
> (Canto XVII, 'Poverty-Richness')

> Transformed the sea's vapour in the form of water;
> Merged in single place in the end though separated in drops. ||38||
> (Canto XXVIII, 'Prayer and World Religion')

Symbol

Gurudeo is the key symbol in *Gramgeeta*, which connotes supreme spirit, regulating spirit, or the mover of cosmos.

> *Guru*, not of bones, flesh; *Guru,* not caste, cults;
> *Guru,* pure knowledge principle of experienced. ||35||
> (Canto XXVII, 'Collective Prayer')

Gurudeo is all-pervading principle, unified force in cosmos, and suggests multiple images, such as *Chaitanyaghan* (condensation of spirit) (XXXVII: 49, LX: 114), *Sacchidanand* (sublime bliss), (XXXVII: 62), *Sadgururaja* (righteous *Guru*, King), (XXXVII: 72), *Sadguru* (righteous *Guru*), *Sarveshwar* (almighty), (LXI: 146), and so, it attains the significance, ramification, and multifariousness of symbol.

Semantic Dimensions

SLT has affinity with tradition which has historical sense and encompasses individual, social, economical, political, ethical, religious, spiritual, scientific, and environmental realities.

Besides the depiction of consensus reality, he dissatisfies with the present and creates his vision of reality to stress what he has to interpret and communicate; his pragmatic vision is experimental, progressive and value-oriented. He deconstructs traditional content and brings peripheral, marginal, and subaltern to the center of the text. Myriad semantic dimensions of *Gramgeeta* have been analysed and interpreted in a comparative vein in the book *Contextualising Tukadoji's Gramgeeta: Trajectories of Tradition and Reality*, penned by the translator and published by Atlantic Publishers and Distributors (P) Ltd., New Delhi.

Being the post-colonial text, *Gramgeeta* imbibes the post-colonial dynamics, projects myriad realities, and encompasses multidiscipline and trajectories of tradition and reality. The translator argues that the critique disseminates the discourse of tradition, history, literary texts, religion, philosophy, mass culture, society, political governance, economy, education, science and technology, and environment; and posits counter discourse of cultural hegemony, cultural politics, monocentricness, dwindling of ethical values, social fragmentation, fundamentalist forces and aggressive nationalism, economic rift, discord with environment, orthodox rituals, and fatalism. Being anchored in multidiscipline and multi-realities, the post-colonial discourse becomes polyphonic. This translation study is comparative cultural product which contributes to post-colonial theory by discovering two components, coordination and conjuncture to bridge ruptures, dissociations, and fragmentations, which post-modernism celebrates.

In this translation, semiotic facets and semantic dimensions, imbibed with cultural ramification, are envisaged to retain the spirit and import of content with the consciousness of form and aesthetic aspects. The attempt is made to render justice to syntax and diction, rooted in Indian culture, through explanations with footnotes; phrases, idioms, and proverbs are transmuted in TLT. The cognisance of semiotic, semantic, and aesthetic aspects are taken in to provide new original to TLT.

I express my gratitude to Tukaramdada Gitacharya and Laxmandada Narkhede, Directors, *Voice of Saint Tukadoji*, Quarterly in English, who rendered me the opportunity to edit it since July 1997, which triggered my critical insight and enthusiasm to delve deep into Tukadoji's literature, and ushered in the translation of *Gramgeeta*, along with its analysis and interpretation in comparative cultural contexts; to S.R. Raut, for the international distribution of the Quarterly; to *Akhil Bhartiya Sri Gurudev Sewa Mandal, Gurukunj Mozari, Atmanusandhan Kendra*, and Adyal Tekdi, for their missionary services; to Universtiy Grants Commission, New Delhi, for financial assistance; to B.B. Taywade, Principal, Dhanwate National College, for motivation and unstinting support; to Sharayu Taywade, Dean, Faculty of Arts, Rashtrasant Tukadoji Maharaj Nagpur University, Nagpur, for his involvement in this endeavour, and Usha Madhav Deshmukh, Professor and Head, Department of Marathi, Mumbai University, who provided cue to undertake the venture sincerely. I am grateful to Sahitya Akademi (New Delhi), British Council Library (New Delhi), Indian Council of Historical Research (New Delhi), Asiatic Society Library (Mumbai), Pune Nagar *Vachan* Mandir (Pune), Pune Marathi *Granthalaya* (Pune), Jayakar Library, Savitribai Phule Pune University (Pune), Osmania University Centre for International Programmes, Osmania University Campus (Hyderabad), Banaras Hindu University (Varanasi), Indian Institute of Advanced Study (Shimla), Center for Religious Studies, University of California (Riverside, California), Ramkrishna Mission Library (Nagpur), and Dhanwate National College (Nagpur) for conducive academic environment and enrichment. My sincere regards are to Anand Patil, comparative culturalist and translator, Professor and Head, Department of English, Goa University, Goa; Usha Bande, critic, Principal, and the Fellow of Indian Institute of Advanced Study, Shimla; Sachin Ketkar, a poet and translator, Professor of English, The Maharaja Sayajirao University of Baroda, Vadodara, Gujarat; and Sunil Sawant, translator, Professor of English, Kisan Veer Mahavidyalaya, Wai, Maharashtra, for their deliberations and suggestions to furnish clues to explore and update the contexts.

My sincere thanks are to P.K.U. Pillai, Chairman, Board of Studies of English; Pramod Sharma, Dean, Faculty of Arts; D.V. Naik, Principal, R.K. Mokhare College; and Urmila Dabir,

Principal, Rajkumari Kewalramani College, of Rashtrasant Tukadoji Maharaj Nagpur University, Nagpur.

At this juncture, I experience the blessings of Deorao Bhellar, my father with aesthetic sensibility, producer of drama troop, Adarsha Kala Niketan, and Radha, my mother with transparency of heart, both abided to black soil in farm, when my tree's leaves rustle, buds bloom, and flowers blossom and permeate vicinity with fragrance.

I acknowledge the interest that Pralhad Ande (brother-in-law), Usha Ande (sister), and Prabhakar Bhelkar (brother) have taken in the venture to boost up my investigative spirit. I am thankful to T.V. Warhekar of International Gurudeo Seva Mandal, Warud, for his missionary zeal, and anticipate the words with warmth of Waman Borade, Anant Zade, Keshav Dahikar, and Anil Zade, who encouraged me.

Without endurance and patience of Sangita R. Bhelkar, Yugandhar R. Bhelkar, Vaibhavi Bhelkar-Zade, Abhijit Zade, and near and dear ones, this challenging task would have not seen the sunlit expanse.

Ratnakar D. Bhelkar

Notes

(a) *Khanjiri,* an indigenous musical instrument, circular shaped, in folk tradition, on the rim of which, the seasoned skin of monitor lizard is stretched, with thin, metallic disc structures in the peripheral zone, prevalent in Rajasthan, Gujrat, Madhya Pradesh, and Maharashtra. With the accomplices of *tabla, tal*, and harmonium, Tukadoji deployed *khanjiri* to sing *bhajans*, which cast magnetic spell on masses. In childhood, he learnt to play on *khanjiri* from Hanuwantibuwa. *Khanjiri* accompanied throughout his hectic schedules and rendered the service for peace and revolt.

(b) *Ekatari,* single stringed instrument used in the traditional music of South Asia, in the devotional practice of singing to maintain tempo rather than providing base note. From Saint Kothalikar, Manik learnt to play ekatari. Also, played by Surdas and Meerabai.

(c) *Bhajan,* a traditional, Indian folk form of singing devotional songs, practised by Kabir, Guru Nanak, Narsi Mehta, Raidas, Surdas, Meerabai, and Chaitanya Mahaprabhau. Tukadoji's identity was his *khanjiri bhajan*, mass communicative mean, in which he infused contemporary themes relating to *bhakti*, society, nation, political scenario, slavery, war, freedom, and constructive citizenship. For more, see Canto VI, 'Impact of Good Company', Canto XII, 'Village Purification', and Canto XXX, '*Bhanjan* Influence', in *Gramgeeta*, (tr.), Ratnakar D. Bhelkar, Atlantic Publishers and Distributors (P) Ltd., New Delhi, 2023.

(d) *Yagnya,* the ritual to lit pyre, out of sacred wooden sticks, with chants, which in the course of time, was associated with animal sacrifices. Salbuldi *yagnya* was the deviation from the traditional sacrifices. Tukadoji alerts:

What makes food available to labourer; a work, the best than *yagnya;*

Otherwise something else not to support by mentioning *Geeta.* ||21||

(Canto XVIII, 'Labour Wealth')

Gadgebaba and Tukadoji, both worked to eradicate orthodoxy and superstition.

(e) *Langar,* community meal, started by Guru Nanak to uphold the principal of equality. It expresses the ethics of sharing, community feeling, inclusiveness, and oneness of all humankind. In their prayers, the sikhs seek the favour, "Loh Langar topde rahin" (May the iron pots of langar be ever warm in service).

(f) *Powada,* a narrative genre of Marathi poetry, a kind of ballad writing; folk form to be sung to narrate valour of heroes/heroines, with *duf, tuntune* by *Shahir,* to motivate. In the modern garb, Tukadoji infused democratic spirit in *powada.* Refer Canto VIII, 'Significance of Propagation'.

(g) *Abhanga,* the form of devotional poetry, composed of *ovi*, which is in couplet, and has *cesuras* at four places and internal lines rhyme. *Abhanga* is composite form of *ovis*, practised by saints in Maharashtra, and deployed in Marathi poetry to imbibe social stratification, discrimination, post-war reality, industrial impact, spiritual desolation, and experimentation by Jotiba Phule, Keshavsut, Bal Sitaram Mardhekar, Vinda Karandikar, Madhukar Keche, Tulsiram Kaje, Sudhakar Gaidhani. Also, see Canto XXX, '*Bhajan* Influence', Canto XXVI, 'An Idol Worship'.

References

1. Said, Edward (1995), *Orientalism,* New Delhi: Penguin Books India Pvt. Ltd., p. 5.
2. Devi, G.N., 'Language, Culture, Translation' presented at the Workshop on Language, Culture and Translation at IIC, New Delhi, from Oct. 31 to Nov. 1, 1990.
3. Quoted in Chakravarti, Amiya (1961), *A Tagore Reader,* Kolkata: Macmillan Co., p. 21.
4. Gopinathan, G., 'Translationa, Transcreation and Culture: The Evolving Theories of Translation in Hindi and Other Indian Languages,' Citesserx.ist.psu.edu.PDF., p. 8.
5. Dharwadkar, Vinay, 'A.K. Ramanujan's Theory and Practice of Translation', *Post-colonial Translation: Theory and Practice,* Eds. Sussan Bassnet and Harish Trivedi, London: Routledge, p. 121
6. Das, Bijay Kumar (2005), *A Handbook of Translation Studies,* New Delhi: Atlantic Publishers and Distributors (P) Ltd., p. 1.
7. *Ibid*, p. 104.
8. *Ibid.*
9. Bassnett, Sussan (2002), 'Preface', *Translation Studies,* London and New York: Routledge, p. 3.
10. Catford, J.C. (1965), *A Linguistic Theory of Translation,* London: OUP, p. 20.
11. *Ibid*, p. 21.

12. Varshney, Radhe L. (2006), *An Introductory Text Book of Linquistic and Phonetics,* Barely: Student Store, p. 337.
13. Verma, S.K., Krishnaswami, N. (1999), *A Modern Linquistics: An Introduction,* New Delhi: Oxford University Press, p. 365.
14. Lefevere, Andre (1992), *Translation, Rewriting and Manipulation of Literary Frame,* London and New York: Routledge, p. 76.
15. Venuti, Lawrence (1995), *The Translator Invisibility: A History and Translation,* London and New York: Routledge, p. 46.
16. Derrida, Jacque, 'What is Relevant Translation?' in Lawrence Venuti (ed.), *The Translation Studies Reader,* London and New York: Routledge, 1999, pp. 423-466.
17. Iyer, K.A. Subramania (1965), *Vakyapadiyan of Bhartrihari,* English translation of Chapter I, 'Brahmakandam', Poona: Deccan College, pp. 48-50.
18. Dingwaney, Anuradha (1955), 'Introduction: Translating Third World' Cultures, Dingusaney, Anuradha and Carol Maier (ed.), *Between Languages and Cultures Translation and Cross-Cultural Texts,* Pittisburgh and Landon: University of Pittisburgh Press, p. 4.
19. Paz, Octavio (1992), 'Translation: Literature and Letters', (tr), 'Irene del Coral', in Rainer Schutte and John Biguenet (ed), *Theories of Translation: Anthology of Essay from Dryden of Derrida,* Chicago: University of Chicago Press, pp. 36-55.
20. Bhabha, Homi (1994), *The Location of Culture,* London and New York: Routledge, p. 38.
21. Viswanatha, Vanamala and Simon, Snerry (1999), 'Shifting Grounds of Exchange: B.M. Srikantaiah and Kannada Translation', in Susan Bassnett and Harish Trivedi (ed.), *Post-Colonial Translation: Theory and Practice,* London and New York: Routledge, p. 162.
22. Interview with Mona Baker, You Tube, June 13, 2017, accessed on May 6, 2020.

23. After, Emily (2006), *Translation Zone: New Comparative Literature,* Princeton: Princeton University Press, pp. 243-52.

24. 'Exploring Translation Theories', the speech by Anthony Pym, You Tube, May 28, 2014, accessed on May 6, 2020.

25. 'Towards an Indian Theory of Translation', Professor Indra Nath Choudhari, www.intranathchoudhari.com, accessed on May 7, 2020, PDF, p. 14.

26. Sapir, Edward (1950), *Culture, Language and Personality,* Barkley Los Angeles: University of California Press, p. 69.

27. Tukadoji (2016), *Rashtriya Bhajanavali,* Gurukunj Ashrama: SriGurudeo Publication, p. 26.

28. Tukadoji (2016), *Meri Japan Yatra,* Gurukunj Ashrama: Sri Gurudeo Publication, p. 148.

29. *Ibid*, p. 145.

30. *Sri Gurudeo*, August 1968, p. 5.

31. The last *bhajan* sung at Pandharpur on July 6, 1968.

32. *Sri Gurudeo*, Sept., 1968, p. 2.

33. *Sakal*, Jan. 7, 2010.

34. Tukadoji (2023), *Gramgeeta* (tr.) Ratnakar D. Bhelkar, Canto VIII, 'Significance of Propagation', New Delhi: Atlantic Publishers and Distributors (P) Ltd., p. 70. (Subsequent textual quotation's are from this edition of the translated text, indicated by Canto/s and Couplet/s).

Dedication Leaflet

Let all village be happy, giving food, raiment and leaf base;
But, to experience pain self, ornamental to village Lord. ||

Build castle by labour, but not your hut apt;
Leap in for freedom, experience joy others. ||

In all nations, let happiness be for such Shankar;
Feel inside to obtain for you human perfectness. ||

So, penned *Gramgeeta* to enlighten village deity;
To relate you as sea-river to all. ||

Let your labour receive dignity, all attention be converged on you;
Let light of humanity be glittered in world by this means. ||

So, dedicate to you; you, the altar of world;
First in the world, thy elevation to be by this mode. ||

This to happen in masses, nature, content my mind will be;
Let everywhere friendship be increased, the motto this, Tukadya says. ||

Tukadya

Right Religion Reflection Quintate

Canto I

Vision of God

The Mover of Universe, the Master of Cosmos I prostrate before you;
Though One but appears myriadly in cosmic forms. ||1||

You, the guardian of the world; the earth surcharged with Your presence;
You pulsating in every particle to stage world play. ||2||

You, the temple, the idol, the worshiper; worship turning in flowers;
You manifests as God in the hearts of devotees. ||3||

Ganesh[1], *Sharada*[2], *Sadguru*, the wish fulfilling tree of devotees;
Thou, God, Goddess, Narad[3], Tunbaroo, became. ||4||

Thou impregnate various arts, song, dance;
When pleased You render fruits of devotion. ||5||

Guru[4] and disciple, You appear different but not so from core;
Conversation facilities between them to colour life. ||6||

When unity experienced by one, pangs of birth and death perish;
Being recognised the nature of spirit, core, real. ||7||

As all illusions vanished, the whole universe becomes *Brahma;*
Whatever he serves becomes offerings for you. ||8||

Your power of perfection has not yet penetrated;
Into our beings an ignorance prevails so. ||9||

With vision of you all doors of knowledge are opened;
And barriers between you and me are collapsed. ||10||

What is alien to one who has vision of you?
The whole universe becomes ours at divine moment. ||11||

We deprived of your vision; how joy can be in other happiness?
In our mean selfishness we strive for heaven. ||12||

Mock at others' lacunas, escape from others' calamities;
Jealous turn we for other's glory, happens this. ||13||

Let others toil hard but we long for false status;
Knock anyone's door for greedy pursuit, happens this. ||14||

When this understood, we realised our ignorance;
Thus, now our mind is focused on Your name entirely. ||15||

How can one be vigorous if surrenders to other?
Time unfruitful though turned to diverse feet. ||16||

For light to pick firefly, to return from forgotten road;
How can one know oneself there dauntlessly. ||17||

Attention flickered though eyes focused on stars;
Same will be our plight on vast road. |18||

You, real firm, immortal, deviating never;
Embodiment of all qualities, receives what strives for. ||19||

For these needs sunrays, visible many roads from distance;
To experience reflection in the form of attainment of motto. ||20||

Vanishes darkness as rises the Sun in the sky;
Manifest You in heart, becomes being cosmic. ||21||

Regales *chakor*[5] when shines the moonlight;
As You embrace, then relieves our pain. ||22||

Swells *Janbuk*[6] with pride till does not see lion;
Devours evil as light Your does not reach. ||23||

Blossoms and smiles lotus in the life giving sunlight;
Like it Your vision blesses beings. ||24||

Water and milk separate by swan's bill;
Realises virtue, flaw as mind grasps Your knowledge. ||25||

Flashes lightening in inky darkness, sees one at distance;
Prevails peace as Your presence experienced. ||26||

Ignorance causes evil, ignorance invites foul weather;
Ignorance prolongs realisation of God, Truth in essence. ||27||

Thy vision, means knowledge, bliss of joy inside;
Existence surcharged with completeness at Your feet. ||28||

O sea of knowledge, full bloomed, self-enlightened moon;
Sage of Heaven! Bless us for complete lift. ||29||

Enriched You are to root out poverty of life;
O Beginner, kneel we before You Almighty. ||30||

Belong to You but departed, though inside, misdirected;
Searched water in mirage like thirsty deer. ||31||

Wretched animals when drenched river-bed;
Relieve us as brings flood water joy. ||32||

Sprouts seed on the earth where gently drizzles rain;
Console long waited being with Thine shower. ||33||

Pray I with all means converging on you;
Duel not to be mind, one to be like salt in sea water. ||34||

Hindrances here many, narrowed due to ignorance;
But, reflection of Your magnanimity will free us. ||35||

Though immerse, fall we, Your look as of black kite;
To provide happiness by all means, will extract out of ignorance. ||36||

Moos a cow for calf path-forgotten, guards an egg a bird;
Cares for kid though performs mother household work. ||37||

Nourishes a black-bee worm, makes like oneself;
Likewise embraces God devotees spreading a web of means. ||38||

Happens this in practice, finds road out when being intense;
While moving on road, realisation of your vast vision. ||39||

Knowing this, pray I to fructify cherished dream of humanity;
Inclined to Your feet single minded for experiencing cosmic presence. ||40||

Everywhere immanent you, joy of true knowledge, detached;
Likewise heart to elevate, then only your devotion. ||41||

As, thus, to toil on the earth our minds expand;
Render us long life to serve the world. ||42||

As pious areas, Pandharpur[7], sitting on the bank of Chandrabhaga;[8]
Surged inspiration inside of cosmic attitude. ||43||

Experienced vision marvelous; how to win the world?
First better to embark on *Gramgeeta*, says. ||44||

World to be known from self-realising one constituent of world;
Creation of family from individual; society from family. ||45||

Village from society, nation from village;
Nations create the world, step by step. ||46||

The first mother home of human beings, our village, home in it;
Progressing in it beautifully to march beyond the world. ||47||

The prime base human conduct, this to maintain best;
To make village, well-equipped; the ideal picture of world. ||48||

Nation to be judged from village being a map of the world;
Nation dwindles down when village devasts. ||49||

Though rivers, mountains make the earth mighty;
But, our village, the basic element of the earth. ||50||

Nation's health collapses if village diseased;
A conscious person to diagnose this symptom. ||51||

Saint, nation, supreme experience delight in rural beauty;
But, attribution of priority to one's mind. ||52||

To diagnose one to know, knowledge is to experience;
Then, happiness to procure of cosmic vision. ||53||

Village is temple to know, people in village supreme;
Service is total worship, a thought to propagate. ||54||

For this the book to initiate, beginning of the conduct knowledge's root;
To erect the foundation pillar of activation. ||55||

Heard this melodious voice on the bank of Bhîma with ease;
Likewise uttered the same the King of Pandhari when meditated. ||56||

Reflected on sage-saints to rejuvenate village;
Nothing new to exhort, old to reframe of God. ||57||

Expounded saints but its reverse implementation in future;
Formed cleavages between man and man by orthodox ones. ||58||

Vanished magnanimity of human beings, emerged castes, sects;
Culminated distribution of works into stratification. ||59||

Sects centers for service but turned into places for differences of people;
Fought like Yadavas though Krishna is sole. ||60||

To root out duality, we to begin service;
With unflickered mind the book penned out with righteous intention. ||61||

One has to select territory suiting one's potential;
Remembering *Guru* the best to be performed. ||62||

Realise literary service as service to channelise masses;
Deeming man as divine, one has to work. ||63||

Whatever known to us to be conveyed to others;
People to be treated as our parents. ||64||

If a speaker treats himself wise and a listener worthless;
In mesh of ego, one is bound to immerse. ||65||

Every one will not pay heed, the past witnesses for it;
As thus, not justifiable to hamper flow of service. ||66||

For self-contentment, with cosmic motive;
Great souls created books with pious motto. ||67||

Story of the world some narrate, concentrate some on nation;
We have to pen *Gramgeeta* focusing on village. ||68||

Krishnageeta[9], *Ramgeeta*[10], *Hansgeeta*[11], *Hanumantgeeta*[12];
Shivgeeta[13], *Avadhootgeeta*[14], narrated some. ||69||

Gurugeeta[15], *Ganeshgeeta*[16], *Pandavgeeta*[17], *Bhagwatgeeta*[18];
Devgeeta[19], *Devigeeta*[20], all written. ||70||

Essence of all to purify the temple of heart;
All beings are to make happy for righteous course. ||71||

Supreme speaks, society is drowned in sorrow;
Knowledge futile which comprehends not rural service. ||72||

Wandered in forest, pilgrim places but his village not progressed;
How can he be called great soul? ||73||

Saint's speech such, our salvation not elevation;
Progressed is he who uplifts people on righteous route. ||74||

Believing in saints, this focus in mind;
Initiated *Gramgeeta* with our intention of service. ||75||

Though not writer intellectual, I know myself;
But, intends to offer our flake rice to heap of grains. ||76||

God, thirsty for love; indifferent to caste, creed;
His grace salivates simpleton, such fame you have. ||77||

Why did He please Kubja though an appreciator of beauty?
Why did turn to Vidur though longs only for glory? ||78||

Why did He incline to *pendya* though lover of art?
What can intellect do where Brahmadeo's ego subsided? ||79||

Pigmy are words to adore the deeds of Supreme;
One has to reflect, working whole heartedly. ||80||

Service is to be as our mode of belief;
Urge to speak here to all. ||81||

One to surrender before Him to become cosmic in the world;
Look into as to make conscious being. ||82||

Bearing this in mind, *Gramgeeta* has begun;
Received blessing, praying saints, great ones. ||83||

Inner voice of saints, great ones, good omen for Supreme;
Initiated conversation to delineate in simple language. ||84||

Here audience asked, wrote about *Gramgeeta;*
Why to incorporate saints honouring with hymns? ||85||

For working all people hand in hand to elevate village;
Why to sing song adoring God? ||86||

Doesn't work function without utterance of God, Saints?
Does righteous work infect without shower of blessing? ||87||

Why should be indulgence of religious stories?
Why attribute to God for the writing performed tirelessly? ||88||

Feeble become people, believing in God;
Bankrupt village became, leave utterance of 'God, God'. ||89||

I heard you but people dependent, lazy;
But, where has as He suggested this? ||90||

Oh! God not born in this mode, then how can He tell others?
Reverses the reality by coward, lazy people. ||91||

Who does nothing shelters in His garb;
To hide one's sin, to remain inactive. ||92||

To illusion in people, to escape from labour;
Evil in the name of God, drowns society. ||93||

As thus, I will not tell it, whatever meditated here;
Not to make people coward, lazy, understand determinately. ||94||

God means valorous, the mother home of justice, moral;
Divine spring of rebellious work, on front in the world. ||95||

He is Superman, ideal of human beings;
His work is to remember, to inspire generation new. ||96||

Highlight on core God not completed here;
Deeming the best in man as God, behave, said to all. ||97||

Initially remembrance of core God; His features one by one;
To make available the means for disciples, so recalled. ||98||

Walk on the road, vast; those who walked, survived;
Fame this engraved on devotees' hearts. ||99||

Friends! village is to be self-reliant, ideal by all means;
For that blessings of ancestors are sought. ||100||

Their blessings mean their speech, to pay need to them;
To fructify them in work performed, blessing this. ||101||

People seek blessings, but does not little work;
Plan turns fiasco; one becomes slave, feeble. ||102||

Our sign of blessing, great beings to guide;
Outlet to be searched out to fulfill motto. ||103||

How can blessings for long life function if one is addicted?
Can one be intellectual despite of study? How can blessing fructify? ||104||

Disfavour I for ever blind, handicapped belief;
Theist is not he who speaks about saints without practice. ||105||

Work motivated at core we are; we favour atheist;
Whose intent universal to make others happy. ||106||

Though one disbelieves in God but advocates happiness for all;
To make man and man complementary. ||107||

All in villages have to be happy, wealthy;
None to be victimised for social balance. ||108||

We will be contended sharing whatever we get;
We will labour, experience joy whatever possible. ||109||

Our wealth not ours, our offspring not ours;
Work energy not ours for personal utilization. ||110||

They belong to village, having body, speech, mind, life;
Atheist whose approach is like this, I support. ||111||

He who makes others happy is not atheist;
Though he doesn't utter 'God', he serves Him. ||112||

We brought God in between but worked for everyone;
Call of time is an urgency for work everywhere. ||113||

To place ideal high, of boundless knowledge before people;
With vast faith the work God is chosen. ||114||

We live for self but He strives for others;
Retained He in mind to water this belief. ||115||

He means not only to receive but to offer;
We adore whole heartedly sect whose belief is this. ||116||

Ultimate motto perpetual peace to experience in being;
For this appreciate we mean as well an end. ||117||

Those who succeeded infusing peace and truth;
Those service idols, saints, ideal forms. ||118||

Cordial respect for magnanimous, sagacious saints;
Who direct 'divine in people' to elevate village. ||119||

God, saints, religion, work for human elevation;
Recalling them let village be upgraded, says Tukadya. ||120||

Such *Sri Gramgeeta* book, *Guru*-discipline-self-experience-accepted;
Saluting God, saints narrated in voice; the First Canto completed. ||121||

Notes

1. Ganesh—Deity in Hindu religion.
2. Sharada—The goddess of knowledge.
3. Narada—The messenger of gods in Indian mythology.
4. *Guru*—Guide, who provides direction.
5. *Chakor*—The bird.
6. Janbuk—Fox
7. Pandharpur—The pilgrim place of Vithoba, the deity in Warkari cult in Maharashtra.
8. Chandrabhaga—The river at Pandharpur.
9. *Krishnageeta*—The text concentrating on Krishna.
10. *Ramgeeta*—The text concentrating on Ram.
11. *Hansgeeta*—A subset of *Uddhava geeta* and the *Bhagwat Purana* proper.
12. *Hanumangeeta*—The text focusing on Hanuman.
13. *Shivgeeta*—The text focusing on Shiva.

14. *Avadhootgeeta*—A mystical text which tells how the Avadhoot is. The word, Avadhoot refers to a mystic who has done way with worldly concerns and standard social etiquette, at least in his or her heart. Such personalities are considered to be free 'to roam like a child.'
15. *Gurugeeta*—The text centering on *Guru*.
16. *Ganeshgeeta*—The text centering on Ganesha.
17. *Pandavgeeta*—The text centering on Pandav.
18. *Bhagvatgeeta*—The text centering on Bhagvat.
19. *Devgeeta*—The text centering on God.
20. *Devigeeta*—The text centering on Goddess.

Canto II

Theological Study

God created the world, Prajapati increases subjects;
Religion narrated for ordering human society. ||1||

The word 'religion', one but its expanse;
Encompassing material and transcendental. ||2||

Order where many animals inhabit;
Contentment to everyone, religion stresses. ||3||

Urge to know self in all quarters of life;
Respect for global family is religion in essence; ||4||

Elevation of self, happiness to others;
Religion indeed, nourished this objective of culture. ||5||

Behaviour where justice, morality equal;
Everyone works with mission is religion. ||6||

Everyone to be satisfied, none to hurt;
To attain self contentment, a core of religion. ||7||

Contentment to all, no sorrow to beings;
It to be studied, actively, asserts religion ethics. ||8||

Diverse modes of works constitute life action;
Shares happiness to everyone though diverse qualities, names. ||9||

No hammer of power, no penalty for pious work;
One has to work, religion insists totality. ||10||

Religious he who works better without power;
Ventures to cope with everyone with one's nature. ||11||

Vaidya or no doctor but remains oneself healthy;
Though no lawyer, justice, power holder, equality with ease. ||12||

No threat of sword, restless self for wrong;
Witnesses God's rein in oneself. ||13||

Where inspiration such in heart, religious real He;
Outer decorum, sign of subsidiary, no religion. ||14||

Purity to be manifested in transient world;
Society to be balanced with one's character. ||15||

Individual religion, family religion, social religion, rural religion;
Empowers national religion for road of success. ||16||

Individual to nourish family, family to society;
Village to nation, nation to world for peace. ||17||

Whatever contributes to this, religion truly;
Treachery to nation, non-religions, same meaning. ||18||

Signs of core religion, sacrifice, non-violence, truth;
Restrain, celibacy, understand with conscience. ||19||

Courage, physical labour, love for each other;
Knowledge supplemented by righteous work for all. ||20||

Religious vision to make entire world happy;
Beneficial it to nourish in every villagers. ||21||

Nation, an element of world, village of nation;
Man, foundation of village, he to be religious. ||22||

Individual religion to know all, family religion to behave;
Rural religion to follow with national spirit. ||23||

Person to person to be religious, not idiosyncratic;
Material and transcendental progress to be of all. ||24||

Everyone has body, speech, organs, intellect, breath;
Medium to uplift them all is religion. ||25||

Such knowledge of righteous religion to receive entirely;
Then life like, it will be lived in the world. ||26||

For this *Ashram* system, the apt tradition of ancestors;
Initially knowledge of religion, then life religious. ||27||

Man came from animal embryo, he to become divine;
For this, imparting balanced *sanskar* subsequently. ||28||

Good and evil, man performs both;
Pious and sin, man has to select from it. ||29||

Conduct to be improved for novel mode;
One to be lifted up assisting others. ||30||

For this religion formed *sanskar; ashram,* four for life;
Assuming life-span hundred; division for flourishing. ||31||

Entering human life, celibacy to be known;
Origin for four *ashram*, foundation of human life. ||32||

Future becomes soothing if one follows celibacy;
Every phase of *ashram* becomes prosperous. ||33||

A way to celibacy originates from contraception;
Growing embryo to be watered with *sanskar.* ||34||

Sanskar not to be adverse on a growing foetus;
As thus, parents to be well mannered with righteous intent. ||35||

Not to speak filthy language, not to see obscene;
Not to be addicted, not to eat spoiled food. ||36||

Balanced diet, meditations, reading to be preferred;
Not to listen erotic songs, with pregnant woman. ||37||

It is to be followed, delivers child later;
Sanskar to be ingrained from infancy. ||38||

Appreciates people birth of new born child;
But, they watch his deeds in time to come. ||39||

Keep they a close eye on what a child plays, sees;
How speaks, walks, sings, sees people. ||40||

As child grows, difficult it becomes to look after;
Nothing wrong to be spoken before him. ||41||

Penance constructive for the best *sanskar;*
As thus, to be taught, memorise, the best subjects. ||42||

Then everyone asks whether have you read?
Why to wander here and there like lunatic? ||43||

Have you not learnt *sanskar* for virtuous nature?
What are parents doing ignoring children? ||44||

Don't you know evening bath purifying for praying Almighty?
Have you not worshipped Thee in morning and evening? ||45||

Then why to wonder in forest? How one can be wise?
Advice for enhancing virtues to become great. ||46||

To have *sanskar*, parents teach good conduct;
To become virtuous, alert in time to come. ||47||

Upanayana sanskar[1] is to be below eight years;
Not to blind by tradition, no decorum. ||48||

Upanayana, penance for knowledge, beginning of celibate;
To mould life, one to be dedicated to *Guru*. ||49||

Guru is to be celibate, secluded in forest;
Celibacy of children to be looked after by him. ||50||

His living, eating, drinking, playing, reading;
Watch is to be of *Guru* on an entertainment. ||51||

Difficult to control if missed once;
Organs function as they conditioned in life. ||52||

In *Guru ashrama*, rules to be implemented with patience;
Applicable this vision in students' hostel too. ||53||

Nutrient food to be eaten when he begins study;
Not to give salty, soar, pungent, spicy one. ||54||

Not to prefer too sweet, fried items;
Or dry, synthetic-mixed food not to be given. ||55||

Simple, fresh food for eating; sleeping, waking in time;
None to touch near when in sleep, awake. ||56||

Meditation in morning, prayer in evening;
Reflection on the deeds of ideal persons in all time. ||57||

Dawn walk, praying to the Sun, *yogasan* regularly;
Swimming and lemon-juice drinking better for health. ||58||

Bath in cold water, morning walk in nature;
Regular reading of the great ones benefits. ||59||

Luxurious living, aromatic perfume, flowers to leave;
Not to use oil, hairs to trim ever. ||60||

Not to look into mirror, not to be fascinated by raiment;
Betal leaf, *bidi,* tea to keep aside totally. ||61||

Not to drink liquor, not to speak deceptively;
Guidelines to understand for intake in fast. ||62||

Self-work to be performed besides working for others;
Brotherhood, sisterhood, religion of service to be taught. ||63||

Not to sit with girls, then how can be complication?
Not to permit to listen song titillating, the company of vulgar. ||64||

Not to be in company of women when he grows;
Ideals of the great persons to be before him. ||65||

No exposure to marriage, no teaching of sensuous song;
Physical exercises to be taught dauntlessly. ||66||

No obscenity to be seen, ideal of daily-routine;
Intellectual feeding to be in morning, evening. ||67||

Tell the glory of celibacy, objective of it;
Tell what to eat to guard celibacy. ||68||

Celibacy means divine conduct, a medium for divine luminance;
Avenue for learning; guarding semen, celibacy. ||69||

Which is other mean as important as celibacy?
Those who practice it leads to be perfect. ||70||

Pleasure and utility, its slaves, God serves those;
Remains skin healthy, shines as the sunlight. ||71||

Provides steadfastness of Bhisma, swiftness of Kartikeya;
Experiences *Jnanyog*[2] of Shukra fearless. ||72||

Vast vision of Awadhoot, might of Hanumanta;
Agile, well-built, resistant body to celebrant. ||73||

Poor, feeble becomes one who hasn't semen powerful;
His body, a breeding house of diseases. ||74||

Who stores semen, success garlands him;
When semen turns weak, death overpowers to victimise. ||75||

Semen has lust of its own, new luminance;
Seed of hygiene, a power of intellect. ||76||

Listen, how does semen form? Forty *sher* of food;
Forms a *sher*[3] blood, two *tola*[4] semen from it. ||77||

If one consumes a sher of food daily, thirty *sher* in a month;
One and half *tola* semen form from it. ||78||

If it destroyed soon, how fatal it is;
Money earned laboriously but spent quickly. ||79||

Celibate deteriorates, monthly income consumed;
What is a serious bolt to life precious? ||80||

Gastric juice formed prepares blood after seven days;
Blood forms flesh subsequently step by step. ||81||

Then fat and bones, nerves too grow;
Then semen forms in due course little-little after a weak. ||82||

Sperms becomes viable after forty days;
But, more food, much efforts to form it. ||83||

A jewel precious which nourishes body;
Ambrosia healthy enhances brightness cell to cell. ||84||

As thus, it to guard to boost up power lustre;
To radiate light as that of the moon and the Sun. ||85||

This to be taught to children youth, people too;
Once mind prepared, life becomes ideal. ||86||

To create ideal, teachers have to teach;
Powerful nation becomes if students mould. ||87||

Life victorious if man continues this for twenty-four years;
Opens avenue for good work in days to come. ||88||

Lives for hundred, the offspring of a celibate;
Disease, weakness don't paralyse them. ||89||

Ideal village will be, strong nation will be;
Entire elevation will be of human society. ||90||

In order to achieve it, *ashram* for celibacy is must;
Activate will be citizens for self as well as nation. ||91||

Life to build for nation, character to mould;
Power of health to retain in body by celibacy. ||92||

Love between man and man, ready for social work;
But, for foundation, concrete life to structure. ||93||

Rules equal to be for boys and girls;
Difference of ages between them prevails at core. ||94||

Women turn *brahmacharini*, educated, luminary;
Their *ashram* at independent place, ideal. ||95||

As long as *ashrams* were, nation was strong, the best;
As addiction, lust increased society dwindled. ||96||

Studentship, the base of religion, for it *ashram* for celibacy;
Elevated will be lives of individual and nation. ||97||

Simple to be rules for *ashram* in rural area;
Friends, educate future generation with alertness. ||98||

I know essence in past, faith, restrain with ease;
Difficult it will be, *ashram* practice in villages at present. ||99||

Luxuries of all increased, living styles changed;
Tunes of passions for material are on *satar.*[5] ||100||

Girls' schools, not separate; no widows without painted faces;
No control left in today's social scenario. ||101||

More fashions in life, misdirected by films, fiction;
Teachers, addicted, luxuriant teach sensuous song. ||102||

Food, drink everywhere; glorious school many;
Luxury is life's target; who care for whom? ||103||

This situation prevails, philanthropist to improve it;
Our village on decline, not to happen this with consciousness. ||104||

Conduct is to restrain, diet to control;
Celibacy to follow strictly, regularly. ||105||

All cause for pleasure and utility, celibacy, knowledge of religion;
As thus, request for audiences not to neglect it. ||106||

If this followed, offspring will be stout;
Hygiene of village will improve, Tukdya says. ||107||

Such *Sri Gramgeeta* book; *Guru*-discipline-self-experience-accepted;
Religion, celibacy narrated here; the Second Canto completed. ||108||

Notes

1. *Upanayan sanskar*—Religious ritual for spiritual birth from *Guru* here.
2. *Jnanyog*—Knowledge-oriented yogic practice.
3. *Sher*—An ancient measurement of weight.
4. *Tola*—An ancient measurement of weight.
5. *Satar*—The Indian string instrument.

Canto III

Ashram Religion

An audience asked the question, celibacy *ashram* narrated;
Religion, the base of life, progress stressed. ||1||

Doubt raised, is it feasible to be celibate for all?
Then whom to perform the worldly activities? ||2||

Answer is simple, who does operate world?
Endless are our worries; says, what will happen of world? ||3||

Oh! why to puzzle for? leave it to Creator;
You practice the discipline of celibacy if possible. ||4||

Be honest to discipline but alleviates collapse;
Sensual distracts attention but maintain home religion. ||5||

Semen to be stored for the twenty-four years;
Will it hamper the functioning of family? ||6||

As a boy attains maturity, turns into vagabond;
Vigour of youth experiences when an adolescent but sorrow later. ||7||

Such skeletal figure, feeble, sinful one;
How can family be happy for ever? ||8||

Such life means sin, such family a trouble;
His offspring means a curse for society. ||9||

World to be happy, elevation of ours to be;
So, the gift of celibacy to be accepted well. ||10||

Not to hinder family life, not to discontinue public life;
By means of celibacy *grihastha ashrama*[1] to follow. ||11||

Bearing in mind laws of nature, *grihastha ashrama* formulated;
By it, individual, village, nation function in an efficient way. ||12||

Disorder in body organs difficult to grapple;
Not to be at loss, better to adopt this mode. ||13||

Marriage indispensable, without which nothing;
Insistence on this is futile indeed. ||14||

One who can control passion, perform righteous work;
It is not binding for him to wed. ||15||

But, more fear for a person, stoic;
Dedication for service not easy as it seems. ||16||

As deaf studies *Vedas*[2], lame climbs a mountain;
Practice of celibacy, a battle fought by blind. ||17||

Difficult it is as it fights against nature;
As thus, its royal kingly path narrated in religion. ||18||

A son learnt theology, became virtuous by study;
Youthful vigour attained by physical exercise. ||19||

Luminant becomes body by an arduous celibacy;
Wedding indispensable in natural course. ||20||

If wedding delays, an illicit relation may develop;
Parents anxious once, son grows adult. ||21||

Marriage *sanskar* apt to forget childhood;
Makes it responsible to know family life. ||22||

What is religion of family holder? which conduct? what essence?
How to work? *Grihastha ashrama* teaches these. ||23||

Uptil now a celibate but today shoulders responsibility;
One has to look after home once tied nuptial knot. ||24||

Education left behind, next to concentrate on work;
So be alert soon, says experienced one. ||25||

With knowledge's wealth, course of life to enlighten;
Conscious to be for implementing religion in family. ||26||

Individual develops family if nature coordinates;
Increases responsibility on one's shoulder. ||27||

To work for welfare of family members;
Marriage *sanskar* imposes bindings of social religion. ||28||

Monogamy to follow, not to see with an evil eye;
It is to learn with firm determination. ||29||

Stigma on family if something uneven happens;
A nuisance is born, other will comment. ||30||

Pious ways applicable for this course;
What saints direct to implement fully. ||31||

Passion not to ignite while glancing at woman in private, public;
Life precious not to spoil adopting evil steps. ||32||

A single wife, an apt in *grihastha ashrama;*
Such person to treat as a celibate. ||33||

Sensual when needful though in *grihastha ashrama;*
He to deem as a celibate too. ||34||

Couple to restrain, intercourse not without cause;
Otherwise both to follow their norms. ||35||

Semen to utilise for productive purpose;
One who practices this is disciplined indeed. ||36||

Oh! though wedded, the slave to passion not told;
Provides it to live with life associated by marriage. ||37||

Wife, not to enhance but to restrain exoticness;
Wealth to be earned for overcoming attachment. ||38||

Once life force concentrated, fame glitters;
The buds of good deeds to blossom. ||39||

Happiness for parents, brothers, sisters, and others;
Magnetises others this mode of behaviour. ||40||

Speech, open, tender; conduct with character;
For life glorious following elders. ||41||

Saints, sages, narrate knowledge, it is to study;
Sage's debt will be paid by performing so. ||42||

Ideal to be an offspring, debt of parents will be paid;
Their names to honour by serving nation. ||43||

World to be served believing God in it;
Share to be for animals, a pious practice; ||44||

God's debt will be paid, in *grihastha ashrama* all lives;
Content wretched, gloomy people with sense of service. ||45||

An apt family, service, being service, village service;
Treasure of meditation to practice for all time. ||46||

If one follows these, important becomes *grihastha ashrama;*
Such mode of it appreciated by saints. ||47||

Restrain, the basic tenet of any *ashrama;*
An ascending order of progress of sacrifice. ||48||

Offspring born, sensual pleasure fulfilled;
Sanskar of sacrifice roots deep later. ||49||

An attachment directs to cater needs of kids;
Offspring to be contented, desires father. ||50||

Whatever he likes, he preserves for others;
Trouble for happiness of others, religion in family. ||51||

Son's virtues, fame are glory of family;
If he becomes vagabond, a blot on family. ||52||

One has to experience trouble to be speculative;
If situation creates, he combats with valour. ||53||

But, no injustice to others for sake of our son;
Other's offspring are as our beings. ||54||

One has to work for all with magnanimity of heart;
Principle this to be learnt in *grihastha ashrama.* ||55||

Kindness for offspring as well as for maids;
No discrimination, it's a religion in family. ||56||

Offspring educated in course, the second born;
Curtailing family after the birth of offspring. ||57||

Many pains to experience if it is not;
Vanprastha ashrama[3] suggested in religion *sanskar.* ||58||

If one follows this, appropriate to call him man;
Those slave to senses are donkey, hare, monkey. ||59||

I have seen, one has married the fourteen times;
Sixty offspring born, stayed at farm. ||60||

A wife on each farm, drives away sparrows;
Wedding means monopoly of these savages. ||61||

This force of life, what a hope from family;
Life turns fiasco, an output of lust. ||62||

Some keeps two, three women; spoil other's lives;
Beastly instinct it is, not *grihastha ashrama*. ||63||

Male has right of polygamy; why not to females?
This thought indeed to drag down for both. ||64||

Prevailed practice to have ten husbands to a woman;
What hell does she experience? She knows only. ||65||

It, ramification of ignorance, complicates with time;
As thus, evil this to be restrained in time. ||66||

Once married with one, no language for second;
Both experience peace, bliss in family life. ||67||

Family, itself incomplete, contentment not in sensual;
Presuming this reality, happiness to experience. ||68||

Both minds to unite, heaven exists there;
Offspring, an ideal renders service to nation. ||69||

An audience said married one must have offspring;
But, a woman was sterile, so marriage twice. ||70||

We disdain it, but how debt can be paid;
Of nation and father, if one has no offspring? ||71||

Once married, but offspring doesn't born;
To others, it a sign for degradation. ||72||

Pay heed; this presumption, insane indeed;
One experiences bliss of freedom by knowledge. ||73||

Having no offspring, *sanyasi*[4], celibate many;
Saint excelled, many beast men drowned. ||74||

Degradation for those without offspring, says some writers;
But, different was connotation of their words. ||75||

In India once, became many *sansyasi;*
No significance given to matrimonial ceremony. ||76||

Many were inclined to do penance;
So, restriction was imposed by writers. ||77||

Offspring to elevate family, otherwise better to be sterile;
This thought stressed with determination in the books. ||78||

Extract reveals, from this, family is for society;
A person who strives, elevates without offspring. ||79||

Strategy for social upliftment not to be halted;
Offspring reliable, complimentary to this though hazardous. ||80||

Oneself knows good, evil; offspring, brothers don't save;
Insists books on this, not to neglect. ||81||

Though no son, others are ours;
Elevated one is if benefactor to all. ||82||

Though money meant for son to be donated for welfare;
No second thought to interfere for righteous action. ||83||

Our home is not ours, universe is our home fine;
Family structure to account this; upliftment by this mean. ||84||

Both have to reflect knowing distances prevailing;
To be practical and speculative though no offspring. ||85||

Deeming son responsible, mind to withdraw from home;
Though no son, journey to begin sacrificing to village. ||86||

Accompanying wife, companion in religions, financial, sensual;
If doesn't respond at renunciation, better to live with son. ||87||

Though wife favours, not to succumb to sensual;
Both have to instill sacrifice, with determination. ||88||

Duties in families over, *vanaprashta* to follow;
Lessons for penance, good behavior to practice. ||89||

Spacious places, temples, forests, saints' *ashramas* to see;
For detachment of mind and body, concentration on work. ||90||

Dedication is serve, spirituality to experience;
Others are to teach, to know worth of service. ||91||

Initiation for service to wipe out desolation in village;
Tireless work with joy in heart for all. ||92||

Institutes of education, *ashrama*, righteous contact, transcendental;
Are to organise entirely for peace. ||93||

Blind, lame, leprosy patient, orphan, old, everywhere;
Ashrama to open for rendering service to them. ||94||

Time for family holder, so concentration on *vanprastha;*
Offspring to look after maintaining celibacy. ||95||

Education of life to transmit for better workers;
Knowledge for all round development to impart in *ashrama.* ||96||

This to perform by *vanprastha*, breaking chords of home;
To behave with detachment for service of all. ||97||

Once sensual appeal is over, detachment springs up;
Understand, this work to perform; education to be given to all. ||98||

Village service is nation service, nation service divine service;
To know this entirely, *vanprastha ashrama* is. ||99||

Third, *vanprastha ashrama*, action line of renunciation;
To control rein of sensual, operated by mind. ||100||

Sannyasa ashrama ahead to break illusion of *vanprastha ashrama;*
Intuition to experience, tendency to change. ||101||

When mind frees from home, renders service to all;
With renunciation one attains transcendental subsequently. ||102||

Sanyasi teaches *vanprastha* what *sthitpradhynas*[5] is;
After cessation of pulse, no attachment prevails. ||103||

Sacrifice in *vanprastha ashrama, yoga* in *sannyasa ashrama;*
Rasa tasted once, nuances of attachment break. ||104||

Realised self, transcendental; life absolute only;
Belief in One unflickers, in forms visible. ||105||

Detachment percolated, freeness from life bondage;
When ingrained in life, full success inevitable. ||106||

He, an inspirator to all; a torch bearer without selfishness;
Render life vision total for entire world. ||107||

Aim this of truth, religion; outcome of all actions;
Extract this sole of this book, Tukadya says. ||108||

Such *Sri Gramgeeta* book, *Guru*-discipline-self-experience-accepted;
Three *ashramas* narrated here; the Third Canto completed. ||109||

Notes

1. *Grihastha ashrama*—The phase of life dedicated to family life.
2. *Vedas*—The ancient Indian scripts: *Rigveda, Samaveda, Atharvaveda*, and *Yajurveda*.
3. *Vanprastha ashrama*—The phase of life in the seclusion of forest.
4. *Sanyasi*—One who renounced the material world.
5. *Sthitpradnya*—The detached state of mind.

Canto IV

Family and Transcendental

Earlier seen the explanation of the four *ashramas;*
Principle in it is perpetual for all. ||1||

If implemented, directs society well;
Attains individual progress, spiritual practice by all. ||2||

Total individual flourish, social situation best;
Everything achieved by *ashrama* in present too. ||3||

Celibacy to follow when an adolescent learning in *guru's* home;
Offspring are to look after marriage. ||4||

Celibacy in religious terrain, family for economic management;
Control of passion in *vanprastha* to free. ||5||

To be detached if offspring are channelled;
Home is to leave for rendering service. ||6||

Service of village, knowledge with tendency of *vanprastha;*
And sense of renunciation for achieving salvation. ||7||

Renunciation bound to be, no salvation without it;
No alternative left other than salvation. ||8||

Sensuality is the world, an attachment is real family;
To go beyond by knowledge is only salvation. ||9||

Destruction of sensuality, its name is renunciation;
Then it is to depoison among ideal people. ||10||

Free from sensuality, no fascination for bondage;
Merges realising nature of self entirely. ||11||

This, being ultimate assumption of world to work purely;
Lies in this the penance for elevation. ||12||

His work turns *yoga*, for those who comprehend this stance;
Condition this of *sanyas* to attain by all. ||13||

The fourth *ashrama*, an oldness, though it is contention;
But, no bar of age for self-elevation. ||14||

Depend all on an attitude, an attitude to condition;
Outer initiation helpful, highlighted it in scriptures. ||15||

Imagined the four parts of life; from delight of senses to sacrifice;
Who does avail life of hundred years without ailment? ||16||

So not paying heed to initiation, the four principles of *ashrama;*
To implement in life in real sense, immediately. ||17||

But, when experienced renouncement, left home at that time;
This not to happen as an insane one. ||18||

Some leave home after renouncement for pilgrimage;
Life depends on others, begging door to door. ||19||

Recurs an anger, sensuality, experiencing sorrow, seeing honour;
These again cast spell of family on him. ||20||

For this to accept initiation for the progress of an apt life;
But, futile it is to pose the decorum of initiation. ||21||

My trust is on *sanskar* but needs its system;
Better to humiliate such initiation. ||22||

Let it be *ashrama* initiation, cult initiation, *guru* initiation;
Penance initiation or work initiation besides religion initiation.
||23||

Initiation moulds mind but requires it to work regular;
Fiasco it turns of initiation practitioner if not followed. ||24||

Initiation of *ekadashi*[1] taken but eats demanding to others;
Seeing such play, people mock treating him lunatic. ||25||

Initiation taken of penance but no ritual regular;
What management of *sanskar* is to operate there. ||26||

Initiation of celibacy taken but no attitude of patience;
Likewise reversal of *grihastha ashrama* happens. ||27||

Tendency to practice *ashrama* phase gone, decorum flourishes;
Which power initiation has without sticking to principle? ||28||

Left house with the motto of *vanaprastha*, started business outer;
Meaningless it is if *sanyasi* fights for honour. ||29||

Wear saffron clothes but lingers anger inside, outside;
Quarrels for a strip of cloth with host. ||30||

Accumulated demanding others, decorated luxuriously cottage;
Sanyasi called he, smearing vermilion; slave he is of the world. ||31||

Pride not left of cottage, love as of cat and dog;
No time for knowledge of Supreme, to tell, experience. ||32||

Which initiation is this? no service is there, no patience;
As animal searches pray, demands for luxury. ||33||

One has to follow regulations who has taken initiation;
Towards evil, action tendency not to tilt. ||34||

Better to live normal, providing justice, doing work;
Name, not be marred accepting any initiation. ||35||

Family life to live happily, it will help to others;
Essence of the four *ashramas* to implement. ||36||

Anxiety of family members and so initiation of renunciation;
Detachment it not, decorum of it, shrinking from duty. ||37||

Experienced a practitioner renouncement and left home;
Bathed in forest wearing a strip of cloth. ||38||

Everyday he bathed, kept cloth on tree to dry;
There a rat tears a strip of cloth. ||39||

Went to village for a strip of cloth, asked what to do?
A rat has become habitual to tear it off. ||40||

To nourish kitten, suggestion was made;
Servants they will become to look after a strip. ||41||

Thought seriously about it, brought kitten;
Created it anxiety to provide food to them. ||42||

People said to domesticate cow but it means care;
Curd, milk, butter, nutrient, we will avail. ||43||

Accepted it too, demanding people, collected cows;
Next trouble in his mind to get fodder. ||44||

Begged for fodder, grass, people sighed;
In addition land is to cultivate on small scale. ||45||

Anticipated it also, procured land lavishly;
Operated labourers to fulfill his expectation. ||46||

Concentrated on it, accumulated money, grains;
Question crept up, how to secure them? ||47||

Who will be an honest, not an idle or a thief?
How to search who will treat work as his own? ||48||

People said, who will decide? Better to marry;
Settlement it will provide to secure money and mind. ||49||

Detachment he lost and recurred the bondage of family;
Sanskar not changed before, a core cause. ||50||

So for detachment, no trouble to leave home;
Needs it brain unbiased, attitude to serve, sacrifice. ||51||

If home is to leave, treat village as home;
Work for entire village deeming as national service. ||52||

In mind, urge for Supreme, strive for village whole;
No food taken without return by one who renounced. ||53||

Wanderer or *sanyasi,* no outer sacrifice for him;
Sense of sacrifice attains detachment in family. ||54||

Detachment means no bondage, no accumulation, no luxury;
Fire of action to lit to serve village. ||55||

In mind other children are to mould as ours;
Penance undertaken to bring up, detached only he is. ||56||

Though torn cloth on one's body but aims for village welfare;
Works spirited to attain it with robust vigour ||57||

Detached he is, who sacrifices whatever lures;
Labours he ever for the service of people. ||58||

Become many self-reliant, provides money donar to other;
Who devotes everything is detached indeed. ||59||

Such *sanyas* to seek by all, first care for one's family;
Once a fruit is ripe, society is to make happy. ||60||

Some give *sanyas* to children, tender they are;
When grow up, commit sin as their will. ||61||

When self accepted *sanyas,* then marriage not to be;
Look for diverse means, nuisance to village. ||62||

Sanyasi so called sounds to be trouble;
Why has society to tolerate such rubbish? ||63||

So improper it, no *sanyas* in real sense;
Vanaprastha, form of *sanyas,* no harm to children. ||64||

Sanyas, the phase of exhaustion, the time for meditation;
Their blessings are to be for all people. ||65||

One who didn't labour, no experience of family life;
How can he be *sanyasi*? wonder it is! ||66||

When direction this lost, village to village face problems;
Those in *grihastha ashrama* all beg for food. ||67||

Some lure children and make them *sanyasi;*
In society, they wonder as fleshy cats in masses. ||68||

No respect for service, no practical knowledge;
Behave and work as their whim operates. ||69||

It is change, no imposition on children;
Study prior is to be for better tomorrow. ||70||

Some have *sanskar* more, some have rich experience;
What to be and not to be, decisions are theirs. ||71||

No bar for them but not formula it is for all;
It will break continual flow of qualities best. ||72||

Realised it by saints and, thus, urged for all;
Not to abandon family for spiritual practice. ||73||

Live in family happily, honour for guests;
Construct simple, mansion, home; earn money by the best transaction. ||74||

Cultivate detachment, serving, helping others;
Immerse oneself in devotion, this royal road by saints. ||75||

Uttered they so and behaved likewise many;
Immortal they became in their areas. ||76||

This to realise, *grihastha ashrama* to bright;
Service for humanity adopting principals of detachment. ||77||

Accompanying wife, both to render service;
This, sign of renunciation, to free from bondage. ||78||

Real *sanyas* in this, otherwise only trouble;
Salvation not of self, not of others, an attached one. ||79||

One indifferent goes to forest, becomes *sanyasi;*
He too, not of any favour for social progress. ||80||

Not understood *grihastha ashrama* and acted as his will;
Whim directed, disrupted actions in society. ||81||

Provided *Geeta* knowledge but people didn't pay heed;
Succumbed to customs and forgot other beings. ||82||

Celibate studies only wonders in woods in *vanprastha;*
Being detached, *sanyasi* treats the world as untouched. ||83||

It, a strategy today, increased load on *grihastha ashrama;*
Everyone has left everyone's task solely. ||84||

Truth, left by everyone, but family person retains it;
Strives hard he and experiences trouble. ||85||

Helpful to everyone but accepts humbleness;
In spite of it, *sanyasi* uttered, "leave the world transient". ||86||

With tolerance, he cares for others in the world forgetting desires;
Retain the dignity of the world providing respect, money. ||87||

One has to labour, self dependent one to be;
Contribution more and more for village to be. ||88||

When saint, king and poor, downtrodden come;
Guest, hungry arrive, *grihastha ashrama* for all. ||89||

Honours for saints, sages; one who come;
With love he bears weight of public work. ||90||

If penalty, pertains to caste, rule he faces it;
Cosmos including ants are dear to him. ||91||

Looks after children, practices *grihastha ashrama;*
Donate food politely, curtailing expenses luxurious. ||92||

Responsibility to care for wife, children, in *grihastha ashrama*;
Tendency to cultivate love for family and nation. ||93||

Ashramas are manifold but focal is *grihastha ashrama;*
On it depends prospects of other *ashramas.* ||94||

Learning and practice of celibacy, waiting for *vanaprastha;*
Criticism of *sanyasi,* knowledgeable in *grihastha ashrama.* ||95||

People say worthless it is though they live in;
How is this mode of family life operable? ||96||

As thus, saint treated *grihastha* as respectable, worthy;
Became father and mother, nourishing others. ||97||

Not refundable their work, only remedy is left;
To guide and educate their sons to settle. ||98||

Children to be taken to *ashrama* as Vishwamitra[2] took Rama, Laxmana;
As Sandipini[3], Drona[4] taught, varied knowledge to impart. ||99||

Village to upgrade, not to come only for food;
If ego swells, passage to hell opens wide. ||100||

Till body remains healthy, needs clothes, food;
World is not meaningless; service is for others. ||101||

Not to be arrogant being *guru*, service to others as self;
Like mother, ignorant people are to teach. ||102||

Everyone has to work, complementary to others;
So as to make load of life bearable, light. ||103||

Children to be taught in *ashrama*, family member to help;
When they grow up, permission to seek by father. ||104||

Travel far or be active in rural progress;
After becoming *sanyasi* too, service to others. ||105||

One has to fill one's belly besides more work;
Means it no reliance on family member. ||106||

One's work, to perform by one, satisfy beings;
None has to depend on others. ||107||

In time to come, service to be for others;
Whatever is left, to be donated to village. ||108||

What service one gives performing one's work;
Depends on it significance of life in the world. ||109||

Tradition it is, which operates how the world to be;
Equal distribution of different works to be. ||110||

Everyone will avail work, no superior or inferior;
The world to beautify as per one's strength. ||111||

Thankful to all, conduct complementary to others;
Be *sanyasi* or family member, rights same to all. ||112||

Family member labours, *sanyasi* points at direction apt;
Is it without substance, former touches latter's feet? ||113||

Can't understand I, whose role has priority?
Everyone in everyone's place is worthy. ||114||

In son's religion son and in father's father are focal;
How can one be higher or lower? ||115||

Kneel down when one misses one's duty;
Otherwise love operable between them. ||116||

Not to look down other, disdainful it is to Supreme;
Faithful woman, greater than egoistic *sanyasi.* ||117||

One has to respect others behaving politely;
No ego centric, extract of *ashrama dharma.* ||118||

No inferior complex, work to perform with conviction;
Helping hand to our village for cooperation. ||119||

Being in *grihastha ashrama* follow the religion of rural service;
Decision to implement for only rural service. ||120||

Earning with labour and its utilisation for righteous work;
Not to earn with futility, succumbing to anyone. ||121||

In villages, religious discourse to be for education;
To enhance the respect of *grihastha ashrama* for order. ||122||

Living in family life, knowledge for transcendental to seek;
Coordination this as saint directed, is rural religion real. ||123||

The essence of family life, a store house of cooperation;
Let we, all enlight splendidly rural religion. ||124||

Rural religion, the major role of *grihastha ashrama*;
Pious water of mega pilgrim place, Tukadya says. ||125||

Such *Sri Gramgeeta* book; *Guru*-discipline-self-experience-accepted;
Narrated transcendental in family; the Fourth Canto completed. ||126||

Notes

1. *Ekadashi*—A pious day in Marathi month, *ashad.*
2. Vishwamitra—The sage in the epic, *Ramayana.*
3. Sandipani—The ancient sage in the age of Krishna.
4. Drona—The ancient *Guru*, the teacher.

Canto V

Varna System

In order to attain *purusharth*[1], follow human religion;
Narrated four *ashramas*, its core *grihastha ashrama*. ||1||

Society in *grihastha ashrama* more, needs different;
In nature too, people differ from one another. ||2||

Though seems same human beings with hands, legs, eyes, ears;
Diversities in characters obvious to viewers. ||3||

Quality of nature changes, thought lines vary;
Sanskar plays its roles to mould it. ||4||

One calm, other angry; one vagrant, other focused;
Some select all those qualities together. ||5||

How can one say, man is same? No similarity in rights too;
As per nature, changes also life style. ||6||

Varied attitudes, varied natures, varied families, varied preference;
Clash with each other, having no knowledge. ||7||

Parallel in nature selected, character diagnosed;
Calm, angry, good natured, trends diverse. ||8||

Three types of nature, include all living beings;
Though vary in feature, in this living world. ||9||

One behaves as quality ingrained in nature;
Everyone's work vary from one another. ||10||

If one deviates from other, how can society be healthy?
How can be progress of an individual and society? ||11||

Religious thinkers thought and considered qualities;
Made everyone complimentary in social system. ||12||

Good natured, calm, mixed, and angry;
Accounting all these, the four sections formulated. ||13||

Structure based on nature, so calls God's plan;
Imagined of arms, body, legs of society man. ||14||

Basically all equal but numerous traits pervade;
One quality nourishes other, human world this is. ||15||

Vary profession with qualities but main four distributions;
As thus, *chaturvarna*[2] called they by sages. ||16||

Kshatriya provides protection, *vaisya* business;
For justice, planning, *brahmin* nominated. ||17||

One, not confined to these, *shudra* he is;
Serves for others and complementary to others. ||18||

Truth, justice, patience, rules applicable to everyone;
But, worship society by performing one's work. ||19||

One having better quality continues his life;
Nourishes also to society, planning of *chaturvarna*. ||20||

Harmonious blend of qualities varied, constructive for all;
How will be life battle? no class conflict. ||21||

Natural variation pervades in all time, all nations;
For peace of the world, the planning of *varna ashrama*. ||22||

But, these are kept aside, attached one became;
Though son behaved like shudra, his *varna* unchanged. ||23||

Not paid heed to quality but birth decided *varna;*
Profession gave birth to caste in society. ||24||

Those learned planned to create quality from work;
Sanskar shaped them to confine *varna* after birth. ||25||

Sanskar was for it, education taught to deal;
The sages in past, tactful, were enough to run social system. ||26||

Family was made institution, teaching since childhood;
Tradition formulated for assigning quality by efforts. ||27||

Farm for farmer, sword for *kshatriya;*
Weighing pan for *vaisya* from childhood. ||28||

Chanting of *mantra* for *brahmin* was taught automatically;
Likewise scope of tradition grew day by day. ||29||

Profession performed by one turned to be nature;
Which became *sanskar* in life too. ||30||

Sanskar moulds their nature, playing, speaking, eating;
Becomes inseparable it with *sanskar.* ||31||

Tradition this discontinued, divided by power, greed;
Discrimination increased to avail power. ||32||

Some calamity, some company, some power, some nature;
Other's business taken in hand for happiness. ||33||

Accepts one the profession of *vaisya*, the business for more interest;
Has not spared his friend too for profit. ||34||

Conscience not operated, focused eyes on profit;
Who is interested in welfare? Impurify good. ||35||

Speak lie naturally; sin, the result of selfishness;
Who will look after this when power not conscious. ||36||

If anyone points at him, rivalry intensifies;
The both business lines fine, moving on same line. ||37||

Villagers oppose and say "why have they to suffer?"
But, they too become lethargic, resisting *vaisya.* ||38||

Chaos everywhere, to be controlled it by *kshatriya;*
But, they too run vagrantly to fill belly. ||39||

Wherever money, respect, *kshatriya* attaracts to;
Who to care for justice, moral? influences money. ||40||

Thieves run after thieves, in the garb of policemen;
Facilitated it to thieves to rob in village. ||41||

Brahmins to provide justice, to engage others in service;
But, they too lured by gifts and respect. ||42||

Then it became norm, *kshatriya* means a threat.
A businessman a robber, people call him *vaisya*. ||43||

Who learnt to divide by intellect, becomes *brahmin;*
Disordered this way *varna* system in village to village. ||44||

Who turned feeble, was expelled as *shudra;*
Hand to mouth he became, condition deteriorated. ||45||

No heed to qualities in *varna*, caste; collapsed system;
Motto basic to *varna* system disrupted. ||46||

Pride of *varna* persisted, qualities crushed;
Sanskar moulded in these ways, setting difficult. ||47||

Earlier scene different, professions complimentary to each other;
Everyone's welfare was in them, no discrimination. ||48||

But, *varna ashrama* in practice proved to be an illusion;
Most of people left their work in *varna ashrama*. ||49||

Brahmin stitches shoes, becomes cobbler a worshipper;
Kshatriya, a service person in the house of *vaisya*. ||50||

Vaisya fights in army; *shudra* performs *katha*, *kirtana;*
Hybridisation of *varna,* says people to this. ||51||

But, caste creeps up though works are different;
Uncertainty it creates, confusing people. ||52||

Father's profession different, not possessed by son;
Not meaningful when son tells his profession as his father's. ||53||

On the basis of work, *varna*, caste to be shaped;
Process it facilitates if one believes in *varna*, caste. ||54||

If this would have happened, people behaved likewise;
How could have one said, *varna* system distorted? ||55||

But, they hesitate to utter, do work reversely;
Lives inactively at the expense of ancestors. ||56||

Though deviated from work, treat oneself superior;
For such status hollow, trends are set up. ||57||

In reality, *varna* for distribution of work, in society all include;
As thus, from *brahmin* to downtrodden all valuable. ||58||

Deeming one higher and other lower, walls increased;
Declination began of *varna* and village both. ||59||

Each profession needs skills diverse, potentials vary;
Different criteria for conduct among them. ||60||

Created ignorance cleavages, higher became who held power;
Base treated by other, acted to purify society. ||61||

Baseness because of evil nature, real elevation by penance;
How can caste, birth a decide higher or lower? ||62||

One who committed sin was punished;
As thus, untouchability crept up for some reasons. ||63||

But, to treat his entire generation, to hide one's baseness;
Not to appreciate other's good, tradition prevailed. ||64||

Oh! Is this justice? It is a symptom of slavery;
How can be reformation of our villages? ||65||

Untouchability is to base on action, species to be one;
Everyone has to perform everyone's share of work. ||66||

Species of all is one but profession differs as qualities of action;
On the basis of nature of work, an identity is to render. ||67||

Otherwise everywhere all *varna*, all qualities everywhere;
But, prime qualities are to be recognised. ||68||

Well behaved born in *shudra's* home; how can he be *shudra*?
Corrupt, born in *kshatriya's* home; how can he be *kshartriya*? ||69||

In a shop, a *brahmin* sat, started selling meat, fishes;
To worship him one goes, is it pertinent? ||70||

Treating oneself *brahmin* avails luxury, addicts to many;
Joins employment, lends money, how can he be *brahmin*? ||71||

To renounce home as tradition and then to tie nuptial knot;
How shameful it is among people? ||72||

Acharya[3] and cook, confine to same caste;
Are they to be respected in the same vein? ||73||

To call *brahmin* to anyone and kneel to respect;
Why not to serve in cobler's shop to clean feet? ||74||

Should avoid self worship, really; those who *brahmin* at core;
To honour all with sense of humanity. ||75||

Working in diverse professions; all are friends, equally;
What is the relevance of the decorum of worship? ||76||

People are to teach to improve whatever is wrong;
As oneself people are to make industrious. ||77||

He is to called *brahmin* where the qualities of *brahmin* are;
In *varna ashrama* such rule, founded from an ancient time. ||78||

So insistence to be on qualities, confine to *varna* on qualities;
Respect for all qualities by nature for all to be. ||79||

Becomes authority of *varna* as he works;
Such rule in practice everywhere to create order. ||80||

Here doubt creeps up, one performs different works;
Then time to time can we call him as *brahmin, kshatriya*? ||81||

Though *vaisya*, but by work meditates in temple;
How can he be *vaisya* at his place? ||82||

One sweeps but prays in temple, occasionally;
On which ground can one treats him as sweeper? ||83||

At that instance he is *brahmin* real, though routine work differs;
As thus, nomenclature at core pertains to one's profession. ||84||

One's focus on business but performs *kirtan* fine;
Is it justifiable to call him *brahmin* by profession? ||85||

Cultivates righteous *brahmin* a land, so deem him a farmer?
This will create time to time, the situation disordered. ||86||

An actor sometime becomes a king; hence does he rule kingdom?
One's art, one's potential; otherwise what is other glory? ||87||

In this, an approach is to know inner inclination;
Reveals a special work, a decisive direction of his life. ||88||

Depending on his special work, quality, area;
Aspect, inner reality, then nomenclature is to be. ||89||

Where his body, mind everything involve;
On such focal qualities, confine him to that *varna*. ||90||

Significance is not to say whatever one's essence;
Prevails in society, it is to honour. ||91||

Action is to structure society well with an appreciation;
Of quality and action, an initiation to seek treating it right. ||92||

Expert has to study principles, their transformation to bring into practice;
Order to set in the dismantled scenario of society. ||93||

To make happy *grihastha ashram*; to cease life's combat;
To live village cooperatively, let an intellect to all. ||94||

An intellect dwarfs when quality clashes with quality;
The function to control, *brahamnya*[4] it is. ||95||

Assistance of quality to quality for successful work;
Regulation of nature's order confines to *brahamnya*. ||96||

To create unity, today needs *brahmin* quality;
Without *brahamnya* impossible it is to happen. ||97||

Learning of collective intellect, equality in all beings;
To tackle odd tendencies, the action of *brahmin*. ||98||

Foresight *brahmin* has, in his home society;
Pains he to set right the fragmentation. ||99||

A pure heart he has, a killer of a wicked mind;
Without violence purifies he the evil mind. ||100||

A donor of power and trick; support for devotion, freedom;
Uplifts the world by all means; decks it he. ||101||

Coordinates he all, treats village service significant;
Never lacks anytime by any mean. ||102||

Focus never flickers, sets whatever disturbs;
Skill for co-working, knows *brahmin*. ||103||

All to coordinate with all; village to infuse with fame, inspiration;
Not to deprive of material and transcendental, villagers. ||104||

Village to make tactful, *sanskar* pure to instill;
Cooperation among all to regulate with justice and morality. ||105||

To teach this, the stories of great ones to tell to alleviate sorrow;
Pointing at their apt, customs to nourish sacrifice. ||106||

The stories of Krishna, Rama's birth, the birth anniversaries of great ones;
Fight for justice in books to teach to be fearless. ||107||

Telling duties of all, inspiring them to work;
By vast means of *brahamnya,* village to harmonise. ||108||

Though *brahmin* in village, rift, quarrel prevail;
Deems it his deterioration, wanton village has become. ||109||

He has left his integrity, so people neglected;
Why has not turned the voice of people towards him? ||110||

When *brahmin* on wrong track, rainless village has become;
Flourished different disgraceful acts in villages. ||111||

What has caused for the change in people' beliefs?
One who has understood this, pure, renounced, an ascetic. ||112||

To experience this influence, an initiation of sacrifice, control;
Hence, needs it penance, to be practiced by *brahman.* ||113||

Sharpness and brightness need to convince old one;
So *brahmin* to chant penance and memorise the righteous books. ||114||

Not to be angry while advising, greedy to change decision;
To control senses, spiritual remedy functions. ||115||

The first he has to sacrifice, then people to teach;
Impact among people to see by this mean. ||116||

One who initiated this, has diminished his sensuality;
Nomenclature of *brahmin* received from the *varna ashrama.* ||117||

One who fails to follow this, yet honoured as *brahmin;*
But, worthless degree it is, functionless. ||118||

To honour an exterior is an offering gold leaf on *Dashera;*
Whose sorrow is alleviated by eating *rui*[5] fruit? ||119||

Brahmin is not caste, it is honour of vastness;
Assuming this, villagers have to perform. ||120||

Experiencing *brahma*, God everywhere, ready to serve;
Such brahmin casts his influence on all of lenience. ||121||

Seeing his character bright, elders showers love;
To everyone he tells the religion of human enlightenment. ||122||

Brahmin confined to untouchables, *kshatriya, vaishya;*
Not alien, his word to anyone. ||123||

He has to think for welfare of all, cement people;
Village to operate with contentment by imparting intellect. ||124||

Unnecessary people don't listen, they are to punish;
But, bad rituals not to allow to function in village. ||125||

Can't survive in cosmos who doesn't listen *brahmin;*
He doesn't perform wrong, the core reason it is. ||126||

His focal motto is peace for all including *shudra;*
An ascetic seeks happiness in villager's happiness. ||127||

So, *brahmin* is rated as the best, mere drum beating it not;
God, mine who receives the kick from Bhrugu[6]. ||128||

Such quality of *brahman* to create, propagate everywhere;
Then everyone will experience the shelter of happiness and peace. ||129||

Quality this of *brahmin* not confines to any caste, anyone to cultivate it;
One who is an ideal, is *brahmin* indeed. ||130||

The quality of *brahman*, righteous intellect, to boost up other qualities;
Prosperity and utility will prevail with virtuous action. ||131||

Comprehension of *Harikatha*[7], politics, alertness, service;
Crux this of the four *varna* to practice by all. ||132||

Public education, protection of justice, nutrition, and manual work;
Whosoever will attempt for these, facilitates *varna ashrama.* ||133||

Work to perform by all as nature, village to embed with beauty;
Everyone to be elevated, Tukadya says. ||134||

Such *Sri Gramgeeta* book; Guru-discipline self-experience-accepted;
Narrated *varna* religion here; the Fifth Canto completed. ||135||

Notes

1. *Purushartha*—In ancient Indian script, the four *purushartha* are *Dharma* (righteousness, moral values), *Artha* (prosperity, economic values), *Kama* (pleasure, love, psychological values), and *Moksha* (liberation, spiritual values, self-actualisation).
2. *Chaturvarna*—Basically, it is distribution of work by profession, on the basis of quality variations; it is not division of labour.
3. *Acharya*—A learned one.
4. *Brahmnya*—A virtue of intellect.
5. *Rui*—A poisonous fruit.
6. Bhrugu—Lord Vishnu bears the mark of the kick of Bhrugu, the Brahmin sage.
7. *Harikatha*—Indian mythological tale of Shrikrishna.

Hyphotic Spell on People Quinate

Canto VI

Impact of Good Company

God created world and His work incomplete;
Given righteous intellect by man to complete it as one's stance. ||1||

Many from One and unity in diversity;
Basic conception, this inculcated in everyone's mind. ||2||

Natural desires, motives, cause for self development;
Manifests man through different forms of individuals. ||3||

Some continue disciples, some create books;
Natural desire to regulate tradition in the world. ||4||

On the earth man lived and flourished in society;
How is it justified, to forget to work for society? ||5||

Man, cosmos related and *sanskar* too with the world;
By self realisation let life be detached, not to disdain the world. ||6||

Let world be truthful, supreme, happy, and beautiful;
Duty important, allotted to man to perform. ||7||

Man has to elevate himself besides society;
So religion assigned to everyone to practice. ||8||

For this only incarnation, for this the drives of saints, devotees;
"Let all world be happy", the motto of their lives. ||9||

If not entire world, our village to upgrade;
The treasure of salvation this will, satisfying almighty. ||10||

No wrong with these; but what is our duty for villages?
No one listens in village; how can we work? ||11||

Everyone works for oneself, wife and offspring, luxury;
But, forgets to work for others to do something. ||12||

Everyone feels, other should listen, but not how?
One doesn't desire to go forward due to this. ||13||

Many to perform but depression if no one accompanies;
Who will face calamity? feel many. ||14||

What to do though we intend to upgrade village?
How can masses be turned to right road? ||15||

I will answer aptly for the question asked;
But, imprinting it on heart, one to behave. ||16||

Saints have uttered same, not only me;
Whatever I trust I will unfold before you. ||17||

One has to be firm, masses are imitative;
Whatever is special, accept without reluctance. ||18||

Others observe the living of a core worker;
They follow his footsteps as a child. ||19||

The worker must have captivity, service, character bright;
Progress, not possible without them. ||20||

To enlighten masses, this formula to practice;
Masses behave as we behave with them. ||21||

Self purification necessary first, body purification, heart purification;
Home purification, village purification by all possible means. ||22||

People observe home thou has shaped;
Follow the same example in their homes. ||23||

One likes if one watches fascinating scenario;
Animal intends to imitate whatever observe. ||24||

In garden saw numerous flowers blossomed, with myriad colours;
Delicious fruits ripened, treasure of beauty. ||25||

Water flows in the beds of plants and flowers;
Pervades, joy prevails diversely of flowers, fruits. ||26||

Greenery under dark shadow, the network of grass leaflets;
Multicoloured butterflies, tender, cast spell on mind. ||27||

Somewhere glitter water as mirror, somewhere the design of stones;
Incline to lie on land wherever soft form. ||28||

The land of different colours, somewhere black, yellowish;
Somewhere white, red, golden sometimes. ||29||

Swing birds on creepers, witness of flowers, fruits;
Though fly in the sky, they know ripe fruits. ||30||

Leap on fruits to taste juice immeasurable;
Whatever one decides, experiences animal likewise. ||31||

Transfuses fragrance everywhere, sensory organs;
Nose, ear, tongue, eyes experience joy varied. ||32||

Whenever one sees, acts to replicate it;
Returns home to decorate one's house. ||33||

Develops garden in yard or plants in the earthen containers;
Embeds one's cottage as one imagines. ||34||

How would have he attempted if a garden he would haven't seen;
Principally, such a man acts as he observes. ||35||

Especially, a child's action echoes observation;
Whatever sees, a child imitates to act. ||36||

Whatever a core worker will work in village;
Children will behave at home, outside, convincing their parents. ||37||

One has domesticated hen and chicks were born;
Other followed the same, his practice. ||38||

Then everyone delighted, they intoxicated in village;
Inclined to monitor the cock fight in village. ||39||

Once cock fight observed, imitated villagers;
Then cock fair for arranging fight. ||40||

Tie knife to cock's legs, fight instigates swiftly;
Game with bloodshed, encouraged by a cruel tendency. ||41||

Told *patil*[1] to incur tax, increase production;
Motivated people in village to arrange the fight. ||42||

What wrong pathetic animal did? a mean for fight;
Lost their lives while fighting, increased the business of sin. ||43||

The chief has directed, other followed that practice;
Seniors too instrumental in organising the fight. ||44||

Concentrated energy on it, respected too succumbed;
As thus, one on one's accord created the place for exercise. ||45||

Children, youth assembled; spirited they became;
Interest created in them for physical exercise. ||46||

Wrestling was arranged first in village, giving away prizes;
Influenced by it, children inclined to exercise. ||47||

In homes, children wrestle; play in with vigour lane to lane;
Youngsters, elders intoxicated by exercise. ||48||

Gymnastic, *mallakhamb*[2], sticks, spear, *lezim*[3];
Sword, sharp belt, field work of exercise. ||49||

Evil practices in village eradicated consequently;
Developed passion to build body for younger, elders. ||50||

Sees everyone the physically built chest, hand;
Thigh, to enhance the beauty of a wrestler. ||51||

Continued open games, smeared a village with red soil;
Declined addiction to cock-fight, drowned into oblivion. ||52||

One triggered off an idea, fed plodder;
Arranged a contest to run with other pairs. ||53||

Attracted in people, a source of an entertainment;
Resulted into *shankarpat*[4] in village to village. ||54||

Purpose it has well, nutrients feed to oxen;
Increase an oxen's strength to work in farm. ||55||

But, setback it has, lags the best work;
Season to run oxen come untimely. ||56||

With sharp point pierces an oxen which run slowly;
Bleed their bodies and pain oxen. ||57||

Kept aside farm work, inclination towards *shankarpat;*
Perform people butcher's work in various ways. ||58||

Tie oxen to cart with ease, pierce them with a pointer;
Beat them cruelty though they don't run fast. ||59||

Fell pray a village to it, not to select good;
Flourishes devil work in village with the fire speed. ||60||

Continued it, *tamasha*[5], one has brought in village;
Drastically changed scenario, prevailing earlier. ||61||

Uttered everyone *lavani*[6] in home, farm, temple;
On everyone's tongue, song sensual all. ||62||

Became *tamasha* popular, received children *sanskar;*
Started parlour, boys, youth as *tamasha* performer. ||63||

Parts everyone hair, gestures with blushful face;
And body gestures, dance children at home. ||64||

Parents appreciate them and girls laugh with fun;
Beat same plates, wooden or metal with joy, like *duf*[7]. ||65||

But, no one pays heed; what will happen?
Drowned entire village in an entertainment by *tamasha*. ||66||

"Drown" *dolak* cries; *tuntune* asks, who? who?
Manjira[8] says "all people" but no one realises. ||67||

Then how can be story, *kirtan*[9], *bhajan*[10] or lecture by saint?
Start youth to mock at right intention. ||68||

Their children followed those who have brought *tamasha;*
Wandered village to village performing shows. ||69||

Difficult for girls to walk, boys tease them;
Increasing frequency of visit at home, trapped many. ||70||

Became *patil* aware of happenings around;
The wind of *tamasha* entered in his home too. ||71||

Brought his brother *tamasha* but ruined his family;
Ran away daughter; son left, drowning other's homes. ||72||

Then he asked others how to ban *tamasha*?
Many told, he himself caused disorder in village. ||73||

Wrestling, exercise made village beautiful, ideal, wonderful;
But, diverse hobbies these, instigated village to doom. ||74||

Fascinating was boys' sport, making of oxen better;
But, this sin caused desolation in village. ||75||

Now time for punishment, all boys play on pipe;
Tamasha everywhere in village with festive spirit. ||76||

Addicted to *tamasha*, one who enters in village;
Difficult has become for *patil* to resist all. ||77||

One favoured hobby, wandering, drinking liquor;
Experienced people zenith of joy in *tamasha*. ||78||

Continued custom, sequently drinkers assembled;
What to ask now about the pathos of village? ||79||

Some perform *dandhar*[11], *tamasha*, some speak vulgar;
No one respects others, young and elders. ||80||

Rush for illicit relation, play of cards for money;
Children started theft, production of liquor everywhere. ||81||

Rush for increased addiction to eat, no rest without it;
Rooted in village many diseases due to meat and liquor. ||82||

Boys part their hair, spit anywhere after chewing betel leaf;
Light cigar and exhales smokes, no fear of anyone. ||83||

Earn labour hard money, spends in liquor;
Children starve, deteriorates life day by day. ||84||

Woman is beaten in village after consuming liquor;
Intensified quarrels, courts' offices crowded. ||85||

Collapse riches also in drainage, anyone beats anyone;
No girls are secure, such happening frequent. ||86||

Money exhausted, village 'elevated' to this level;
Drunkard caused chaos in the entire village. ||87||

Village chief drank wine, others followed him;
Then the whole village tilted towards the drainage water. ||88||

Follows in playing cards, theft and illicit relation;
First, the village chief succumbs and then villagers. ||89||

People who are dwindled, had imitated someone;
So, other people followed the same footsteps. ||90||

First, he had behaved, then told others;
So, masses attracted towards him to imitate. ||91||

The conduct of village is known from workers;
We treat workers as the breath of village. ||92||

Village flourishes if the four behaves well;
Though so called chief selfish, entire village likewise. ||93||

Village, a pure mirror, reflects what it receives;
Our village performs whatever is seen outside. ||94||

What I spoke in beginning, delighted when saw garden;
Likewise, I behaved and it happens for everyone. ||95||

As thus, I request whatever ideal one prefers;
Its impact can be created and retained in our life. ||96||

Frail, one raises voice for donation of land;
The same wave is surged in village to village. ||97||

How many people ask for donation excluding pleasure, luxury?
Rich-poor forgetting selfishness, donate land with joy. ||98||

People follow in homes, whatever leaders behave;
On the shoulder of a leader, responsibility lies. ||99||

So what is to be done, it is to be planned;
Likewise one has to improve oneself. ||100||

One has to be alert to do whatever is good;
With foresight, a work is to be undertaken. ||101||

If done casually, purpose will be not attained;
Disorder in an entire village will prevail. ||102||

So, in village, a work is to commence to bring fame;
In the village's boundary, evil work is not to enter. ||103||

One has not to tolerate if anyone commits it;
With mature stance, the evil rituals to be uprooted. ||104||

Because one experiences as one's contact;
Hence, conscience to operate to nourish the best qualities. ||105||

The best sport, the best work, the best art, the best beauty;
Whatever will dignify a village, is to pick up. ||106||

If any addiction forays, it is to be eradicated;
Support of heads in village is to be consistent. ||107||

If disagreement prevails, offsprings dissatisfy;
Elders have to clarify them to understand. ||108||

The best remedy in all to change surrounding;
This new passion to nourish by workers. ||109||

Worker is he who has no greediness of any sort;
He has to treat his village as salvation. ||110||

Then village witnesses his ideal, entire village improves;
Village relies on the chief, Tukadya says. ||111||

Such *Sri Gramgeeta* book, *Guru*-discipline-self experience-accepted;
Narrated the essence of village life; the Sixth Canto completed. ||112||

Notes

1. *Patil*—An administrative head of village.
2. *Mallakhamb*—An erected, wooden pillar for physical exercise.
3. *Lazim*—Indian dance form in which the dancer has light musical instrument in both hands.
4. *Shankarpat*—In village, a competition of the running oxen with small wooden cart, *chhakara.*
5. *Tamasha*—The folk performance in Maharashtra with dramatic action, *chonka* (a string instrument), *dholki* (a small drum), in which a male performs a role of female character.
6. *Lavani*—The folk dance form in Maharashtra, which titillates viewers.
7. *Duf*—The round musical instrument with strings leather cover and tiny, round metal sheet on circumference.

8. *Manjira*—The two round bronze plates, when strike on each other, create music.
9. *Bhajan*—A devotional song sung in chorus.
10. *Kirtan*—Narrative presentation of religious theme, accompanied by musical instruments.
11. *Dandhar*—The folk drama form in Maharashtra.

Canto VII

Strength of Behaviour

A conscious person asks, we understand public ways;
Accept truth that chief, leaders elevate village. ||1||

But, they succumb and other create nuisance;
How can our voice outstand before their drums? ||2||

The Goddess of justice on thorne but caused injustice;
Tell, tell where is balanced system set up? ||3||

For good contact, *pandit*[1] is called but created chaos;
To whom wise is to be called, turned an idiot. ||4||

For freshness, singing is arranged but heard pathos;
Cried, insisted for more to fill one's belly. ||5||

To teach riding, called a rider but injured after fall;
How can others ride horses if they have to learn? ||6||

Looked for a servant deeming an honest but deceived;
Now on whom and by whom has one to trust? ||7||

To teach, invited a teacher but misbehaved he;
Situation prevails to educate teacher himself. ||8||

To provide medicine brought doctor but poisoned a patient;
Tell, tell, now who will treat with care? ||9||

Tell, what arrangement is to be made in our village?
To whom to call with confidence in such strife? ||10||

Collective responsibility whatever falls on shoulder;
With determination, it to follow without selfishness. ||41||

No one to hate or praise, an ideal conduct to operate;
With love, trust to behave with women, children, old ones all. ||42||

Words to value assigning importance to time;
Other's pleasure, sorrow, injury, welfare are to feel. ||43||

When people will notice this, others will treat as righteous;
Consequently, the glory of the work will enhance. ||44||

People will know thy behaviour inside, outer;
Other will start treating thee as an ideal. ||45||

Friend! People will experience pleasure in thy company;
They will experience joy to listen thee. ||46||

They will say to follow him what he directs;
Death they will embrace to keep their words. ||47||

Think first whether to take an initiative or not;
Decision is to be firm not to retrieve in dream too. ||48||

One who works for people has to keep aside shame;
One has to witness his self treating work as truth. ||49||

Reluctance to welfare, happiness of all;
Sinful it is to behave in this way. ||50||

Beginning is to be such to percolate in masses;
In heart and senses so as to reconcile. ||51||

Subsequently, to step experiencing contentment in work;
Answer to give to rivals with politeness. ||52||

People are to be taught to speak, speaking oneself better;
With love, sweetness to pour in words. ||53||

Not to speak so as to make other irritate;
Not to answer without listening fully to others. ||54||

Our speech with love, other's with an anger;
But, an attack to tolerate with patience. ||55||

Though anyone is angry, it is to face with smile;
In our own way, answer is to be given with peace. ||56||

In mind, doubt will creep up time to time;
Bearing this tediousness, one has to march. ||57||

Once determined, others will assist in venture;
Facilitates it, the process of operation. ||58||

Resolves everything in due course, assemble people;
One who has involvement, is to be selected. ||59||

Companionship is to be developed for winning confidence;
Work is to be assigned, as one performs. ||60||

With some persons, good work is to be initiated;
Then pious work of village service is to be carried out. ||61||

No other alternative to channelise our village;
To elevate village, treat this theory as chanting. ||62||

Listening my answer, a question was asked;
What will happen of village if more days require? ||63||

Means you have suggested, are difficult;
Who will practices *yamniyam, asana,* meditation all? ||64||

Time consuming it is, our organs will lose vigour;
Who will look after village whether good or evil? ||65||

Desire will be unfilled if one meets an end;
How can we predict who will carry out work? ||66||

Suggest any remedy which will set well;
Expenses whatever we will bear for it. ||67||

Friend! Listen, village to be beautiful without thou;
To trust in such desire, lunatic it is. ||68||

My village to be beautiful though I burger;
Discordant this seems to be your saying. ||69||

What is another option besides purity of an individual?
No other measure I perceive to restore village well. ||70||

Thou will say to improve by power, formulate rules;
Others will shoulder off; let selfish people as they are. ||71||

Who will listen this? Though spoke whole heartedly;
Masses will realise it, abusing us. ||72||

How can village be elevated if this permitted?
Futile if one forgets, individuals build village. ||73||

Show willingness to give money for public welfare;
But, still people deceive after giving money. ||74||

Say to deliver lecturers but people also learn lecture;
What will be outcome if man doesn't change? ||75||

At core, it requires heart, affliction towards service;
Without decorum, village will be paradise. ||76||

No time he has, improvement will be along with;
Initiating people to be taught, teaching one's mind. ||77||

Utter, utter an answer, are thou ready soon?
If no, don't waste out time otherwise. ||78||

With despair he spoke, though limit to desires;
What will remain for offspring? What benefit of mine? ||79||

What for this arduous task? let people continue;
What should we die experiencing sorrow? ||80||

Listening, I expressed, you are culprits;
Besides this seek our assistance to drown. ||81||

Village thou immersed, in spite of it dared to ask;
Received a blow in this way, entire village, nation. ||82||

I understood now, nation is trapped by them;
Deeming as wise, thou damaged village. ||83||

First, those who spoke and came for welfare of village;
Drowned they our village entirely. ||84||

Words your mere decorum, felt I you to whip;
Otherwise perform honestly what direct. ||85||

Didn't retrieve he, entangled in an attraction, illusions myriad;
Desiring any profit said he, came to meet me. ||86||

To village, saint, sage, intellectuals, activists come;
My earnest interest to assimilate meaning they unfold. ||87||

We discuss what books, *puran*[3], we read;
Who, so called wise, glance at them superficially? ||88||

Always we discuss what we listen I trust;
In time to come, our emotions also will be moulded. ||89||

Thou insist time to time, tell to initiate;
To think over this needs more years. ||90||

Pained I was entirely listening his verdict;
Felt I, Supreme created such people too! ||91||

With folded hands I expressed not to have his company;
Much knowledge given to thou by thy mentor. ||92||

Idiots are better than him, they listen atleast;
With righteous intention, they say to attempt for better. ||93||

Thou seem literate idiot, experience happiness hurting others;
How to appreciate this? If did, shameful it is. ||94||

But, instill on mind, it doesn't benefit thou;
But, who will satisfy, adopting such means in practice? ||95||

If any wise one encounter me to ask, in this way;
Hampers it the work of village service. ||96||

Glaring they are in speech but awesome in work;
Tell me, how can village be upgraded by this? ||97||

Without rendering service, they expect leadership;
Desire for respect of *sanyasi*, adhering to wife. ||98||

Speak emotionally with *sadhu*, intellectual before an idiot;
Accompany an addict, succumbing to addiction. ||99||

Expects he respect everywhere, accumulation of wealth;
Transaction without experiencing any strain. ||100||

Deception to realise, literate idiots call them scientist;
Incurable his disease is, treating it for long. ||101||

Village to save from him, goodness is to infuse;
For simplicity, openness, social reformers to work. ||102||

The means I suggest, whosoever are in village with this intent;
In the beginning they have to work with missionary zeal. ||103||

Those who outshine in speech but lags behind in practice;
Are to interrogate tactfully, accompanying villagers. ||104||

No involvement in intellectual discussion, our knowledge power lacks;
To such illusion my people not to succumb. ||105||

Purity, pity, courage, signs of knowledge, *Geeta* says;
Pandit is he who practices, wishing welfare of all beings. ||106||

One, mine competent worker, greater than lakh speakers;
Practicing this speech finely, village to be reformed by action. ||107||

When talk for welfare, say to work collectively;
Take a container to load with soil, on head. ||108||

The best way is to involve all in work;
An ideal will become village, seeking help for righteous work. ||109||

How can one be respected if life isn't ideal;
How can an ideal be created in the world? Tukadya says. ||110||

Such *Sri Gramgeeta* book; *Guru*-discipline-self experience-accepted;
Narrated the conduct for village upliftment; the Seventh Canto completed. ||111||

Notes

1. *Pandit*—A learned one.
2. *Yamniyam*—Yogic practices in *hatyoga*.
3. *Puran*—An ancient narrative script.

Canto VIII

Significance of Propagation

One, attired as *sadhu* utters, people don't listen;
Influenced they are by others, though good our conduct. ||1||

Inclination natural towards evil, fascination in culprit's hand;
Doesn't grow mango tree with labour, grass does without. ||2||

Experienced I this, people don't accept though told;
How to act? Misguided people don't pay heed. ||3||

So, I pray, laws are to be inducted;
By fine imprisonment, masses are to be elevated. ||4||

Said, listening his words, then government turns into God;
Why to sing *bhajan*? Better to polish the boots of an autocrat. ||5||

Saint speaks with love, government with an imposition;
Though their target, subsequently, sounds same. ||6||

By oppression people fear, behaved they rightly for an instance;
And they searched out ways numerous to commit sin. ||7||

Not this track of saint, *sadhu*, speak they with the warmth of heart;
Once convinced by their thoughts, people don't forget up to an end. ||8||

Sadhu to pray for Almighty, enlight entire masses;
Such are means fine of *sadhu*, saints. ||9||

Initially propagator as *sadhu* wandered village to village;
Guard uttering "*alak*" home to home at dawn. ||10||

His love functions, people wake regularly;
Cleanliness visible outside and purity of mind. ||11||

Fear to commit sin, arises by stories, *kirtana;*
Masses proceed on right road without an imposition of laws. ||12||

In world, some are without knowledge and they imitate;
Ideals of great lives are to follow. ||13||

Same are analytical, behave accordingly when convinced;
Needs it an interpreter and propagator competent. ||14||

Some succumbed to greed, work where profit is;
Heaven's door to show them eliminating sorrows by servicemen. ||15||

But, some don't listen words pertaining to fear;
As without imposition, animals don't walk on the right track. ||16||

Who has to teach them? Who will mould an idiot's heart?
As thus, power to operate, this means enhanced. ||17||

Understanding money, punishment, difference, politics diverse;
Intend to purify masses by the measures of laws. ||18||

Village structure by law, behaviour as directed by law;
Help to render to people as pointed by law. ||19||

One will be punished, who will violet law;
To regulate it, a king, a power holder, a leader are to be appointed. ||20||

But, propaganda in people, a king as the part of Vishnu;
Then only law operates, the technique of propagation in it. ||21||

Nation is a pious God, law is an equation for management;
Sin it is not to follow, an indispensable the technique of propagation. ||22||

Propaganda emerges out of faith in power, law, and flag;
Without it, fear, ever, never binds to rule. ||23||

Not due to a king's fear, after full propaganda in masses;
Behave people self consciously, the best experience it is. ||24||

Likewise many commit sin always keeping aside law;
But, step doesn't divert if propagation percolates into thought. ||25||

In retrospect, power rules, propagation encompasses life;
Power adheres to body only, law blind a beggar. ||26||

Propagation influences mind, affects inside and out;
Elevates man by rule to turn into village, a pilgrim place. ||27||

Not possible this by power; reversely, miscreants avail benefit;
Poor, well behaved suffer, sometime it happens. ||28||

Benefits availed by an arrogant, of laws made by power;
And weak, simple one dragged behind, this happened. ||29||

As thus, law is not everything, not best than propagation;
Lesson of humanism to everyone regulates with it. ||30||

King ruled and left, their laws perished;
Assembly of power desolated but saints rule. ||31||

Immortal is saints' propagation, still on mass psyche;
Ruling relentlessly to elevate lakh beings. ||32||

No cudgel of power, no fear on righteous road;
Points the sun of propagation to perform one's work. ||33||

When this awareness falters, punishment, discrimination function;
In such way, the ballads of anomalies' were sung more. ||34||

Though punishment abolishes injustice, progress people;
Prisons are not decreased; crimes are not lowered. ||35||

Knowing this, righteous one says to light flame in heart;
Then human nature will elevate, world will be an ideal. ||36||

Those who say, village will not be an ideal without power;
Their words are imperfect, one has to notice. ||37||

Needs it righteous propagator, lovable, simple, polite, and believer;
Without power he serves people with service, love. ||38||

Oh! Great is people power, one who will organise it;
With work, will create mark in heaven too. ||39||

Without taking sword, Buddha ruled the world;
Reason influential for this is propagation influential. ||40||

Whatever has happened in the world, caused by propagators;
Stumbles work pertaining to no propagator. ||41||

The best technique of propagation, the nerve of rural welfare;
Hurdles everywhere due to no propagators. ||42||

The Sun sets where a propagator turns back;
Pervades the network of darkness, as despair. ||43||

Where propagation reaches, a village appears paradise;
Behave people there reconciling to justice. ||44||

Propagator animates corpse, weak experiences the proud of work;
Cause spoilage and welfare, both, propagator. ||45||

Propagation is an art, retains it in heart;
Technique of propagation, a remedy to feed belly too. ||46||

Propagation sells unreal, makes God out of stone;
It beats drum of war, rains ambrosia too. ||47||

Nature of some to propagate wrong to fill pocket;
Experience some joy exploiting people. ||48||

But, an ill behaved propagator, ends himself driving other to death;
Caused it disorder in village, violence in the world. ||49||

Instead of his propagation, poisonous, influential should be;
Our propagation, truthful and elevated, then reform possible. ||50||

Until heart is not poured, propagation is at surface;
In the life of propagator, colours are to be infused. ||51||

Friends! To make village ideal, the best propagator requires;
Possible it is then to operate work well in village. ||52||

Sits the queen fly, other honey bees hover around;
With the passage of time, nature turns beautiful. ||53||

An audience asked question, which are qualities;
Of propagator who will propagate in the entire village? ||54||

What is a propagator's behaviour? What are living, nature, speech?
What are aim, strategy, means for village? ||55||

Pay heed to answer, whatever qualities a propagator need;
Adapting them in practice, people will elevate with ease. ||56||

To bright the village's future, need propagation, energetic;
Needs integrity, truth, character, politeness in propagator. ||57||

Core signs of a propagator, to work without power;
To elevate village with self purification, know s/he. ||58||

No attraction for power, no greed for wealth;
Spring of self, love incessant moulds mind. ||59||

A propagator, simple natured, killer of evil tendencies;
Mind, pure than water, non violent. ||60||

Fearless in speech, ready to proceed for labour;
Conduct ideal two is of a propagator. ||61||

Routine of a propagator, not to waste time;
Whatever suits to service, performs all s/he. ||62||

Gentle radiance in eyes, luster infused in speech;
Detachment, sacrifice, in with ease, the living of a propagator. ||63||

As stalk detaches from ripe fruit, a propagator's mind is;
Everything, bondage to senses has diminished. ||64||

No vigour in senses, orientation towards service;
Equivalent to him, rainy season, winter and summer. ||65||

But, no despair in a propagator's mind, ever smiling face;
Full of vibrant force to inspire work always. ||66||

No restlessness, though hill of calamity falls;
Labouring hard to full extent, tracks well people. ||67||

No house for a propagator, everywhere is his home;
In world, all people are his family members. ||68||

No greed for power, no awareness of prestige;
No lingering to demand money for self utilisation. ||69||

For righteous work, asks for money, land, respect too;
Without reluctance, long for sole dedication, breath too. ||70||

Nothing for personal, whatever does with thought of others;
Life is to dedicate, the intention of service. ||71||

All endeavours for everyone, soul, Supreme;
To tie knot of humanism with contentment. ||72||

One urge is remained, masses are to elevate;
Man's devastation is to wipe out. ||73||

Everyone's prayer to be one, complimentary to human conduct;
Living, same everywhere pious, for all. ||74||

Efforts for this, ventures accepting calamities;
He feels to sacrifice his living for it too. ||75||

Strategy this of *sadhu*, saint, these means of a propagator;
The pinnacle of propagation, truth, sainthood. ||76||

Real propagators, *sadhu*, saint; communicated they essence of the world;
What is real; what is unreal in the world? ||77||

Creates it propagators, propagator knows truth;
Listens doubts, anticipation, the whole heartedly. ||78||

Moment when consciousness has inspired mind;
Strengthen it with rigorous study, good contact. ||79||

Assimilates it with meditation, directs it mind;
Power once fuses in words, straight it moves. ||80||

The best person once paid heed, accepted it as mission;
Propagation of a propagator moves fast like wind. ||81||

Propagator propagates with propagation with rapid speed;
Before reaching any vehicle, propagation runs. ||82||

Whomsoever he encounters, he expresses himself;
Not necessary like a cloud to see who will accept it or not. ||83||

Whether seen torn-broken, rich-poor;
Whether intellectual, educated, laughed, fawned; not halt for propagation. ||84||

Whosoever be of any sect, supports himself;
Propagation flows, patching holes, spotted. ||85||

When seen a mask with eyes, speaks a propagator;
Like a parrot he utters, yes or no, all. ||86||

His work continues though people told to stop;
Again walks with short pause, paving way for Ganges of words. ||87||

Propagator's words reflective, intersects at doubt, with precision;
Though not biting, pierces core of healthy heart. ||88||

If any rival abuses, with smile he tolerates words;
With sweetness, he attempts to decipher his stand. ||89||

Tolerance, his mission; no words unreliable on his lips;
Though debate arises, seriousness is not lost. ||90||

Not hurting anyone, retaining tolerance;
Convinces a propagator his principle, in routine. ||91||

With sweetness mind moulds, dedicates for village service;
Shapes tendency in an apt, mould in all possible means. ||92||

Set in disordered home, bridge cleavages;
Many kinds, many plans in mind of a propagator. ||93||

Sometime by *bhajan*, sometime by prayer, impart thought;
Sometime by telling story consoles mind, a propagator. ||95||

Somewhere *kirtan*, religious discourse, *tunbadi*[2], *powada*[3];
In fare, festival involves a propagator. ||96||

Somewhere by work, somewhere lure by art performance;
Somewhere the move also by an entertainment. ||97||

Somewhere inspiration through exercise, sometime in party;
Sometime initiation is through wedding also. ||98||

No stone unturned in birth, death anniversaries, ritual;
Works in every possible modes, as time demands. ||99||

Somewhere in tailor's shop, somewhere in barber's saloon;
On platform outside, everywhere propagation functions. ||100||

Continues in *bazaar*, speaks same in *tamasha* too;
Miraculous power operates on a propagator's tongue. ||101||

Some sit near parents, moulds members in family;
In which way, a propagator functions, none tells. ||102||

In work, song, laugh, addiction, variously;
In routine style, the words of propagation harmonise. ||103||

A propagator child among child, youth to guide young;
To provide experience to an old, content reflective s/he has. ||104||

Service renders among boys, both cultivates art among girls;
Youths, male and female, work for village service. ||105||

Relations prevail with addiction but to shape his mind;
Never cards upset in imagination, of a propagator. ||106||

Diverse arts in his blood, as time demands;
Performs s/he art with different hues for propagation. ||107||

With conscience inside, propagates s/he with sweetness;
Feels as hypnotic spell casts on village by a propagator. ||108||

A propagator such liked by all, attracts others;
People run when called to work for village. ||109||

Wanders with ease in village, people flock together;
Function they as directed by a propagator. ||110||

Such propagator, a magician, sea of people in his/her hand;
Simple s/he is, a creator of new world. ||111||

A propagator speaks with everyone, knowledge manifests in him;
In every cell of him, detachment is ingrained. ||112||

Being this attraction, pulls in people like birds;
To make village self reliant, a propagator is indispensable. ||113||

Unflickering determination he has; happens what he decided;
By practicing various means, achieves he success. ||114||

His propagation massive power; operates any time, anywhere;
Without propagation not a single word uttered. ||115||

Known to him, what to do; doesn't know what not to do;
'No', not known to him, in his lifestyle. ||116||

Slight information to him what is not in our village;
Whatever he takes in hand fulfills it. ||117||

By tact and skill in masses, creates he what is not;
Spirit of righteous work infuses s/he life to life. ||118||

Propagation for which s/he craves for, completes it;
If not, one should infer, a death of a propagator. ||119||

So the base of village is profound propagator;
Whatever lacuna exists, fulfill it in village. ||120||

In essence, where a propagator is, another *Pandhari*[4] it;
Make it to dance with zeal, people, mind, stones too. ||121||

Select such propagator to flourish village with glare;
For service, *seva mandal*[5] is to establish. ||122||

Famous becomes s/he who has moulded village such;
A work of propagation is to initiate for it. ||123||

Spoke time to time, bound I to propagation;
Servant I became of all for propagation. ||124||

Firmly, for village creation, core base is propagator;
Created *Gramgeeta* for this, Tukadya says. ||125||

Such *Sri Gramgeeta* book; *Guru*-discipline-self-experience-accepted;
Narrated the significance of propagation; the Eighth Canto completed. ||126||

Notes

1. *Alak*—To know, to realise. Niranjan is divine form.
2. *Tunbadi*—Flash-shaped dry fruit utilised in presenting folk-song.
3. *Powada*—The ballad form in Maharashtra, presented in chorus accompanied by musical instruments.
4. *Pandhari*—The pilgrim place in Maharashtra, where Vithal and Rukhmi are worshipped as idols by devotees.
5. *Seva mandal*—The assembly of like-minded people for village service. Tukadoji founded *Gurudeo Seva Mandal* with the missionary zeal for mass elevation.

Canto IX

Power of Service

Audiences asked, understood importance of propagation;
But, not possible for all to practice it. ||1||

Difficult to get an ideal propagator, if available difficult to continue;
Which is the second road for village upliftment? ||2||

Listen answer of this, I have seen the village beautiful;
Disciplined, peace, facilities, dedicated people there. ||3||

But, experienced surprise, searched whose work is this?
Whose skill has culminated into fruitful result? ||4||

A leader has to come forward, when called by people;
Uttered he, "I am a serviceman humble; was in thy class". ||5||

Wonder-struck I; how has he done work?
He can't speak well; doesn't have skill more. ||6||

Simple look he has but passion in the heart for work;
Liked by all because of qualities of service. ||7||

Not propagating but service fascinates village;
This crux of understanding one receives there. ||8||

Service speaks without words, makes all people happy;
Hearts their wins easily, enhances affection. ||9||

Propagating by all means, *sanskar* it causes;
But, decision without service doesn't last long. ||10||

Mind to control by service, to mould after unfolding;
In life, work, not lasts only due to an advice. ||11||

Oh! Though a propagator doesn't speak, people like him;
Fascinates villager, his love for service. ||12||

Wherever he walks, works time to time;
Humble people become when see him. ||13||

Though not talkative, a speaker, an advisor's apt;
More is his influence than an orator, *pandit.* ||14||

These people elevate village, bright the name of nation;
Though not known to others, wild flower exhales fragrance. ||15||

Though erected palace, of massive height to viewers;
But, relies they on the foundation stones. ||16||

Though not visible the foundation stones, significant they are;
As importance of service in the nation elevation entirely. ||17||

Lures the other's mind to whom a service renders;
With magnanimous heart, he will donate everything. ||18||

Heart pleases when rendition of a melodious song before a deer;
Then without consciousness, everything can be procured. ||19||

Energy accumulates with service, happens what one speaks;
By him or others, all works fulfill. ||20||

Once the restoration of people's trust, rendition of service to God;
Then what is deficient? Gets he whatever expects. ||21||

Only resolution sufficient for serviceman, wish fulfills;
Happens everything what he intends by different means. ||22||

But, not for luxury, when a serviceman presumes;
The glory of service he will experience till an end. ||23||

When tilted to luxury sensual, service ceases;
Onward, onward, leads this it to ridicule. ||24||

But, who deems service as wealth without return;
God he has become, at every home his worship. ||25||

People don't ask for wealthy, not recognise power;
But, worship with heart, at the feet of serviceman. ||26||

Honoured due to service, all adorable people in the world;
Became demon after quitting service, killed by God. ||27||

Saint Damaji[1] served, occasionally by robbing granaries;
Gods also respected, paid this debt. ||28||

Here God returned debt, means Narayan[2] pleased with;
Wealth supplied in return by someone. ||29||

How can one tell, who will meet whom?
Though work is good of mass service. ||30||

Performing all work, penance, visiting pilgrim place, forest;
One has to serve people for righteous fame. ||31||

Charity at pilgrim place, righteous meal, food, money for *yagnya;*
From the stance of service good mirrors in it, otherwise an illusion. ||32||

Not to give to needy, expense more at pilgrim place;
It will not render good to thou of mass service. ||33||

Pilgrim place, a treasure of good, and sinful, rural animal;
To him, at pilgrim place only water and stones, say saints. ||34||

Water in *kawdi*[3] from Ganges at Kashi to pour in thirsty mouth;
In it good prevails than pilgrim place, says Lord. ||35||

Labouring self, others to make happy;
Good it is to make happy rural masses. ||36||

When one serves as this, breaks the bondage of the world;
Friendly Lord embraces him, not to deviate. ||37||

Service is wealth, treasure will not cease in life to come;
Increase cosmic consciousness, worshipping village with service. ||38||

So says, serve, the best this road;
One's birth is to lift along with village. ||39||

When one performs service, elevates being;
Upgrades the village by all means. ||40||

Everyone serves, some for family, masses;
But, doesn't facilitate it the elevation of village, I will tell. ||41||

Everyone ready for service, transaction by service;
Service has varieties but different is crux. ||42||

I am *patil* of village and so renders service;
Calls oneself serviceman but squizes poor. ||43||

A pair of oxen, hungry, which was working;
Says he without mercy to drive cart for *sahab*. ||44||

Worked till noon and didn't go to home for meal;
In spite of it called for worthless work. ||45||

Kill the pair of oxen, workers with hunger, but pleases *sahab;*
His mode of service is this, *sahab* expresses gratitude. ||46||

A wedding at our home, but appears calamity to villagers;
Eat those who elude work, laborious one neglected. ||47||

In village delicious sweet food served to *seth*[4], *savkar*[5]*;*
Exploited poor, no respect for them. ||48||

Calling, "Come! sister-in-law", assembled women;
Keeping aside daily work, worked day and night. ||49||

Work ended well, appreciation for a landlord;
Type of service it is to send workers with an empty belly. ||50||

People work at night as an officer arrives to village;
To renovate village they labour hard to the last extent. ||51||

Only to labour by others, stands he at distance;
At end, pat on his back, people far away. ||52||

Made village beautiful labouring male, female;
Spreads his fame as the leader with zeal of service. ||53||

Expensed wealth and built temple gracious;
Known as generous but doesn't know the crux. ||54||

Exploited people first, accumulated a heap of wealth;
Constructed then temple, then earning doesn't dwindle. ||55||

Became rich by stealing, courageous in donation;
Demised poor working, not known to others. ||56||

Place the photographs of servicemen as ideals;
Massive service this is, food donor, a beggar call them. ||57||

Some perform *bhajan* for God, longs for status;
Deceives innocent, simple, deeming oneself serviceman. ||58||

Collects fee as whim operates from all corners;
Says "we will build charity home", at last lives he. ||59||

First collects fund, pouring knowledge deep;
Planning in detail, public work on massive scale. ||60||

Unfolding benefits various, instigate people;
At last, self-fishiness mingles in the garb of service. ||61||

Same performs *yagnya*, speaks for world peace;
But, enjoys lavish dish, treating all servicemen. ||62||

To assist people well, organises charity programmes;
Seeks some servicemen interest in name, enjoying luxury. ||63||

Service for hobby, otherwise who labours?
Experience some contentment whenever receives status. ||64||

Some served but flung away due to non-inclusion of name;
Picked up quarrel asking "what is ours?" ||65||

Some transact, glared the eyes of elders, younger by service;
Destroyed life from inside supplying corrupt products. ||66||

Met me *tamasha* performer, calling harlot to dance;
Posed he as if working tirelessly to dedicate service. ||67||

Rationally some supported black marketing, corruption;
People difficulties readily to solve, by this service. ||68||

One assembled beggars, left village to village;
Snatched he their money, as service rendered. ||69||

Some serve with mind, body for long time as desire;
But, work only to click photo and then abscond. ||70||

Some went for travel, wandered to all corners;
Then after fulfillment of selfishness, sat at home. ||71||

Some ignited people, fragmented saying service;
Attaining the purpose of selfishness, united innerly. ||72||

One has progressed in dedication of service for power;
Atleast, procured power to serve others. ||73||

How many years consumed in service? Now needs power;
To progress more, squeeze other people. ||74||

Some initiated service but availed service of others;
Disabled him whose service he has sought. ||75||

Came *sadhu* for service but behaved like a bridegroom;
Upper hand he has, instead of his service. ||76||

Deceived people like this, alert they are to be;
Harmful service it is, without thought. ||77||

Like it service ought not be, cooperation to nourish;
Needs to fulfill without intent of greed. ||78||

All to be contented, serviceman and served;
While giving, receiving both, let them be satisfied. ||79||

Service not to be deceptive, inner and outer different;
It not to be artificial like the paper flowers. ||80||

It not be for status, serviceman, not selfish;
Who disrupts social peace by destructive service. ||81||

Real service is detached work, crux for other's happiness;
Who sacrifices oneself, serviceman indeed he is. ||82||

Who forgets his home, village belongs to him;
With sense of dedication he will serve. ||83||

Who entangles in his home, can't provide public benefit;
Though he is soft spoken, people don't pay heed. ||84||

Whose selfishness increases, professional, he becomes;
Why will people pay respect, after observation? ||85||

For selfishness, *sadhu* becomes a leader too;
Runs risk of life, everything for selfishness. ||86||

But, started doing detached service, who escaped from this;
Glittered as serviceman in all people. ||87||

Worker has to know this, restrain selfish motto;
Then for service one has to step further. ||88||

Serves the Sun for all but doesn't expect return;
Persistently works thee with service. ||89||

Renders tree, shade, flowers, fruits to all;
At last devotes his life for works, service. ||90||

Served some earlier by offering money, grain, kingdom;
At last, sacrificed their bodies to fulfill service. ||91||

Became his service legend, fame motivated others;
It to be adopted by us to serve. ||92||

Myriad forms of service, comprehending it to serve;
One to serve as per one's interest with dedication. ||93||

Food service, labour service, knowledge service;
At last, life service by providing medicines. ||94||

Transaction service, righteous religion service, core service of self, great;
Attains truth of all services in service of self. ||95||

Service of self, not of senses; pure treasure of knowledge it is;
Village is to be elevated by righteous contact. ||96||

Service is not one, service is each work;
But, in it, doesn't include an accumulative tendency. ||97||

Non-accumulation, real service it is;
More significance of service is than this too. ||98||

We have to be as the earth to lift poor ones;
Contentment serviceman has to seek in it. ||99||

We to give, we to give this to meditate;
As *yagnya*, one's labour to contribute for service. ||100||

Trouble to experience by all, success to be by all;
One has to presume, one is not someone. ||101||

Service not for status, innate inclination it is;
Its complete fruit, an inner contentment. ||102||

Cleaned our village, everyone is pleased;
All are delighted, its fulfilment. ||103||

Dignitaries have come, decorated village beautiful;
Projected the names of workers, real serviceman he is. ||104||

Drifts back for labour, come forward for fame;
Laughs people differently, ridiculing a leader. ||105||

Who has greediness, jealousy, an anger, rivalry;
His service, mockery of real service, deem it. ||106||

Who wishes other's welfare, seeks joy in it;
Presume I, serviceman he is in era to come. ||107||

Progress of life is this, others to treat as ours;
In practice, to implement, one has to be humble. ||108||

All burden on us, real service it is;
Though difficult this penance, our burden not to be. ||109||

No threat of our arrival, but sorrow of one's departure;
In village, serviceman to be of such magnetic quality. ||110||

Otherwise fear family members when serviceman comes;
How to arrange for him? express we poor. ||111||

When serviceman comes, receives family support;
In his presence, joy to experience for young, elders. ||112||

Feel of *Dashera, diwali* when he arrives;
All to be satisfied with cooperation. ||113||

Ideal he to be in living, speaking, performing *bhajan;*
Mind involves in righteous work all time. ||114||

Hurdles tell people, serviceman serves them;
Works for them in numerous ways in their lives. ||115||

Efforts in myriad modes to eliminate evil;
Conscience inside maintains, core service it is. ||116||

Knows not about himself, whatever performs service it is;
No word of self-fishiness, happiness through work done. ||117||

At home, outside, love for all, at far distance;
Propagates he message with an attitude ideal. ||118||

Let be different parties, sects, castes, opinions varied;
In the fabric of service they will be interwoven. ||119||

Serviceman to nourish by people to make village best;
Love to infuse in all by serviceman. ||120||

Such serviceman indispensable, serviceman to be at home;
Without serviceman, family, village, not best. ||121||

Words so spoke, service, the most mighty;
With serviceman, an entire village will be happy. ||122||

Audiences! Know importance of this, supremacy of public service;
Pour in heart principle, march to serve. ||123||

Not requires for it, art, skill; honest affection feasible;
Turn, turn to this road, all, Tukadya says. ||124||

Such *Sri Gramgeeta* book; *Guru*-discipline-self experience-accepted;
Narrated the means of service; the Ninth Canto completed. ||125||

Notes

1. Saint Damaji—To render service to people, he opened the doors of grain-storage.
2. Narayan—The name of God in Indian context.
3. *Kawdi*—A devotee carries *kawdi* on sholder, the mean to transport water as a religious ritual.
4. *Seth*—A rich person.
5. *Savkar*—A money lender.

Canto X

Organisation Unity

An audience, service oriented, with heaviness of heart;
Listen my pathetic story for once, spoke. ||1||

After plucking the fruit of village elevation, with service;
No other *mantra*[1] is with us besides mass hypnosis. ||2||

True it indeed, experienced we with determination;
But, some selfish people turn jealous of service. ||3||

Some intellectual, respected, influential in government;
Need they leadership in village for selfishness, here, there. ||4||

Intend they to keep people under control to serve purpose;
As thus, play diverse strategies wearing the garb of service. ||5||

Give some rare objects, others some fascination;
Procures love, encouraging addicted, village bully. ||6||

Becomes entire our service feeble sometime;
In their net, an innocent people are trapped. ||7||

Happened this in our village, the serviceman made it best;
In future, an unfortune impends by this way. ||8||

Planted in court yard beautiful creepers, watering with labour;
Blossomed with fruits, kissing the sky. ||9||

As storm roared, dropped fruits, flowers, yellow leave;
In no time, creepers too squashed to ground. ||10||

Why one will not dishearten, who nourished them?
All of sudden a beauty of home is lost. ||11||

Likewise village cared with strategy, nourished children;
Love flourished in each other with service qualities sportively. ||12||

But, intruded a village divider to fulfill selfish motives;
Misdirecting illusioned mind, formed clevage. ||13||

Erected decorum of service, intruded flatterers;
Blamed serviceman whenever a wrong takes place. ||14||

Valiant they are to trigger off arrow pin-pointedly;
But, village was crushed creating rift. ||15||

Numerous differences, upheaval by different parties;
Sometime hidden, sometime openly started they work. ||16||

Confused the masses, love power, topsy-turvy;
Pervades everywhere the attitude of fragmentation. ||17||

Some righteous people built village, some village bully spoiled it;
Various ludicrous shows performed in our village. ||18||

Selfishness surged, everyone projected as king;
Entangled entire society in various inducement. ||19||

Hook sheathed under allurement but a fish sees only allurement;
Likewise people illusioned due to seduction. ||20||

Some are humble, cleans an officer's boots too;
But, inner intent passionate to take the rein of village. ||21||

No one cared for service, crazy for power;
Village shattered by contesting elections. ||22||

Elections in village, people doubtful among themselves;
In practice, they are hurt due to many parties. ||23||

Likewise happened, adhered some to caste;
Status gained ridiculing others, promises given as one likes. ||24||

Some offered feast, captured votes by providing liquor;
In vehicles they have brought, trapping an innocent people. ||25||

Adapted these means, elected threatening others;
Says opportunity for serviceman to serve than all. ||26||

Means, basically impure, how can consequence be pure?
Wealthy, exploiting people, creating rift in village. ||27||

Committing sin of any kind to satisfy greed for power;
Trampling mass power under feet for selfish motto. ||28||

Leading to wretched state, growing differences;
Depression for righteous one as if death occurs. ||29||

What to tell now? How to elevate village?
Only to see what happens, feel with depression. ||30||

Such question asked by an audience, heard I from heart;
Friends! remedies I will tell as my conviction. ||31||

Not to discourage though scenario is real;
To increase strength of evil, despair will be cause. ||32||

What have we to do? speak people wise;
But, understand, village will devast by these qualities. ||33||

Why not to presume he, not the chief of village?
All conscious people to venture with determination. ||34||

Such strategy to be, admirable for workers;
To create village, efforts to direct to full extent. ||35||

Not to sit at home when resistance operates;
Though Ganges fears viewing mountain, not merges with sea. ||36||

What is appreciable to swim in dry tank?
Essence lies in the swimming resisting the waves of flood. ||37||

As thus, adhere to duty to restore the village character;
No one to lash in village by storm. ||38||

Presuming the village service as the service to God;
Village is to prepare for service by all means. ||39||

Objectively intellectual discourse others to convince;
By propagation, village intellect is to mould. ||40||

Without mass enlightenment, poverty in village will not vanish;
Once people understood, evil can't create obstacle. ||41||

To assist this work, help of some prominent villagers to seek;
Strength will enhance to disarm the village's rivals. ||42||

With or without cooperation of power, righteous people to contact;
The foundation of village state to be on truth by serviceman. ||43||

Longing for justice and interest for village service;
Organisation to be made firm to enhance day by day. ||44||

Conscious ones to be selected, an intimate to be picked up;
By the great ones, the work of village elevation to be operated. ||45||

Practiced, an audience said, assembled righteous people with stern efforts;
But, not to set properly once disrupted. ||46||

Oh! to beautify village, a committee was formed;
Insistence was on to conduct an election for leader. ||47||

Who has to elect the village's leader? Who has to give priority?
To whom rein is to give for the village administration? ||48||

Decided an election but added it fuel to fire;
Or, a tank of kerosene was poured in fire. ||49||

Fire was blazed, turbulent flows of opinions;
Jealous of each other, wise people. ||50||

Everyone deems oneself wise, no one listens;
Oh! alas! alas! no limit to uproar. ||51||

Beating at home, an irritating wife beats husband;
Say children, wise they are, learnt books. ||52||

Whom to treat a leader? thought everyone in village;
No consensus with brother; what to do? ||53||

Experience this of an audience, prevails in village to village;
But, misplaced the basic set up here. ||54||

Surfaces dirt in hand with stirring of turbid water;
Chaos natural where no inner drive for service. ||55||

For this, organization to set up of service-oriented people;
No queue to be there other than them. ||56||

In village righteous persons one by one to search to link;
The assembly of spirited serviceman forms with efforts. |57||

When honest, righteous work dauntlessly comes before public;
Consequently, determination will be to direct village. ||58||

When moral power of service, influential for village welfare;
Then can't withstand resistance there principally. ||59||

Dominating others, luring for treachery;
Hurdles in righteous journey will wipe out. ||60||

If the chief of service organization elected, an apt person;
Magnificent village will become in all means. ||61||

An audience said, fine this but the wind of election blows in village;
Village our succumbs to its different drives. ||62||

Opposition due to selfishness, poses by a leader in village;
By diverse sources creates they discrimination in mind. ||63||

There what we have to do? How to elevate village?
Pay heed to the query of an audience to satisfy. ||64||

Whatever narrated real it is; experience in village to village;
For this, with reflection, a remedy to search out. ||65||

The present mode of election, faulty it is basically;
As thus, an apt approach to be revealed before villagers. ||66||

To which extent, an election, responsibility of life lies?
Without confusion real nature of election to convince. ||67||

Direction we visualise when thought step by step;
When the principle of election comprehended, chaos will cease. ||68||

See! why leadership only to serve village?
Then apply the test of service, leader at core will come to know. ||69||

Who strive for village? Who wake up at dawn?
Who sweep, taking broom in hand? ||70||

Who works for poor in a day with simple living?
Who wander on feet to serve village? ||71||

Who is morally strong? Who doesn't like discrimination?
Doesn't succumb to village fund as hobby. ||72||

Who look for everyone's happiness, sorrows? Who works for service?
Signs these are to know to elect. ||73||

Or, allot duty to all, order you strictly;
Observe who serves restlessly for village. ||74||

Then real leader he is, blind will also select him;
Why decorum we need glaring here? ||75||

Every element in village, man everyone to know him;
Who are evasive, serviceman, an initiator? ||76||

Who serves village? Who inroad for prestige?
Whenever situation creeps up, it is to unfold to villagers. ||77||

Blushfulness, shame not to be, disorder it will village's work;
As thus, person reliable to project without dilemma. ||78||

Who has affection for village, an idol of work knowledge;
Being elected, village happy he will make. ||79||

If not, quarrel will take place, reinless will be village scenario;
Then righteous one will be at distance, advantage to selfish people. ||80||

To select qualitative person, appreciated by all;
Deeming him leader, rein to hand over to him. ||81||

Otherwise leader they presume, look for supremacy;
Turning oneself into tiger, makes village to starve. ||82||

Deliver some speeches, rift creates in party;
Disjoint minds once united, prepares ground for pique. ||83||

No need of such leader who is no valorous;
We consider him not as friend but foe. ||84||

Who has elevated village or work ideal of community;
Power to speak better he has, understand we. ||85||

Speaks relentlessly whenever chances to get money;
Towards him no one's mind to incline. ||86||

Not to take to heart wherever such leadership prevails;
The honest server, the head of village he is. ||87||

To speak one, behave another; to conceal one, to reveal another;
Harmful it is for village, an audience to comprehend. ||88||

Though consumed poison for fear or drank milk to a serpent;
End is bound to be though closeness with tiger. ||89||

Not to behave like this, honest servers those who are;
To be elected, collectively by all people. ||90||

Care for everyone for society; who is reliable among people?
Who will look after village all time? ||91||

Leader he must be, not to succumb to anyone;
Luring to money, village authority he not to be. ||92||

Leadership due to service, all have to speak this;
Not to nourish the filthy game of party politics. ||93||

For relation, party, sect, caste, poor, rich;
Transaction, shame for others, not to vote. ||94||

On our vote, indeed future of village or nation relies;
Single vote of immense significance, gravity to know. ||95||

Vote, a weapon two sided, if not employed aptly;
Reverts it on us in the end to attack. ||96||

Upper hand a nuisance will have, if received the support of votes;
Makes village feeble if not voted rightly. ||97||

Voting, not an entertainment, voting not skill in market;
Election, an opportunity pin-pointed for future. ||98||

Though election as *swayanwar*[2], in whose hand rein to give;
Test apt to apply for it consciously. ||99||

As wound to lick, disciples selected by Ramdas[3];
Looking in the test for death as by *Guru* Govind Singh[4]. ||100||

When a runway exhausted some, out some;
Some runners, excellent, come to know by this mode. ||101||

Likewise in election, all have to look his work;
Whose work has more worth, he to elect. ||102||

All to convince this, chaos will diminish;
Receive servicemen the opportunity by this means. ||103||

Then listen his words only, all villagers to assemble;
One who speaks tracklessly, to be warned by villagers. ||104||

Organisation once formed, initiates village elevation;
Animates the garden of children, elders with love. ||105||

New flowers of ideas blossom, grow into delicious fruits;
In village, dream will be reality of village state, beautiful. ||106||

Dust someone will throw but enters in his eyes;
Happily entire village will live, Tukadya says. ||107||

Such *Sri Gramgeeta* book; *Guru*-discipline-self experience-accepted;
Narrated the road of village state; the Tenth Canto completed. ||108||

Notes

1. *Mantra*—Magical spell.
2. *Swayanwar*—A ceremony of choosing a bride in ancient India.
3. Ramdas—Marathi saint poet of 16th century, who wrote *Dasbodh*.
4. Guru Govind Singh—Religious preacher of Sikhism in 18th century.

Village Creation Quinate

Canto XI

Village Security

God service only village service, the treasure of everyone's happiness;
But, to disturb the mission in village some devils are. ||1||

A gentleman queried, garden blossoms in village;
But, miscreants light fire, what is remedy for ever? ||2||

Built up we organisation, elected gentleman;
But, helpless we are, before evil people. ||3||

Though shown an ideal life, convinced by propagation;
Or, rendered service requisite to them day and night. ||4||

But, don't pay heed, becomes angry when advised;
Defeats workers time to time posing obstacles. ||5||

Extracts evil out of good, spreads infected air;
Calamity he brings for gentleman by diplomacy. ||6||

Killer of pen, outspoken; dead hearted, village bully;
Agents for disputes, rich, influential, in their hands. ||7||

Seeking support of power always trap they;
Terror people experience, what to do? ||8||

Friend! whatever nature of disease, tell medicine to cure;
For implementation needs a planner with skill. ||9||

Feeble becomes truth, so untruth surfaces;
For powerful service, truth to be more stubborn. ||10||

Listen peacefully, how to boost up power of truth;
Lazy or depressed gentlemen are not to be. ||11||

Though terror in their minds but like thou some are;
Restless in heart to wish for good. ||12||

Those who like service, preserve treasure of truth;
Assembling people, such active organisation to nourish. ||13||

Time this of mass strategy, energy intrinsic all in people;
Can bow down empire, the power of mass determination. ||14||

Grass rope controls an elephant, ants injure a serpent;
Tore tiger, lion when skilled wild dogs united. ||15||

What can't organisation do? Sea forms when drops accumulate;
Village garden blossoms with flowers, fruits of organisation. ||16||

Basic incantation of village welfare, to assemble gentleman;
Organisation, formula of village's energy to create village state. ||17||

What village performs individual cannot do, told with skill;
Though authority doesn't respond, village can alter it. ||18||

So, requires powerful organisation to eliminate injustice;
Providing village justice to secure. ||19||

Strong organisation in village to unfold our sorrows;
No one to treat with injustice, the function of organisation. ||20||

Collectively people to nominate, an honest, good one;
Sacrifices, courageous, with character glorious. ||21||

Becomes soldier pious serviceman in village when time demands;
No calamity when in village such conscious pillars are. ||22||

Whenever crime in village, immediately to inform;
With involvement of all to set in order disrupted. ||23||

Cooperation to be of everyone, conscious in village;
All have to assemble when call given. ||24||

If one commits crime, he to be taught by all;
Punishment to him by village when not responds criminal. ||25||

Falls pray to greed a mature, snores posing decorum;
By pinching only he is to wake. ||26||

At the end, black it is though wash coal with soap;
Bright it turns when burns in *agnisanskar*[1]. ||27||

So, by boycott, non-cooperation, support to be withdrawn;
Pressing of nose, immediately opens mouth. ||28||

All have to pursue, one intends to spoil village;
Free him from village, when not follows power. ||29||

Better to collect the best and disdain evil;
Not to favour the growth of evil tree. ||30||

All have to work for this, though tedious it is;
For service it is to tolerate, though risk of life. ||31||

If village is ready, heaven it will become;
No *tutari*[2] back of power holder. ||32||

Such action and behaviour, store of justice village will be;
If conscious is gentleman, ingenious. ||33||

Fortune smiles of village when behaves like this;
Numerous hurdles are otherwise its fate. ||34||

Listening this one spoke, thy favoured peace;
And thy too chased those who are misbehaved. ||35||

Good and evil, in both same God;
Where is service, when one is penalised? ||36||

Pity, forgiveness, and peace, the wealth of pious;
Is gentleness in treatment when cruel against rival? ||37||

No one has to lure if one listens this;
Village to be elevated with thought, conscience. ||38||

Yardstick indeed is how to judge a pious one;
Village to be alert knowing this at the first sight. ||39||

Conscience to be, to whom render service?
Deceived they are, who have no vision as this. ||40||

An honest servant he needs to continue black marketing;
Who will receive return by rendering them service reliable? ||41||

People served *sadhu* and saint, worked day and night for truth;
No longing they have for kings, palaces. ||42||

Many kings ruled in the world but not all worshipped;
Treated they saints, gentlemen as gods, in the temple of heart. ||43||

So vision to form whom to render service by whom;
Then to leap into service, religion this of human beings. ||44||

Pity to be in heart, love for help to others;
Whenever finds, lacuna is not to be left. ||45||

Forgiveness, heart peaceful, dauntless behavior with trust;
Cruel we not to be though body ceases to breath. ||46||

But, when cruelty demands, hard one to be than stone;
With conscience this to bear in mind. ||47||

Otherwise shown pity but bounds on ourselves;
Pity, it not if destructs village. ||48||

Money given to beggar but spent in wine, drug;
Tell, what is meaning of pity by this mean? ||49||

Come some thieves to village in the garb of *sadhu;*
Rob they in night, changing garments. ||50||

To tolerate this, to leave him deeming *sadhu;*
Such adoration of pity not to be by valorous persons. ||51||

Religion of donation, religion of pity, the essence to understand;
Work not to be whimsical, complimentary to laziness, voice. ||52||

Turned *buwa* renouncing home, wandered door to door;
Drowned all good conduct by such qualities. ||53||

No innate tendency to labour, no sacrifice for virtues;
Roam hypocrites wearing garb to defame saint's name. ||54||

Though religion of donation, provision for sinful act;
Conscience to maintain by donor religion. ||55||

Demand *madhukari*[3] but plays openly gambling;
In *math*[4] secrete of liquor, opium, *bhang*, girls. ||56||

Donation to these people, village to drawn, defame;
Tell, which God has told this religion? ||57||

Pity, the crux of religion but it, guarding of animal;
And elimination of miscreants, speak saints. ||58||

Security of gentlemen and destruction of vicious one;
This, the work-sign of incarnation coping with justice. ||59||

As thus, one who has caused injustice, pained poor;
In village, his resistance to be. ||60||

Otherwise openness to miscreants as if free donkeys;
To leave wicked, showing pity, no religion this is. ||61||

Resistance bound to be for injustice, understanding its nature;
Call to be given to organisation once realised precisely. ||62||

Injustice, myriad kinds, some of money, prestige;
Some stimulate addiction, immortality, among people. ||63||

Outlet to search out not to practice misconduct;
By thinker, such religion real to realise. ||64||

In heart, preciseness of justice to infuse;
Stance of pity, on one hand and specter on other. ||65||

Such, a painted cave, reality of a man, worthless to pose with gold;
To die in the hands of thieves, without valour. ||66||

Some are innocent, lost they the pride of humanity;
Lunatically treat people them holy. ||67||

Who can't secure mission, no pride of justice;
How can we deem him holy one? ||68||

One who robbed by thieves, deceived by village bully;
Humiliated by another woman, how can he be virtuous? ||69||

Who is too lethargic, startle by seeing police;
Who can't know his right, virtuous he is not. ||70||

Feeble he is, coward, non-progressive, an ignorant;
Who has not glare of *purushartha*[5] for security. ||71||

Anyone can lift him, compel to drink liquor, opium;
Drinks being an innocent, what an innocence such? ||72||

This stone, without an intellect, no knowledge of good conduct;
Being dumb, static, treat people him serious, silent. ||73||

Who doesn't deceive by other's deception, real silent he is;
No indulgence in gossiping, chatting. ||74||

Dislikes other's hate; doesn't tolerate other's pain;
Runs for cooperation when other are in trouble. ||75||

Leaves the place when listens adverse of others;
Not to speak irrelevant, say he to people. ||76||

No criticism at back, speaks face to face;
As crystal, his heart, courageous, pure. ||77||

Dislikes filthiness, sings good of gentlemen ever;
For good contact, his life longs forever. ||78||

Behaves with brotherhood, shares with others;
Links with people skillfully to enlight. ||79||

Not to be an egoistic in happiness, not to fear in calamity;
With justice to behave, to treat other people. ||80||

Who has implemented this, speak peacefully, piously;
Welfare they cause, understand we. ||81||

Instead of this, feebleness comes, village deteriorates;
Out of joint it is, to control by anyone. ||82||

So, needs strictness of justice, conscience in pity too;
Service this logically, which elevates by all means. ||83||

Abolishing evil person without hate, cause for his progress;
Operation surgical by doctor, pity is his. ||84||

God in all, no harm for him, transaction of truth;
Village to make beautiful, worship it is. ||85||

Love for all, enhancing qualities, honour;
Eliminating nuisance all in our village. ||86||

The world is God but disdain our nature;
As thus, miscreants under control brought by saint Tukaram. ||87||

How can be catastrophe there, where devotees of Hari are?
Presuming this they put their lives to task. ||88||

Our pilgrims, *Warkari*[6] faithful, pillars they are to combat;
Threat to rivals as if all are Shivaji. ||89||

Seeking inspiration from them, army of justice to erect;
As if nuisance in our village on the verge of an end. ||90||

Liquor, opium, drug, gambling, prostitution, evil work;
Trace not to find in our village. ||91||

For it some righteous villagers have to eradicate addiction;
Many tiers of the best qualities have to nourish. ||92||

Assembling gentlemen in village unreliable tradition to cease;
Not to persist which provides harm to village. ||93||

Pierces iron-point to oxen, some reinless farmers;
Fulfills their desire extracting blood. ||94||

In the name of God, some kills living beings;
Practice this to cease, improving people's sentiments. ||95||

By body intoxication, some deceive, some lure people;
Teach illusioned opinion, penance; conscious to be for it. ||96||

Help to others, hurdles to eliminate;
From all aspects, an apt service is to seek. ||97||

Priority to give to an obstacle in village service;
Arrangement to make by giving our land too. ||98||

Needy to be cooperated if not service this by all;
Without deception, service to render whatever possible. ||99||

All have to involve in the marriage of son, daughter;
On their parents, burden not to impose. ||100||

To give to bride, bridegroom, all have to bring little;
By all means meal to look after. ||101||

Help by little extent, religion realised by villagers;
Likewise cooperation to be on all occasions. ||102||

Uplifts village as increases cooperation subsequently;
No problem for any man in village. ||103||

Service this once infused in life, no lacuna in village;
In spite of, the section of servicemen separate to be. ||104||

Ready to be all rural youth, if impends any calamity;
Keeping aside their work, all have to run for. ||105||

For fire, drowning in well, cholera, fainting;
To run every time, their duty is. ||106||

Planning this for village service, enlighten village army;
There, in heaven's paradise, blossoming with ease. ||107||

By such organisation, luminant glory village will experience;
Village state, treasure of happiness, Tukadya says. ||108||

Such *Sri Gramgeeta* book; *Guru*-discipline-self experience-accepted;
Narrated sect of village security; the Eleventh Canto completed. ||109||

Notes

1. *Agnisanskar*—Fire lighted for ritual.
2. *Tutari*—Indian curved pipe instrument to initiate action.
3. *Madhukari*—Food demanded from door to door.
4. *Math*—The place for spiritual practices.
5. *Purushartha*—The four *purushartha* in ancient script: *kam* (action), *arth* (wealth), *dharam* (religion), and *moksha* (salvation).
6. *Warkari*—Pilgrim who travels every year in the month of *Ashad* to Pandharpur in Maharashtra, the place of the deity, Vitthala.

Canto XII

Village Purification

A gentleman asked, what is in village state?
Prevails here and there confusion of disorder. ||1||

In books, poetry, description of village, glorious more;
But, reluctant to live when peeps into reality. ||2||

Dirty roads, in pond water accumulates;
Without city, no work is completed there. ||3||

Says 'turn to village' but no facility there;
Are they houses? Pig houses, dovecot they are. ||4||

No entertainment there besides *dandhar, tamasha;*
Why have we to describe village saying it the best? ||5||

Friend! Heard your words, convinced I by whatever apt;
Their reasons to be listened by audiences. ||6||

When lazy becomes workers, tilts towards luxury;
Distance it increases from work in village boundary. ||7||

No problem once committed mistake but error continues;
Invites death it for state; what about village? ||8||

Workers in dark, then what barrenness to see in village;
Begins chaos of miscreants, people confused. ||9||

Vatandar[1], *ijardar*[2], *gramjosh*[3], *veskar*[4];
Did wrong when they held village power before. ||10||

After committing error, search to way out;
Behaves as they will with fun for disruption. ||11||

Some constructed houses, protruded platform on a road;
Extended roof, obstacles for vehicles. ||12||

Some left drainage open, its flow on a road;
Trapped human beings, animals in his vicinity of house. ||13||

Accumulated sanitary water increased mosquitos, germs;
Restless neighbours become due to infectious diseases. ||14||

Tied some cattle on road, but fierce they are;
Discomfort to passerby, hard to narrate. ||15||

Placed some stones on door, upturned cart passing;
Knocked upon, fell down some in darkness. ||16||

Threw some wastage, dust, glass, nails many;
Pinch them to passerby, what to tell? ||17||

In cars, officers go, some wear shoes;
None asks to poor though feet are injured. ||18||

Threw rotten fruits, legume, husk, peels on a road;
Looking here and there, threw ewer piece by a mother. ||19||

Road covered with excreta, corners with dirt;
Everywhere garbage; encircled village by dirt, rubbish. ||20||

Fence rots in every house, thorns on a road;
Didn't know to clean who have brought thorny branches. ||21||

In village, weeds in barren land, shelter for snakes, scorpions;
Broken small fortress, horrible, no step to clean. ||22||

Constructed some wells but not repaired them;
Increased dirt by washer women, foliage in foul water. ||23||

Threw mud, ugly, on a road, from wells, drainages;
Sharp edged chips, broken tiles, dead rats too. ||24||

Cattle-shed encroached by riches, platforms on a road;
Woods, bricks, stones too on road. Who will speak? ||25||

In village, judge slept, "What to tell? Relative, friend ours"
Not thought over it, closing eyes; turned village load heavy. ||26||

Situation such strange in village, experienced;
At this instance, in village, good track to be. ||27||

To repair this, wise men to orient to village;
Being the ideal village, the foundation of nation. ||28||

Whosoever became wise in village, progressed by power, trick;
Turned to city, so leaving village barren. ||29||

Sweeper cleans city, likewise labourer, outcaste in past;
Were sweeping village lanes fine and then of *Patil* only. ||30||

To keep holy God's way, realising intention of devotees;
Idols were placed but garbage there too. ||31||

In many sects, practice of circumambulation dear was;
Vanished it is now, only unfateful is left. ||32||

On auspicious festivity, *dindi*[5], procession *dahikala*[6], were;
Entered now there, disorderly, dance, song, *dandari*. ||33||

No principle understood though *dindi*, procession are;
Door to door, home to home, increased dirt more. ||34||

Sometime *bhajan*[7] invites visiting home to home;
Broken *veena*, two *majira, mrudang* not functional. ||35||

Then left musical instrument other, balance, tune approximate;
Somehow they manage as in marriage, thread ceremony. ||36||

Chaos causes all loudspeaker, conch, bells, kettledrum;
Disturbed once, how can be balance in village? ||37||

Scenario such is; disturbed *kirtan*, meetings are;
"Render pity *Rukhminivallabha*"[8] says, no self consciousness. ||38||

Palanquin of village temple proceeds, everyone expresses;
What emotions? makes fun glancing at women. ||39||

No discipline in walking, strange hurry of people;
Concern of no-one with others for anything. ||40||

Listens none to anyone, attempts to come forward;
No education to them how to walk on a road? ||41||

No discipline to walker as if cattle walks;
Forgotten people healthy walking of a man. ||42||

Dashes on a road, smashes figures of many;
In circumambulation, operates push forward and backward. ||43||

Circumambulation now such, mockery of it indeed;
What use of it when no cleaning of dirt on a road? ||44||

So, *Ramdhun*[9] procession for recreation of village;
Rise of work through the institute of *Sevamandal*. ||45||

Friends! *Ramdhun*, not of today, tradition it of circumambulation;
Planning of work in circumambulation, *Ramdhun* it is. ||46||

Presume I village as body, piousness it to maintain;
In village, joy will prevail everywhere by it. ||47||

As we bath, village is to clean;
All people to strive for village prosperity. ||48||

We to be clean and observe dirt in vicinity;
How can be purity there? polluted body and mind too. ||49||

Hence, shop, home to clean, drainage, road too;
Then procession of *Ramdhun,* fine to arrange by an elder, an older. ||50||

Before *Ramdhun,* village to be clean, beautiful;
No uncleanliness to be seen in home, anywhere. ||51||

To assist it, cooperation to seek of service spirited;
To whom preference for service as mission. ||52||

Collectively, village cleaning of drainage, narrow channel;
Roads all to clean by self and others. ||53||

Dirt accumulated to take away out of village;
No spreading elsewhere, properly to arrange. ||54||

Excavation for manure in an open land out of village;
Urine, excreta of cattle to deposit in it. ||55||

Char latrine[10] to make, not to see dirt;
Better to manage one's dirt by oneself. ||56||

On river bank or among trees outskirt for nature call women go;
Hesitation, dirt will be at bay by *char* latrine. ||57||

After nature call, dirt to cover with soil;
To utilise, turning urine, excreta into manure. ||58||

In all village, such practice to follow whatever told;
Pleasure for the earth, contented with manure. ||59||

Otherwise he, irresponsible fellow, utilises farm as his will;
Like monkey, spoils manure and nutrients both. ||60||

Oh! This system of nature to comprehend by all;
Food turns manure, from manure production of food. ||61||

Whatever we eat, form flesh, flood, and fluid;
Manure is whatever left to disperse on the earth. ||62||

Leads to production, manure, well protected;
Without manure, an erosion of land causes. ||63||

When urine, excreta, bones merge in soil, enhances fertility;
Produces many corns' cones after sowing subsequently. ||64||

But, no knowledge for anyone, understood not village;
Disorder of excreta of us besides of cattle. ||65||

Burn the cakes of cowdungs, deprive of benefit;
Wealth in cowdung, religious books' speech are. ||66||

Accumulating dirt, urine in village, it to cover with technique;
Land all in village to manure by it. ||67||

Dirt it will eliminate, destruction it will protect;
More grain production will be, more benefits in one. ||68||

To know this needs committee, by different ways;
Public to enlighten to increase production. ||69||

Land encircled by whatever weeds, acanthus, bunions, cassia tora;
Motivating all to turn them into manure to increase productivity.
||70||

Plenty manure, plenty water, plenty labour, plenty seeds;
Plenty production, sky soaring, to see in village. ||71||

Service this real, liked by God core;
Why to exaggerate ego unnecessarily? ||72||

All to clean village for hygiene well;
Through dirt, manure, new glory will come up. ||73||

After cleanness of village, *Ramdhun* to be louding names;
To infuse holiness besides cleanliness in atmosphere. ||74||

At dawn, collective chanting of names for happy state;
For it *brahmamuhurta*[11], *ramprahar*[12], Veda says. ||75||

Asked audience, how can be *Ramdhun* in circumambulation?
Initiate it will *bhajan* of God to maintain hygiene. ||76||

Listen the mode of *Ramdhun*, the first purification of village;
Which will bath village, healthy. ||77||

Suryanarayan[13] before departure, sweeping and sprinkling;
Cleaning road by all villagers, the mansion of joy to create. ||78||

Sprinkling water here and there, *rangoli*[14] on roads;
To be placed the photographs of saints, great ones. ||79||

Archway of mango leaves to beautify open space everywhere;
The display of our labour on door to door. ||80||

Assembling all servicemen, *Ramdhun* to proceed;
To be embedded the first row with skill. ||81||

To plan children in children rows, youth in youth rows;
Older people in senior rows, with the ease. ||82||

To walk women, girls separately, beauty to be on road;
Intermittently planning is to be of singers. ||83||

On sideways, servicemen to walk in uniform full;
Discipline they to maintain in row, two in each. ||84||

In one's hand bell, strokes on round brass plate;
From the scheduled place, begins *Ramdhun* in planned mode. ||85||

'Raghupati Raghav Rajaram, Patipawarn Sitaram'[15];
To be uttered first by singer, then to be followed. ||86||

Tune to be with restrain in line, discipline;
To be sung the patriotic songs by singers. ||87||

Songs some to be on village, some on devotion;
Some on character-oriented for ever. ||88||

While passing in squares, doors, with silence;
Loud acclamation to be to reverberate in the sky. ||89||

With acclamation of *Gurudeo*, chanting of the mother India;
Utterances of sages, saints, enlightenment with joy to be. ||90||

Respect with folded hands, the images of great ones on roads;
Not to be halted in road, leaving *Ramdhun.* ||91||

Round to complete at *Gurudeo* square halt to be;
Coming forward, servicemen to be lined in row. ||92||

Then spaciously in que, people have to stand;
Children in children rows, youth, seniors likewise. ||93||

Separate que of women, systematically to arrange;
Union of people to beautify in square or open space. ||94||

Then suggestion by initiator to implement whatever spoken;
To plan prayer, speech, salutation as per schedule. ||95||

In speech to stress, people have to clean;
In village, behaviour to be with cooperation. ||96||

When increases dirt, contaminates also mind;
By this mean, hampers the complete progress of lives. ||97||

All to be cleaned, disciplined, and loved each other;
Engrossingly village to be heaven. ||98||

Acclimating after speech, all people have to turn;
Ramdhun to close suggesting to walk peacefully. ||99||

Servicemen have to depart, pleasing their minds;
By planning, heaven descends in village. ||100||

Remedies searched being not known to people to walk;
Including poor, rich, all to learn. ||101||

Rows with two in each, one after another;
Purify the *Ganges* of *bhajan*, integrate organisation. ||102||

Learn walking, speaking with ease; sitting, standing with discipline;
Knows to play an instrument with song in the royal court of village. ||103||

Repairs home and home enhances love for beauty;
Abolishes tendency of uncleanliness, boosts up cooperation. ||104||

Strengthen the feeling of "We one", eliminates laziness;
Experiences no one hesitation, chances all to express. ||105||

Nourishes affinity for all, pleasant all people live;
Ramdhun such is, the school for cooperation. ||106||

Plan such to be taken, village to be rebuild;
To all it will provide joy, Tukadya says. ||107||

Such *Sri Gramgeeta* book; *Guru*-discipline-self experience-accepted;
Narrated village bath-*Ramdhun;* the Twelfth Canto completed. ||108||

Notes

1,2. *Vatandar, ijardar*—The chief executive officer of the village.

3. *Gramjoshi*—The chief Brahmin who looks after religious practices in village.
4. *Veshkar*—The village sweepers.
5. *Dindi*—The musical procession of devotees who play on *manjira* (two small round brass plates when strike on each other create melody) and *dholki* (Indian horizontal drum which is played on both sides).
6. *Dahikala*—The mixture of curd, flat rice, pulse, chilly, cucumber prepared to serve devotees on religious function.
7. *Bhajan*—Indian folk form of religious singing accompanied by *manjira, mrudung, khanjiri.*
8. *Rukhminivallabha*—Vitthal, the deity in Karnataka and Maharashtra.
9. *Ramdhun*—Circumambulation to village with religious utterance in morning.
10. *Char latrine*—Economical latrine by digging land and covering by side.
11. *Brahmamuhurta*—An apt time to begin.
12. *Ramprahar*—Dawn time to chant holy name.
13. *Suryanarayan*—Salutation to the sun, the life giver.
14. *Rangoli*—A design by hand on floor by white powder.
15. *Raghupati Raghav Rajaram, Patitpawan Sitaram*—In the rhythmical mode, the utterance of name, Ram, who is the protagonist of Indian epic, *Ramayana*, the husband of Sita, the benefactor of downtrodden.

Canto XIII

Art of Village Creation

Where work, wealth enters, knowing this formula;
Than city, our village to beautify. ||1||

Forgot people this, misfortune due to laziness;
Prevail misery, poverty everywhere in village. ||2||

Arrived machines, paralysed industrial skills in village;
For work, to city, skilled persons have gone. ||3||

To city, intellect of village, prosperity of village have;
Labour power, handicrafts too have gone. ||4||

Remained chiefly farming in village, continues it somehow;
At different end, the flow of special intellect, power, wealth. ||5||

Wander highly qualified, an energetic for employment;
How can village be elevated, if not industries, farming? ||6||

If they pay attention, though small industries and farm;
Nourish all definitely, unemployed, wretched, none left. ||7||

Because, raw materials at village, provide livelihood;
Situation deteriorated in village, no refining of raw materials. ||8||

At low rate raw material, price four times when refined;
How can villagers be happy? Empty bellied though producer. ||9||

Total self reliance, the core mean of their happiness;
No depending on city, all have to work. ||10||

Planning the best intellectual skill, strength of power;
Self reliance to enhance, shedding laziness of all. ||11||

Here and there love for self reliance, some work at home;
Others to help with detachment, doing one's work. ||12||

At home, children to work—farming, work, business to do self;
Wife, children to be happy, labouring hard. ||13||

In hand, the mean for industry; reflection on the name of Rama;
Great is this religion of village people. ||14||

Each element of village, artist, serviceman to be;
Who will décorate village making one's home beautiful? ||15||

Life of labourer graces as God's presence;
Being selfreliant, cooperates to village. ||16||

The first step, work at home; the second, outer management;
The next, village cleanliness; hobby to be with joy. ||17||

Such, nature of labour to enhance naturally;
Forms of different arts to learn with labour. ||18||

Art, an ornament of human life, but in it reflection of life must;
In heart, seeking contentment, life to continue. ||19||

All art such to be, otherwise wasteful it is;
Without purpose, an animal born and left. ||20||

Identity of man due to art, otherwise who asks?
Whether you are poor or rich, no one asks. ||21||

Though anyone is wealthy, artistic he to be;
In it lies wisdom, lies of rich persons. ||22||

Otherwise all in home disordered, not known to sing, play;
But, hire they singers freely, night sleepless without. ||23||

Poses their festival great, to celebrate *navaratra*[1];
Singers artistic for this brought to deity. ||24||

Don't understand we, so called to listeners;
Modulations in song they listen, we only laugh. ||25||

What use of this mode of which we have no sense;
Better to learn any art than this. ||26||

Though ours is blue pigeon, good other's swan;
But, parrot of art, self reliant to call by everyone. ||27||

Oh! At least single art of life to know to a man;
Then 'man' he is, otherwise chaos in life. ||28||

The art of sweet speaking, the art of cleanliness;
The art of manual labour, an indispensable in life. ||29||

Writing beautiful letters and lines, clear reading of books;
Never visible excuse little anywhere of artist. ||30||

To be straight in life, the essence of simple purity;
Sign of cleanliness in heart, the religion of artist it is. ||31||

Know art everyone, none is an exception;
Conscience necessary to present before masses. ||32||

By self-labour, home to make an ideal;
Though cottage it is, paradise to appear. ||33||

Constructed mud-houses but beautiful more than lime;
With less money, the design of house is made. ||34||

In village bricks made; moulded, baked earthen pot, goblet;
Produced tiles, containers in our village. ||35||

Made wood straight by sharpening, infused creative energy;
Learnt art our carpenter in village. ||36||

In village, made hammer, nail, anvil, axe, enclosure, sickle;
Spade, hoe, sling, the items needful for life. ||37||

Breaking stones created flat slab, sharpened it straight;
Look beautiful all after fitting in house. ||38||

Broom, mat, weaving strips, cots, doormat, leather, container, rope;
Made beautiful sowing pipe, plough in new style. ||39||

Spined separating cotton, weaved fine cloth, sweater;
Made, nose-rope, mouth mask, rope, net. ||40||

Planned some farm, boundaries, dam, beds in the field different;
Seem they straight in row in farm. ||41||

Trees in row, straight, beautiful, pure green;
Performs work, owner himself with his hands. ||42||

Garden, surrounding house, grew trees on drainage water;
Saplings of fruits, flowers, creepers, vegetables ever. ||43||

From outside water not seen, water flows inside;
Smoke out from chimneys, not accumulates cow urine in shed. ||44||

Purity in house, cleanliness in behaviour;
The place allotted for every object seem an apt. ||45||

Written names of the objects, not to ask for while talking;
Entering house, one knows where the items are. ||46||

Whatever is before door, decorated with the art;
Created they in village by the artists. ||47||

Not seen hired pride, decorum by foreigners;
Objects numerous brought from foreign countries. ||48||

Whatever see, are from our village or state, nation;
For that venture all people appreciate us. ||49||

Beauty such we have to bring in homes;
Experiences pleasure when anyone observes with keen sight. ||50||

Art to be based on labour, progressive self-reliant work;
Complete urge in it, enlivens life of nation. ||51||

Ornaments body someone's art, someone's cleanliness at home;
Decors someone's art village amateurly. ||52||

Decors village human art, village's art enlivens state;
State's art embeds nation with individualities. ||53||

Knows better such artistic skills to man;
But, in an artist's mind, planning is to be. ||54||

Otherwise, on head foreign hat and raiment of *khadi* down;
Maroti's head to Ganesha, happens this. ||55||

Built someone beautified hall, delight to viewers;
But, his toilet set was defunct. ||56||

Came home to know, entered in lavatory;
Inside scattered dirt, no cleanness to see. ||57||

Then seen kitchen, peeling of onions, potatoes, there;
Ash rubbish in *chullaha*[2], no brooming to clean. ||58||

Split in corner, dirt on backside of cupboard;
When unfolded fine carpet, waste, papers below it. ||59||

How is an artist? Peep inside far a while;
No cow-dung wash from seven days seems to be. ||60||

Made everything fine but stigma on it this much;
In the art, such lacunae not to exist. ||61||

Multi-faceted art to be, serene fully inside and outside;
Then wealth runs whenever one touches. ||62||

House decorate with such art, made beautiful our life;
But, beauty does not persist if village disorders. ||63||

As leucoderma on body, appears it misfit;
The ideal, systematic village to be by our art. ||64||

Sevak-mandal in village to realise 'on tongue Ram, in hand work';
For village service, the celebration of work relentlessly. ||65||

Roads to be repaired by weekly labour donation;
By absorptive pit and narrow channel, drainage-water to be blocked. ||66||

On road for one side traffic, narrow has become lane;
Weed, thorns, bushes grew; all to be managed. ||67||

An accumulated water on road, to be cleaned;
In new style toilets to be made for all. ||68||

Cleanness in river, lake, arrangement for strong platform, *ghat*[3];
Principally for more production water to be used. ||69||

Roads, wells, houses, cattle shed are to be beautified;
Place to place, urinal, channels to be made. ||70||

On both sides of road, plantation to be;
Dustbin to be kept after intervals to dump garbage. ||71||

Village beautiful from all sides, wind to blow inside;
Dirt not to be seen in any house while looking. ||72||

Though house is dilapidated, one has to go there;
Renovated it to be, deeming it ours. ||73||

House, without windows, dark, suffocated, sultry, dwarf not to be;
Cattle shed inside, not to be spotted. ||74||

Stones, platform to be repaired; corner, an open land;
Not to be disordered, crooked situation. ||75||

All have to dig-lines with thread;
New roads spacious to make to please people. ||76||

Roads to mark with stone, word; ways to be clean;
Village to pull if anyone hurdles, unfortunate. ||77||

Thorns fence, grass weed possibly not to be in village;
Waste piles, dust particles not to be scattered. ||78||

For thorny branches, grass heap, weed, threshing;
Pottery making, pit for consecrated fire, secure places to assign.
||79||

Dead cattle anywhere; dirt, flesh, bones in village;
Not to happen this, places specific to be for burial. ||80||

Everywhere information board to be for guidance;
Roads, squares to decorate with great names. ||81||

Where darkness on road, an arrangement for light;
On all sides, to be made by workers. ||82||

In village, school to open arrangement for;
Market, small place for selling, necessary for convenience. ||83||

Otherwise, bazaar in village, no discipline to shop;
Kept good anywhere, prevail chaos everywhere. ||84||

Push people each other, pickpockets some;
Not understood the mode of humanity. ||85||

Looks youth at wrong places, speaks words crooked;
Walks here and looks there, cause it jerks to people. ||86||

Scatter someone good, leaves bullock-cart, inland short stump;
Wander freely sheep, cows; arrange chillies in between. ||87||

No row of shops, arranges goods anyone anywhere;
Causes it inconvenience to seller and purchaser. ||88||

Group of flies there, listens, no one to anyone;
Swing of earning money everywhere with an enthusiasm. ||89||

May ask someone, "Why this?" says a shopkeeper, tax they give;
Who can instruct us? Tell, tell. ||90||

There all to repair wherever this happens;
Collectively telling with love, not to enforce. ||91||

When people listen not to us, repair to be by assembly;
May be presentation before government to renovate village. ||92||

Principally our committee to be, to keep bazaar beautiful;
Weight, measurement, items, place, mode to be in order. ||93||

To protect crops, army of monkeys not to enter;
Committees various to be formed for different works. ||94||

Inclusive village structure to be, entertainment to nourish emotions;
Subsequently, villagers not to recall of city. ||95||

Lectures, *kirtan*, art troops, debates, *powada*, plays pure;
Entertainment such with novelty to function in village. ||96||

Beautiful garden to be facet of it for psychic peace too;
To enhance pleasure, myriad colours, plant, creepers, bushes. ||97||

Playground, swings to please children, youth;
Forgetting walls of caste, creed, they to run naturally. ||98||

Rest-house in village to be, for guests, an enthusiastic, good;
Doors open to all to rest there. ||99||

There beautiful well to be for drinking water, cold;
On all walls, proverbs to be aphoristic, fine. ||100||

Beautiful to be wresting ground, roam children sportively with joy;
To learn lesson of an ideal wrestler, players. ||101||

Fine bodies of children look as if pleasant rose;
Garden blossoms with colours of son's honest. ||102||

Beautiful library to be with books knowledgeable;
To rise refined intellect in villagers. ||103||

To know in village, what happens in world;
Fresh newspapers, radio to be there. ||104||

Likewise the handwritten monthly to make calligraphy fine;
Boost up it the appreciation of writing, painting. ||105||

To know easily news and thought, blackboard to be in square;
As if Jnaneshwar's wall, knowledge it will provide. ||106||

To empower illiterate, adult education to be;
Numbering to be on houses, placing name plates. ||107||

Villagers who know medicines for cattle, help to render;
Folksongs various to be collected from sources. ||108||

To keep hygiene well, for welfare of all beings;
In village, health home is to run in village. ||109||

Plants, creepers, nodules, roots to be used for medicines;
By naturopathic means they are to provide. ||110||

Doctor to practice to neutralise snake's venom;
To heal, to join bones, utilising such medicines. ||111||

Maternity home there to be, where hospital for men;
The indispensable need of both, villagers experience. ||112||

In village, doctor, midwife to be trained;
Providing them with new means of knowledge. ||113||

In village, post-office is to be to know the present;
To facilitate communication by letters. ||114||

Such all facilities, people can do with determination;
Being self-reliant completely, cooperating others. ||115||

Wastes everyone much time, labour power, and an intellect;
Utilising them engrossedly, happy will be village. ||116||

Being village the ideal fully, paradise than city;
Lures beautiful life all, Tukadya says. ||117||

Such *Sri Gramgeeta* book; *Guru*-discipline-self experience-accepted;
Narrated self-relied village creation; the Thirteen Canto completed. ||118||

Notes

1. *Navratra*—The festival of godess, Durga.
2. *Chullaha*—U-shaped mud plastered structure to cook food.
3. *Ghat*—The structure on shore of river, with stairs for rituals.

Canto XIV

Village Hygiene

An audience, an ardent believer said, though village systematised;
But, difficult to eradicate hurdle by God. ||1||

Though village turned in city, what is powerful before Him?
What happens though village turned in city. ||2||

Frowned god-goddess, caused cholera;
Impossible it to cure anyone by an expert doctor. ||3||

Worship to perform to please goddess;
Whether village or city, can't be happy without it. ||4||

Friend! listen the answer, god-goddess or Supreme;
This incarnation of grace, no frown in their heart. ||5||

Frown they on wicked with thought of elevation in heart;
Not to say, God to him who tortures innocent. ||6||

All are His sons; why torture to anyone?
Action ours trouble us, our foes we are. ||7||

Dirt on all sides, germs are created in it;
Grew from it epidemic of various diseases. ||8||

No disciplined behaviour, no purity in diet, no walking;
Impure air, water, eliminate people. ||9||

Anytime, anything to eat; anytime to sleep, wake;
Surface up seven minerals in the form of diseases. ||10||

"Eat at hotel, go to cemetery", say wise people;
In addition, addiction of pungent as fiery ghost. ||11||

No rule to anything, which patient splits where?
Contingency due to food, prevails disorder everywhere. ||12||

Spreads it diseases, increases diseases contagious;
Victimise thousand people, causing an infection. ||13||

Then 'frowned goddess' some say; call some for an incantation;
Deeming it due to outer cause, waves lamps. ||14||

Treat it some, a black magic, an evil; controls some ghost;
Kills patient without medicines, with nonsense. ||15||

A devotee, an incantor, a black magician operate differently;
Among people, pose opinions various for belly. ||16||

Vows, high-sounding; worships before goddess;
Slaughter male buffalo, goat, hen ignorantly. ||17||

Created God living beings; not passionate to kill them?
Play their roles intermediators to satisfy their hobby. ||18||

Saint pleased gods; who have butchered?
Say Chokhoba, Chakradhar, Ramakrishna, "delightful He in faith". ||19||

Sacrifice of animal God needs; illusion, false pride ours;
Without wiping out ignorance, life not to be happy. ||20||

Though village or city, thought and conduct disordered;
Restless due to diseases all people are. ||21||

To make village healthy and fine, each home to be improved;
And more than it, an ideal to inhabit at home. ||22||

To become individual an ideal, inclusive, needs daily schedule pure;
All life healthy and fine will be of village. ||23||

Disciplined each day to be, improves it life complete;
Healthy will be village; pleasant all gods, goddess. ||24||

Basic crux of discipline, stout to be decision;
On it relies the progressive steps of material and spiritual. ||25||

Formulated rules by man to facilitate life all;
But, negligence once leads to false direction. ||26||

Not slept at night once, then why to wake up in morning?
Breaking rules, all day was spent in laziness. ||27||

No fear, care of others, not spoken people at home;
Though wake up he next day at ten in morning. ||28||

For some days continued it, habitual he to wake up late;
No change later on though whatever remedial steps. ||29||

Why to happen this? Better to wake up in morning;
With determination, home members have to wake up sleepers.
||30||

Sign it of fortune to wake up late, say some;
What lacuna a fortunate has to feed his belly? ||31||

Presuming it lazy he became? How can he be fortunate?
If sleeper is fortunate, is not a patient more fortunate? ||32||

Sleeps he all time; drinks, eats on bed;
Is he more fortunate? Tell, tell. ||33||

Reverse is definition of fortunate; is it honourable to wise?
O friend! Fortunate he is who wakes up in morning. ||34||

Labour creates wealth, sleepers provide harm;
Additional labour to others, lowers our enthusiasm. ||35||

Sleeps house owner though the Sun at noon;
Still sleeps though the sunshine, tilts on sides. ||36||

Turns servants lazy; says, sleeps house-owner;
Then how can we perform work going there? ||37||

Darkness impends like this, bark dogs;
Cry, weep children; sleep women. ||38||

How can house be pious? Makes body lazy after awakening;
Prevails disorder, constipation increases. ||39||

Lead they to all diseases, turn to doctors time to time;
Hampers work, enters misfortune in house. ||40||

Air hygienic at dawn, nourishes life for ever;
Pleasure a season provides at that time to all beings. ||41||

Wakes up an entire forest, blossom all flowers;
Wakes up all animals, birds at dawn. ||42||

Milking of cow, buffalo at dawn, contains it more nutrients;
Makes blood immune, the wind at dawn. ||43||

So wake up at dawn to see time heavenly;
After waking, meditate where thou sits. ||44||

Meditation at dawn means new inspiration to progress in rising day;
To perform, work in full swing, the prayer for God. ||45||

One who determines at that time, reflects not to happen evil;
Progresses he with good *sanskar*, speedily. ||46||

So, meditation at dawn to infuse with natural enthusiasm;
Then natural call, routine regular, valuable. ||47||

Nature's call, mouth-washing at dawn cure gaseous problems;
Creates new vigour gaining purity. ||48||

In morning, inhale air to calm inner organs;
Then bath by cold water to fresh one's mind. ||49||

Importance of cold bath more, makes it skin beautiful;
Body always active, fresh with an enthusiasm. ||50||

Improves mind if brain part remains cool;
Experienced this by many great persons. ||51||

Patient to be treated if one baths with warm water;
Harmful for body if this habit continues. ||52||

Collective meditation, prayer to be after bath before the sunrise;
Barrack, temple clean to search for meditation. ||53||

Golden glare of dawn, decor of beauty to watch;
Enhances nature's peace, gift to benefit invaluably to *yogi*. ||54||

Say people, *yogi* to meditate, why early waking, meditation to them?
Words these, not true ever of anyone. ||55||

Enters yogi in trance, *yog* for the righteous path;
Yog of life's luminescence, possible in morning time. ||56||

Besides meditation, daily habit to walk necessary;
With oxygen, body and mind remain pure, clean. ||57||

Some run, some walk, some practice *asana*, *suryanamaskar;*
Some sing, meditate; such scene let see in morning. ||58||

Some have to read; body, mind to mould;
By this routine, the entire life becomes beautiful. ||59||

Though at home, *ashram*, journey or pilgrimage;
Curriculum to complete regularly in morning. ||60||

Home, *ashram* to clean, cleanliness on path everywhere;
Cattle shed of cows, buffaloes to clean like mirror. ||61||

Servants, others to cooperate but everyone to work;
Mother, other women to do work swiftly. ||62||

At dawn, sees everyone sprinkling, smearing, *rangoli;*
No dirt inside, outside; winds up work everyone. ||63||

In village, where this happens, presume *Laxmi* is lured;
Prevails kingdom of hygiene in that village. ||64||

Increases life span where cleanliness in morning;
No living being in sleep to spot there. ||65||

So in regulation, such not to commit mistake;
Behaviour our to control again and again. ||66||

Once comprehended, hygiene, fortune prevails in family;
No need of medicine to body; increases new luminescence. ||67||

In past, performed morning, noon, and in evening;
Prayer in three times to instill *sanskar.* ||68||

Apt it for all time, so morning meditation regular;
And evening prayer to be performed by all. ||69||

Before and after sleep, at the juncture of day and night;
And becomes deep noted *sanskar*, determination at meal. ||70||

Among people, at meal, praying for *Hari*, uttering *Geeta;*
Good feelings in heart makes life pure. ||71||

An audience asked, "after urging for God";
What and how are the fruits, tell us? ||72||

Meal means intake of nutrients, why song of God?
Why not to make fun for pleasure? ||73||

Listen answer of this, meal means *sanskar* on body;
Call it *yagnya* massive, fire burning in liver. ||74||

Pleasant at meal, pious meditation;
Likewise infuse pure virtues with food. ||75||

Pious incense, fragrance, pure atmosphere, disease destructive;
Rangoli, others, place to be clean. ||76||

Meal without cleanliness, deems it unclean;
Cleaning hands, legs, sufficient meal to be for more energy. ||77||

Some work before meal so as to rest for all;
Work it facilitates, collectively all people. ||78||

Some to place *aasan*[2], wooden platform; serve food, water;
Some to light incense stick for fragrance. ||79||

First, after sitting, utterance with dignified voice;
Shantimantra to sing after serving with seriousness. ||80||

Then offering to *Brahma*, intake of food with respect;
Shloka, sweet words to speak while eating. ||81||

Sipping of water before meal, it's purpose to ignite fire;
Circling of water, dedication its crux. ||82||

God created food; food it, God's grace;
Debt to recall, on which everyone's life relies. ||83||

Public their offsprings, they too get food;
For this offering to cosmic God, *yagnya* of food. ||84||

Food means *prasad* of the earth mother, with happiness to taste;
Food in which labour of farmer unfolds. ||85||

With respect it to eat, the best *shloka* to sing in village;
No talk disturbing to make furious at the time of meal. ||86||

Though humour, no obscenity to be crept in discussion;
No trace of food to be left after meal. ||87||

Lovely, inflammable, pure, food of different types;
Realising our appetite one to proceed. ||88||

Same righteous one says, food created for digestion;
But, the nature of appetite to understand. ||89||

Some food causes disease, some food stimulates desire;
Some food responsible for evil impressions. ||90||

Some eats limestones, meat, insects too;
But, their nature, temperament vary accordingly. ||91||

What to eat by man to enhance humanity?
This to know by a well behaved person. ||92||

Pure, nourishable food to take, to create thoughts pure;
If food, inflammable, lovely, eaten; behaviour moulds likewise. ||93||

Some prefer liquor, meat, passion it instigates;
Infections different cause they, contagious too. ||94||

Certain it is, food creates digestive juice;
In body, flesh, fat, semen are formed without doubt. ||95||

Thoughts inspire in mind as qualities in blood;
In blood composition, mirror cruelty, courage, dullness, intelligence. ||96||

Besides mixture in blood, creep up hereditary qualities;
Pertain some impressions to habits of eating and drinking. ||97||

Some turn due to contact, some to nature of land;
Mould living being, because of persistent efforts. ||98||

Though this true, the core is food and drink;
Form and reduce blood, the fresh of living beings. ||99||

Food to be the best for body having the pure blood;
Intake of not apt food influences brain, organs reversely. ||100||

Reinless becomes erotic desire, wind blows outwardly;
As cattle fights, man behaves likewise. ||101||

One to eat accordingly without doubt to perform cruel work;
From consequences one has to suffer aftermath. ||102||

From core of heart, one who feels to be humane;
Has to eat pure food all the time. ||103||

One has asked question, what pure food is for poor?
What he has to do for life? ||104||

Friends! pure food available easily, grow it in farm;
Vegetable, *chapati*, procurable with little efforts. ||105||

Sunlight produces roots, vegetables, fruits;
Nutrients they all are for hygiene. ||106||

Simple, fresh, digestible, pure food it is;
Sweets, breeder of disorder, impure it is. ||107||

Crude grain powder, on which poor people rely;
Pure means nutrients to body, hygienic with *sanskar.* ||108||

Fried, spoiled food not to eat besides soar, salty;
In meal, intake not to be of excessive sweet. ||109||

Not to eat sweet, fried, spicy, always;
Favour not to be for pungent, of all. ||110||

Clean to be pure food, fresh, delicious, and juicy;
Leafy vegetables, fruits different, tasty originally. ||111||

To eat r*abadi*[3] condensing milk, to make *puranpoli*[4] by pulping;
To eat *bhajepuri*[5] fried, food of irresponsible one it is. ||112||

Prepared *rava*[6] after sieving, infused *khawa*[7] more;
Tongue appreciates it but stomach doesn't operate well. ||113||

Some enhanced the art of eating, eat some rice excessively;
Pour tamarind water cup by cup on rice. ||114||

Some eat *ladu*[8], *pethe*[9] excessively; *rabadi*[10], *halwa*[11] too;
Calculating money, some measure edible items. ||115||

The ill digestible it becomes, disorders the entire;
Different ailments enter to provide pain. ||116||

Eat some for taste, push inside though no need;
Then causes illness of cholera, an ill digestion, an accumulation. ||117||

Suffer some from gases in stomach, foul smell of an ill digestion;
Laugh saying people, "why does intake liberal?" ||118||

Diet against nature, no cognisance of time;
Sour, oily, odd mix, such poisonous diet. ||119||

Eat some people this, take medicine after illness;
How has poor money? *Vaidya*[12], house to house. ||120||

Says doctor, no exclusion; due to it root of disease remains;
Observes patient daily when approaches to death. ||121||

First to eat for pleasure, then to digest with medicine;
Such nuisance, why to create reinlessly? ||122||

Useless it is to eat such, to take medicinal powder to digest it;
For what does destroy digestive juices? ||123||

What does a *vaidya* perform when disorder increases inside?
No return in consuming medicine, spending money. ||124||

But, people insist, offer to eat being well-wisher;
They to deem as harmful, discipline to maintain for diet. ||125||

Regular, *satvik*[13] food to eat, simple, fresh, vegetables;
Milk, curd in diet, making meal medicinal. ||126||

In all meals, the best meal in which cow milk preparations;
Intake of ambrosia to deem it for body. ||127||

Intake of cow milk daily, principally core changes;
Energy, agility, intellect, hygiene always in hand. ||128||

Healthy life will be more, short demise or epidemic;
Will not step in village, Tukadya says. ||129||

Such *Sri Gramgeeta* book, *Guru*-discipline-self experience-accepted;
Narrated conduct based village hygiene; the Fourteenth Canto completed. ||130||

Notes

1. *Laxmi*—The Goddess of wealth in Hindu mythology.
2. *Aasan*—Seat.
3. *Rabidi*—Semisolid product of milk.

4. *Puranpoli*—Sweet chapatti made of powdering pulses.
5. *Bhajepuri*—Fried eatable.
6. *Rawa*—Powder form of wheat.
7. *Khawa*—Fatty product of milk.
8. *Ladu*—Sweet preparations.
9. *Pethe*—Sweet preparations.
10. *Rabadi*—Sweet preparations.
11. *Halwa*—Sweet preparations.
12. *Vaidya*—Ayurvedic treatment giver.
13. *Satvik*—Not spicy, oily, pungent.

Canto XV

Improvement of Cow Race

An audience asked, a scarcity of milk prevails;
How can be curd, butter of cow for all? ||1||

Corrupt milk providers pour water in buffalo's milk;
Sells milk treating it as cow's milk with more money. ||2||

Where are cows? Sparingly visible for selling if saved;
For footwear, boots, calves too are killed. ||3||

India, the nation of shepherds, worships cattle;
But, cows turned into manuals, no notice towards them. ||4||

Same purchased by butcher, some are elsewhere;
Rest is waste, remaining stuff of cow all. ||5||

Costly is fodder, no avenue to escape;
Half strived a man is; how can cows be domesticated? ||6||

Listening to his illustration, said, anticipated thy saying;
But, in this, the entire setback of ours. ||7||

India, the agricultural nation, needs cow race for farming;
No pure nutrient essence elsewhere besides cow milk. ||8||

No poverty was when cow race was flourished;
Not were plenty of diseases prevalent. ||9||

Maintained quality of soil by cow dung, cow urine;
Reservoirs were filled in villages, with grains. ||10||

Land and cattle, reservoir this of production;
New animals form one co-business in every house. ||11||

Everywhere milk products, subservient to food grains;
Lived aged people healthy and without diseases. ||12||

So cow treasure, the name apt for cow cattle;
Happy was entire India when cow race protected. ||13||

But, later on negligence, ruling party also responsible;
Become cows victim, scarcity of them due to it. ||14||

Turned we to buffalo, started enjoying tea, coffee;
So we, deprived of cows, besides others. ||15||

Contented once eating animals who lost for ever;
Then how milk, offspring, fodder for them? Such happened lunatically. ||16||

Filled belly after selling cow? What is left for every day?
Experienced happiness who nourished cow, feeding less to self. ||17||

Self protection in cow-home, the narration of ancestors;
Scarified their lives many valorous persons for them. ||18||

Shri Krishna and Shivshankar, Vashistha[1] and Datta Digambar;
Dilip, Shivaji ready for cow service; saint, devotee of cow. ||19||

Those renounced everything, *bhiksha* on palm, residence among trees;
Guru such unattached too rendered service for cows. ||20||

In cow's body, all perceived God, Goddess;
Faith their was such, cow, the base for nation. ||21||

Cultivates cow-dung farm, renders farm happiness, wealth;
So, narration prevails, wealth in cow dung. ||22||

Health better by milk, where is left doctor?
Moulds milk nutrients intellect, beauty, and knowledge too. ||23||

Eliminator of gastric ailment, provides nutrients cow's butter milk;
Solace to eyes, forehead by butter as the Moon, the Sun in eyes. ||24||

Mansion of hygiene cow is; labour, her direct offspring;
Practice of cow service, the easy avenue to nation's happiness. ||25||

As thus, to improve cow race everyone's duty is;
Some remedies to search completely. ||26||

From village a butcher takes away cows, watching scene;
Sorrow to experience by all to bring cows back. ||27||

Such mediators are to expel or engage in some work;
By possible means, seller and purchaser are to turn towards good. ||28||

Can by this way he become rich? A seller to understand;
Manure, urine they provide; service to cow, never fruitless. ||29||

If cow mows in morning, rises up with cow urine;
Place has become pious, one has to conceive? ||30||

Cows to domesticate, who has farm;
Cow she is, whose cow dung, urine useful. ||31||

Cow like mother to look after;
Not to create much files or mere skeleton. ||32||

Nourishing with fodder, oil cake, grain powder, cow to make healthy;
Patting with love at home, she is to be pleasant. ||33||

An ideal bull in village is to produce well built ox;
Beautiful co-venture will be to cultivate farm. ||34||

Experiences joy more when sees the best cows, bull;
Show children enormous power after drinking milk. ||35||

Pure beauty it is, touch gently children cow mother;
Drinking milk remain engrossed them in game. ||36||

Increases milk of cow race, progress climb ladder;
Eating *laddu, pethe* unnecessarily swell belly. ||37||

Artificial milk butter, not equal to cow milk products;
Flourish diverse diseases unconsciously, artificially. ||38||

Happier will not be farming, with machines only;
The best way to keep village wealth in village. ||39||

For this place at home to care for cow, cattle;
Animals many to see fresh to get milk, curd. ||40||

Need of milk, curd to be fulfilled in village;
Cow, calf at every home, fortunate to village. ||41||

Cow security home for those who don't keep cow at home;
Facility for poor people, there to get more milk. ||42||

At same place, place for cow security, but cows' frail;
Engulf money, kill cows without fodder. ||43||

Such cow security home ought not to be, which hurts man;
Seeing cow, bull, people have to be pleasant. ||44||

In it, provision to be for milk, curd, for wealth of people;
Dry worship is not to be in home or village. ||45||

Providing them fodder, their weights to increase;
Keeping an ideal cow, strong bull, the best breed to enhance. ||46||

In village, to graze herd of cows, needs large posture;
As rivers, lake, group of wells, spacious. ||47||

The best bull to be supplied with fodder amply;
After fertilization, gives birth to cows. ||48||

Cow security home, this real, otherwise cow slaughter house;
Can it be cow security home by enclosing them in *wada*[2]. ||49||

If no pasture for cows, it to be demanded from government;
Or, to be donated by landlord in village. ||50||

Cow security home to be studied, different experiments too;
Information to be given how other nations have flourished. ||51||

For eradication of cow race diseases, hospital in village to be;
Immunity to be understood for benefit of all. ||52||

In villages, cow to worship, centres for cow service, cow milk;
Taste for younger, elders for cow milk to inculcate. ||53||

All to be done, possible but improve pure diet;
Impossible seems to have right-mind without it. ||54||

Without pure diet and water, hygiene in village out of reach;
How wealth can be if in body no power? ||55||

The best milk, the best bull, the best farm, the best choice;
The best workers massive with power. ||56||

Respectable they became who mould villages;
Without work died they posing themselves. ||57||

Without work futile wealth, without work futile power;
Ceases in various ways, imparts sorrow to life. ||58||

Eating much nutrient food, increased fat;
Caused diseases to provide pain. ||59||

So, important work is, exercise for health;
If sweats body, germs are killed. ||60||

Exercise, healthy friend, to retain this formula in mind;
Laziness deemed as rival everywhere. ||61||

Without exercise pure food too turns harmful;
Exercise, ignition of food is; digestion of food feasible. ||62||

Expels exercise inertia, pours sportiveness in body;
Blood circulation well in body, liveness develops in thought. ||63||

Muscles powerful by exercise, larger span of life by it;
Without exercise trouble more acidity, cough, gas. ||64||

Increases it resistance, an attitude for self-reliance;
An exercise increases an inspiration to work more. ||65||

Such exercise for all, envisaging its utility;
This not mere territory of wrestlers. ||66||

Some are after exercise to become wrestler;
Shown strength of body power to glare people. ||67||

For award strive some by all means;
Beats some each other for money. ||68||

For service body to work, village to secure by truth;
Weak to lift up by art of wrestling. ||69||

But, no heed to this after engulfing sweets;
Waste energy in evil work, many exercising people. ||70||

On some well built body, raiment silky, soft;
Anxiety ever for one's food, nutrients only. ||71||

Leadership given to him for village service;
But, his tongue operates without doing anything. ||72||

Conscious not to fold his cloth, aloof he remains;
Work others but doesn't leave his place. ||73||

May be expert in wrestling but of no helpful when needs;
How can he be deemed as wrestler with justice. ||74||

Wrestler is he real who developing his physique;
Like Hanumant dedicates himself for service. ||75||

Only to lift on knee, to knock, to win in wrestling, to digest;
To warn younger and elders, not signs of exercise. ||76||

To follow scheme of service, to serve for life;
Exercise indispensable for all which provides energy. ||77||

Not necessary, only in exercise home exercise is;
The best exercise it is, which assists in production. ||78||

To lift with weight in hand, better to pull water;
Grinding, breaking, digging, all hygienic are. ||79||

Wasted time valuable in playing temporary games;
The fruits of labour better than them. ||80||

Grinding, breaking, the best for exercise hygienic;
Body remains vital, such essentials one avails. ||81||

Saves wealth more, increases labour power;
By these means in village, aspirations will fulfill. ||82||

Rendering public service, the fruits of hygiene we will get;
What difficulty, where? Treasure of happiness village will receive.
||83||

Our farm our labour, using cow dung, urine, fine;
An ideal farming will be, no want of production. ||84||

In home to home, an old, male, female will work;
In spite of it, they experience pleasure in life. ||85||

In work itself, the fruit ripe will be availed;
Strength of health, nature will give to all people. ||86||

Company of plants, the essence in the sunlight;
Labour in pure air, an ambrosia to all. ||87||

Be it be village or city, no disease will prevail;
Every person will behave like this. ||88||

At distance from an addiction, laziness, mis-conduct;
Requires in village element each beautiful. ||89||

Virtues to bring in practice wherever found;
Progressive individual will be, village life will improve. ||90||

Let life be glorious, convenient all works be;
Whatever one performs, to be continued in same way. ||91||

At the places of meal, sleep, meeting, work;
On special event, at casual places, with good thoughts to behave. ||92||

Sanskar and pure mind, hygiene and piousness;
Converging on these, purity to mirror in life. ||93||

For this, in food and conduct, the daily routine to be followed;
Experiencing by villagers, life to elevate. ||94||

Work to perform so as to prevail pure beauty;
In it, honey of happiness heavenly, Tukadya says. ||95||

Such *Sri Gramgeeta* book, *Guru*-discipline-self experience-accepted.
Narrated cow products, exercise; the Fifteenth Canto completed. ||96||

Notes

1. Vashistha—The ancient sage.
2. *Wada*—The old palatial mansion.

Village Reformation Quinate

Canto XVI
Raiment Wealth

Whatever righteous work acceptable to God, told by saints;
Real beauty of life to bring it into practice. ||1||

Pure diet, pure walk, pure company, transaction;
Pure reading, *Darshan*[1], an apt conduct with righteous people. ||2||

To mould life pure such, no sign of superstition;
Purity adheres to nature's law, experience of perceiver. ||3||

Provides purity to life—peace, happiness, slave to it;
Glitters life myriadly by beauty influential. ||4||

Reinless act, mean thought, *rajas*[2]-*tamas*[3] diet-thought;
No order in routine, on the earth paralyses his happiness. ||5||

Slave to tea, *chiwara*[4], *chirut*[5], destruction of body, mind, money;
Misdirects one's life and village too. ||6||

Keeping life straight, pure, becomes it beautiful, hygienic;
Pure to be man's consciousness of raiment. ||7||

Glamorous clothes some wear, cloth after cloth some put on;
Inside frail though decorates one's body. ||8||

Narrow mouth, bones visible, depth of chest reveal they;
What happens though cloth of sizzling silk? ||9||

Unnecessary decorum, on forehead, a fragrant layer;
Powder, comb, mirror, *chirut* in pockets. ||10||

Addiction makes mouth bony, oil hair frequently;
Combing hair says, "look beautiful we". ||11||

Body frail, old, inflected with scabies, ring worm infection;
Hidden all these with clothes to appear beautiful. ||12||

Which beauty is this? No sunlight passes there;
No content of celibacy in corporeal frame. ||13||

While walking cross legs, stumbles when touched;
Talks exaggeratedly treating oneself hobby seeker. ||14||

Speaks as if one weeps, no stool without intake of medicine;
What's use in placing ring in finger, of small diamond. ||15||

Pale corpse decked with flowers or scarecrow in farm;
Looks stranger alone in crowd, raiment not such to be. ||16||

Or, wore gorgeous clothes but not washed;
Put on time to time for worship, the same *pitamber*[6]. ||17||

Why art to practice if makes ludicrous and harmful?
Our living simple to be as one's capacity. ||18||

Beauty of qualities to infuse, beautiful pure cloth to wear;
Khadi, products of village industries to wear. ||19||

Always clean, washed to wear; body to cover with single cloth;
Air in nature, sunrays to touch the body. ||20||

Layer on layer, blind imitation of cold countries;
Medicinal quality in body if sunlight touches body. ||21||

Gold, pearl, silk, cosmetics multiple;
Body's freshness, hundred times better than these. ||22||

Beauty to be of blood purity, vigour of celibacy;
Clean, disciplined conduct in home, outside better. ||23||

Art to be of built muscles, high chest, an erect body;
Hygiene, self-respect, an ideal in every sense. ||24||

Competition for costumes, turned difficult in today's life;
What greatness is in the increase of need, anxiety, disease? ||25||

Glamour of outside items, an expression of inside lacuna;
Significant if it becomes, collapses humanity's value. ||26||

Man to be beautified by humanity, Gandhi's cloth excels wealth;
Peacock-feathered coronet, flute of Shri Krishna, fascinate world. ||27||

Knowing this in mind, pure to be in diet-walking;
Naturally, service better of home, village, nation. ||28||

An ideal before people, joy for equality surges up;
Uplift of village industries in natural course. ||29||

Doubts an audience, here, simple living, high thinking;
Not operable today though this, formula of sage's life. ||30||

Costly cloth, glaring living, influence people today;
Simple, pure one lingers at back step. ||31||

It, like offering Laxmi to sea, seeing *pitamber* of Vishnu;
Poison given to Shankar, looking at his strips. ||32||

Avail today anything expensing money, justice, power;
Fame, honour, greatness, such experience of all. ||33||

Friend! this illusionary experience tells, "money is God";
Sorrow aggravated in life today by this mean. ||34||

Presuming, prevails this everywhere, competition in people;
Shows decorum, excels one another, dwindles more and more. ||35||

Cloth, white more than cotton; ornaments, yellow more than gold;
Reached to pinnacle artificiality for fascination, new forever. ||36||

Cleanliness and piousness, purity and neutrality;
More dear artificiality has become, literacy it deems. ||37||

Spray instead of bath, sprinkling of scent on clothes;
Though dirt but beautiful to be seen cloth new, ever. ||38||

New fashion, glare, increased subsequently;
If coat stitched costly, pant needs equally. ||39||

Needs increase day by day; rich wealth, not sufficient;
What work do workers then poor there? ||40||

Indulge some in corruption, dacoity by some openly;
Increase injustice, torture for money. ||41||

Conduct some clearly but entangle due to it;
Flicker attitude their also, prevail unrest everywhere. ||42||

Some starve at home,. doesn't provide milk to children;
But, maintain decorum intact to pose supremacy. ||43||

Some say, no business, no wealth without it;
But, understood by all secrete of everyone. ||44||

Why to insist then? Why not to incline to good path?
But, no realisation of that road? Obsession for wealth. ||45||

Says, procures money everything, salvation, kingdom;
Saint, fame, even worship of God. ||46||

But, this verdict lunatic, money departs near and dear;
Troubles for money only, drives it to hell. ||47||

If money earned with regulation, expensed with conscience;
Provides happiness to a man in life. ||48||

Otherwise venom money is, not permits peace for a while;
Makes an ape to a man, unstabilising his mind. ||49||

Anxiety in earning, labour different like beast;
Burns body, mind, life every time of a man. ||50||

Anxiety for security, fear of thief, fire;
Passion for an epicurean attitude, turns man like a beast. ||51||

Restless his mind when sees money such;
How to spend money? Can't sleep he. ||52||

Salary earned, spent in watching film, *tamasha;*
If money left, no way out good before him. ||53||

Drinks wine, opium; expenses some in gambling;
Needs some in distribution for infidelity. ||54||

In excitation some quarrel on road;
Benefits lawyer to treat oneself superior. ||55||

Eats food spicy, oily; disorder in stomach, head;
Running for doctors, spends money for it. ||56||

To show greatness, arrange party, give donation;
Purchasing unnecessary entity, cheats oneself while laughing. ||57||

Some people earn but not sufficient to them;
Expenditure more, take debt; consciously runs risk. ||58||

As spends money after debt, pays no heed to earning;
Impends hazards at home and out, "what to do?" asks. ||59||

Experiences one anxiety, doesn't move time forward;
Instigates mind, unrest to steal, for mischief. ||60||

No intellect for wealth, no sense for calculation;
Tongue habitual for food and drinks inclines to theft. ||61||

Stigma on the ancestors, humiliation for parents;
Turned offspring as rivals, no one speaks good of. ||62||

Left religion for living, performs work nauseating;
Various illicit deeds he does and instigates others. ||63||

Rich some devil indeed, makes slaves to others by money;
Commits sin, motivates others to do for self. ||64||

Some earn money by deception, utilise it for self;
At the end, they are deceived, heard fame of many. ||65||

Youth of some bounces up, weds for ten, twelve times;
Money consumed and debt, no one supports. ||66||

Then wives hammer on, bring money from anywhere;
What to eat at home? What for wedding? ||67||

Some exaggerated, every thought left unnoticed;
No heed to family, harlot kept at home. ||68||

An ape, he turned, his face people don't see;
Near and dear laugh at his deed from distance. ||69||

Some adopt for money but no money in hand due to quarrel;
Though remained, adopted friends waste it. ||70||

Some practice vow, Oh God! If male child is born;
Gold, silver I will offer, equal to child's weight. ||71||

Male children born to some, distributed sweets in villages;
Estate lost in the celebration of a child's birth. ||72||

When children born more wept he, cursing himself;
No coin left, begs to people. ||73||

Some saved from this but consumed money at home only;
Organised marriages of son and daughter, wasted money in fire-work. ||74||

Set up *pandal* massive, not cared for finance;
Enjoyed people delicacies, *ladu, jilebi*[7], *basundi*[8]. ||75||

Some inclined to decorum, *vratabandha*[9], *sanskar;*
Whatever money, exhausted for the birthday of child. ||76||

Some celebrated anniversary of father, lost entire money;
At last, who will give bread in the name of father? ||77||

Some escaped from this but entangled in festivities;
In *diwali, dashera*[10], *holi*[11], money consumed whatever he has. ||78||

Doesn't expense money, some for bad work;
But, run after they for false status, providing money. ||79||

Though cracks in farm land, for an honour turned to court;
Though estate spoiled but fight for an abusive word. ||80||

To earn fame in people, gives feast to officers;
Provides delicacies, various gifts, whatever need. ||81||

Sold some houses to establish one's reputation;
Died their children turning beggars in future. ||82||

Contested some election, bankrupt by losing their money;
No reliability in the world, invited sorrow. ||83||

Sold some farms, built bungalow roadside;
Enjoyed luxury in city; at the end, no food for belly. ||84||

Constructed some house for business but money consumed;
In future, inconvenience for food; no mind for business. ||85||

Visit some native country and foreign, collect various items;
At the end, their fiasco, left their tall talks. ||86||

Succumb some to *sadhu*, their visit to home often;
Miracle they do, all say; expense money for it. ||87||

Do service, give donation, offer sweets different;
Donating costly raiment and container, turned himself beggar. ||88||

Then asks to fake *sadhu* restlessly for wealth;
Encountered with deceivers, depressed at the end. ||89||

Spoke false *sadhu* sweet for return but forgot home later;
Who ask for penniless? Meets nemesis at the end. ||90||

Treats devotion for miracle, so hindrances more;
Lost their households, cheated by false *sadhu*. ||91||

Went some to pilgrimage, brought wealth with them;
Beaten up by burglar, dacoits; looted their money. ||92||

Pathetic they were, returned begging;
Made condition such of money seekers. ||93||

Without good thought, money don't direct to positive cause;
Increase desires as wealth accumulates, no decrease in habits. ||94||

Wealth necessary for life, an initiator for all works;
In family, needs gold time to time but wealth of thought more. ||95||

Surface low qualities when humanity is forgotten;
Pious people say at face, disdain at back. ||96||

At the end, transaction pure of man, nourish honour in heart;
Activates thought of each others welfare by self essence. ||97||

Human religion all to practice but not to turn beggar;
Life to be duty oriented, positive action to be performed. ||98||

Better to do which perpetuates, treated fair by the righteous people;
Better not to be miser, not to spend lavishly. ||99||

As per capacity, programmes to organise, occasionally not to be miser;
But, not to spend money excessively, resorting to penury. ||100||

Not to turn beggar for material gain, stretch legs looking at bed;
Behave which suits an occasion, considering effect lasting. ||101||

When succumbs to emotions, his conscience crumbles;
Perform strange acts, any thing, saying 'no cost to hobby'. ||102||

Show magnanimity in vain, not caring for consequences;
Having no money at home, incurs debt for hobby. ||103||

In future, destroying oneself, drives children to beggary;
No progress of anyone, why to do this? ||104||

Everyday money to earn justifiably, save turn by turn;
Some to be spend out of it for family when needs. ||105||

Reliable guest to honour, with him bread to share;
Visitors are to welcome as per our capability. ||106||

One to experience sorrow in others, happiness in other's joy;
Occasionally by mental justice we to withdraw. ||107||

We earn, we eat but whatever left to be given to village;
With discipline, an expense to be to the least extent. ||108||

Earning, not wealth; whatever saved, wealth;
Becomes individual prosperous, flourishes village too. ||109||

More expense on small items, saving if constrain;
Drop by drop lake forms, then provides peace to mind. ||110||

Oil granules contain oil; moment, moment make life;
Bit by bit accumulate money, grain, useful in time. ||111||

No additional piece of bread so as to cause starvation;
Little trouble, more progress; pleasant end by this way. ||112||

Conduct this to be in village, needs to minimise;
Detachment to increase subsequently by everyone. ||113||

Conduct with restrain saves money more in village;
Village will be paradise by all means. ||114||

In village, the era of truth to be; happiness in it, heaven indeed;
Our tastes of senses leave step by step. ||115||

Engross in nature of perpetual joy, knowing self colour;
Being becomes unified at immortal place at the end. ||116||

Right conduct, right thought, ideal, great of patience;
Sadhu, *saint*, Mahavir[12], won the world by this road. ||117||

Pure conduct, fruit of thought, in service of individual village clean;
In village, all happiness will be, Tukadya says. ||118||

Such *Sri Gramgeeta* book, *Guru*-discipline-self experience-accepted;
Narrated simple living, with restrain; the Sixteenth Canto completed. ||119||

Notes

1. *Darshan*—Sublime philosophical vision in Indian thought, i.e., *Upanishad darshan*, Boudha *darshan*, Jain *darshan.*
2. *Rajas*—Stands for passion.
3. *Tamas*—Stands for grim, destructive.
4. *Chiwra*—Pungent eatables prepared from flattened parched rice.
5. *Chirut*—Wooden pipe to smoke.
6. *Pitamber*—Clean cloth to wear at the time of worship.
7. *Jilebi*—Circular-shaped coily sweet.
8. *Basundi*—Liquid milk product.
9. *Vratabandha*—Thread ceremony of male child.
10. *Dashera*—The festival in which the leaf of *apte* is given to others as the sign of respect.
11. *Holi*—The festival of colours.
12. Mahavir—The pioneer of Jain religion who emphasises upon control of desires, not to hurt others; avoidance of bad company, not to accumulate more wealth; patience, love, and non-violence; and avoidance of greed. He hammers on differences between low-high, woman-man, and *shudra-brahmin.*

Canto XVII

Poverty-Richness

An audience asked, "our village has wealth";
But, doesn't people experience happiness? Happened this. ||1||

What progress of work? Dispute aggravated in village;
Operates class conflict among rich and poor. ||2||

Cleavaged society in two, one doesn't listen to other;
Lost their trust in each other. ||3||

Now, what to plan? Whose greatness to convince to people?
How will be our social structure beautiful? ||4||

Listen to this query, decision is bound to be;
Without it collapses the basic foundation of village. ||5||

Dispute between rich-poor will ruin village;
So an obstacle to be eliminated by responsible one. ||6||

Unique animal in God's home, no rich, no beggar, any one;
This lacuna in social structure man created. ||7||

No division basically, all this play of greed;
No difference visible when both understand. ||8||

Two teams for play but started fighting, forgetting game;
Rivalry between them pertains to an ignorance. ||9||

One has more glass balls, belonged to him, says he;
Then ceased other's game due to one's greed. ||10||

This, the mode of world, home, and society;
Disruption of family by an ignorance and greed. ||11||

Made caste for work, caste remained forgetting work;
Birth born caste retained in the name of *varnashrama.* ||12||

Happened same of eco structure, shareholders all of wealth;
But, no honour left, other died of hunger. ||13||

One remained poor servant, one became more prosperous;
This, shackle of all ignorance troubled all. ||14||

Deposit kept with one, enjoyed he without thought;
After sometime, deposit's owner was kept aside. ||15||

Worshipper assigned in temple, eclipsed he temple;
Utilised he temple for wife, children. ||16||

Turned some devotee at pilgrim place, ruled temple;
Then made mean for business, showing rights by children. ||17||

Ample land given to distribute to settle village;
But, prosperous he turned squeezing workers. ||18||

Brought security person for wealth, saw he weak owner;
Snatched himself money by power, tricks. ||19||

Occurred this of poverty-richness, distanced labourers;
Here owner they became, who were money receiver. ||20||

Limited money to workers, consequently more money left;
Sin it is to utilise it but made it justifiable right. ||21||

Real name to false, enhances money glory of money;
Treasure it is of an ancestor, what right of workers? ||22||

Now, not understood, who asks to sermon, *kirtana*?
Sugar particle to ants, says donation it is. ||23||

Exploited thousand lives to increase diseases in them;
Then opened charity dispensaries, treating oneself religious. ||24||

Looking at today's labour, no bread to him;
Works he day and night, what religious owner is! ||25||

Lives he in palatial house in city, drives vehicles, children to theatre;
Learns an infidelity, an addiction, theft; squeezes peasant in transaction. ||26||

Applied some their brain, increased wealth disproportionately;
Not given a *paisa* to worker after his demise. ||27||

People in village died without food, let them die, says;
Who saves life? Money, medicine all false! ||28||

Accumulated money this way, no utility of it for society;
Proved they are as burglar, self-centered, aloof. ||29||

One who has more land, doesn't feed belly of labourer;
How is he fortunate? The most miser he is. ||30||

Mansion desolate, single wife, single offspring;
But, no neighbourhood, what a honour of a miser? ||31||

Animal like behaviour of many, suppression by the aristocratic mean;
Work by threatening, in future harmful it will be. ||32||

Poor men cry, rich men are dacoits, say;
But, their eyelids closed, not open by any mean. ||33||

Some remedy to be for this, for it two avenues possible;
Law or religious mode, to warn by service. ||34||

Turn people angry, when no one pays heed to this;
Then a call for blood revolt, increases a threat deep. ||35||

Some break house to steal, some by dacoity;
Some slain others including children in day time. ||36||

Why this phase to arrive? Some plan to search out;
Poor and rich both will live better. ||37||

Thoughts with others to share, our equal share to keep;
No one to be angry, this to be done by village. ||38||

Thine money, our labour; thine intellect, our action;
As one's horse, other's rein to be. ||39||

Life structure like it at core, many hands with single;
Collectively, our place to receive honour. ||40||

None functions excluding village, everyone has everyone's work;
Illusion his increases after work performance. ||41||

A carpenter makes pillar, constructs mason wall;
Arranges a potter tiles for the roof of hut. ||42||

Moulds a blacksmith nails, blades; a labourer builds house, front yard;
Where would have *gosavi*[1] lived if this not done? ||43||

Makes a cobbler boots, supplies a weaver cloth to him;
Stitches a tailor cloth proportionate to him. ||44||

Grows a farmer grains, chilli, vegetable, onions;
Equips his house joyfully with labour of all. ||45||

Share all hands in all, ramification motivates to live;
Understanding this who behaves, is an intelligent indeed. ||46||

But, entered negative thought, no one respects to another;
We give money to all and so they work, says. ||47||

Real significance to labour but trust in money;
Is it difficult to cope with, though money without work? ||48||

Dug out stones, soil; shaped slabs; constructed walls;
With touch of labour, wealth it turned. ||49||

Let woods, sticks be in forest; no building, vehicles without labour;
Wealth without labour, cowry shells, procured they too with work. ||50||

Conscience, real knowledge, all have to understand;
Support complete to all, religion this of rich. ||51||

In village, those rich, their wealth, village's property;
To behave understanding this, helping others occasionally. ||52||

Whatever additional we have, to be given to neighbour;
With unity all to live, deeming it village religion. ||53||

Wealth, blood of poor, let rich be behaved understanding it;
Labour, treasure of village, so it to respect. ||54||

Following this by all people, class division will be abolished;
To prepare mind, *sadhu,* saint have to work. ||55||

And conscious, government to be, to mould proceedings well;
Among people, the wind of education to blow. ||56||

From little boys and girls, grades of poor and rich to be scrapped;
All to look equally by the actual practice. ||57||

Equality, not in words, in wealth, respect, education to be in practice;
Those who divide, to be expelled, dividers in village. ||58||

Those who don't listen, have to teach lesson by law;
Then structure to base on equality, with honesty. ||59||

As offspring equal to father, rich and poor equal to king;
This cleavage to bridge, an administrator's religion it is. ||60||

But, where government succumbs, subjects on fire;
Then who ask to whom? See disorder everywhere. ||61||

Saint, *sadhu* too slaves, lured by offerings;
Then collapses mountain's cliff on society. ||62||

No caretaker of citizens, turned spark completely into fire;
With scream the earth will devast. ||63||

Though all citizens are imprisoned or killed;
Can be productivity without labour? Everyone to labour. ||64||

Why this to be happen? All have to awake before;
Work of village to be looked after well by us. ||65||

Money to earn with the best transaction, to use for the best work;
Transaction to be for the welfare of each other. ||66||

No miserliness so as to submerge village in debt;
When an occasion demands, no cooperation to people. ||67||

No expense of money without thought, no deception with poor;
In transaction, both modes to be equal. ||68||

Dispute not to be at peak, sympathy to stimulate;
No opposition to be for this by anyone. ||69||

All to behave with involvement, all to work in unison;
No rich-poor to be seen outwardly in life. ||70||

It to be seen with quality, intellect, work;
Though these kinds to be; sense of equality not to leave. ||71||

Receives society education this, a fortunate day it is;
Then no fear in future to fragment consciousness. ||72||

Shapes revolution when increases guides in society;
Ends it illusion of differences of parties consequently. ||73||

Change they will bring, sowing seeds of the best knowledge;
Sanctify they will Mother India for more esteem. ||74||

Let this good thought be in all, rich-poor to bridge;
Prospect of society not better now otherwise. ||75||

Indispensable it is to understand, for it time waits;
Like this it will not stop, with speed it will attack. ||76||

So, my insistence is to carve the caves of social attitudes;
Among people, the ornaments of collectivity to glitter. ||77||

Cooperates rich only by expensing lakh of rupees;
But, it will not end attitude of differentiation. ||78||

Realising dignity of labour, trust in work to highlight;
By self-labour, labour of workers to alleviate. ||79||

All complementary to be each other, the formula this of religion;
Is this you to tell? Wise people! ||80||

Without it collapses village, like animals some work;
Wander some deeming them tender, as nescient. ||81||

Say some, we are rich; what less is with us?
Earned more our father, operating at home. ||82||

Deep ignorance this is, not understood they essence;
In time to come, wealth, land will leave, of labourless. ||83||

Without work, who will avail rest?
Towards labourless all will turn without rein. ||84||

So, exhorts to learn work, not to be dependent;
Money of our right, taste its sweetness. ||85||

Flourishment of non-labourers today, their trouble tomorrow;
So, trick to understand of industry. ||86||

Wisely to behave learning all skills;
Opens then avenue to fill belly without hesitation. ||87||

Arrow of words will cease when literate will do this;
Disloyal they will prove us otherwise. ||88||

We have to labour, thou to be in luxury;
Which leader will say, "equality to maintain"? ||89||

Love same for all, rule same for all then;
As per capacity all have to labour. ||90||

One has to work, another to rest;
Dishonest it is for welfare of nation. ||91||

The world is of workers, the farm of toilers;
Laxmi to be slave of those who labours. ||92||

Today's tendency this is, need for society;
Why elders to experience hesitation for it? ||93||

Intellectual, literate, sage, rich, intentionally;
Have to work, the sign of greatness. ||94||

Convenient it will for all, fastly people will work;
Shame will vanish completely due to glory. ||95||

Involvement of intellectuals in work to turn knowledge in practice;
Flourishment of farm, prosperity of nation. ||96||

Shameful for man to experience pleasure without work;
To fulfill needs of lazy one, a great sin it is. ||97||

Labour degrades, if anyone speaks this;
Deem him anti-national, a nuisance, sinful. ||98||

Why shame to feel to do our work;
On contrary pride to experience of our work. ||99||

Work system to operate as our mode of grasping;
Seeking education with constructive mind he to proceed. ||100||

Valuable all works, their suitability equal;
Took away food waste by Shri Krishna, pulled cattle by Vitthala. ||101||

Less none's eligibility, all work necessary;
Remuneration same everywhere generally for work. ||102||

One farm labourer, others mason, carpenter, blacksmith;
Tailor, washer, potter, cobbler, all useful. ||103||

Some do waste sweeping, other of medical treatment;
Some worshipper active in temple, equally useful. ||104||

Some intellectual speak on legend, some direct to misdirected;
As per temperament nature, made plan consequently. ||105||

But, respect for all, conduct of the world to be;
Who is *brahmin*? Who is *mahar*? Equal all in work. ||106||

High-low in work, who to decide in practice?
Significance of every work at its place. ||107||

All are needful all time with ease;
Incompleteness reveals the ship of world in absence. ||108||

Taking rope of chain to tie wooden pieces;
If breaks single ring, all disrupt. ||109||

Like it speed of work; work to be for all;
Then the world will survive if labour equally. ||110||

Whatever competency one has, to be utilised for nation;
One who is wise in whatever work, has to render service. ||111||

Ample contribution to give, of whatever one has;
With whatever strength, an intellect one has, one has to labour. ||112||

If this work done, an inner realisation will be;
Will reach to house of contentment, otherwise calamity inevitable. ||113||

Oh! Awake! Awake rich! Officers! Intellectuals!
Literates! Sages! Call for revolution. ||114||

Enlight village to village, diminish differences completely;
Light the lamp of village elevation, Tukadya says. ||115||

Such *Sri Gramgeeta* book, *Guru*-discipline-self experience-accepted;
Narrated the our wealth's worth; the Seventeenth Canto completed. ||116||

Note

1. *Gosavi*—One who wanders in village for *bhiksha*.

Canto XVIII
Labour Wealth

An audience asked, "We heard in *Geeta*";
Action fused in cosmos; without performance action takes place. ||1||

An action to everyone, an action is body's religion;
There purposefully to work, this speech contradictory. ||2||

Thou say to labour, ego it will nourish;
Better action among people, facilitates with ease. ||3||

Doubt this of an audience eludes people often;
But, this not the stance of *Geeta*, pure. ||4||

An action fused the world is, who is without work?
Some work everyone performs as usual. ||5||

But, different kinds of work, some pure, hateful, mix;
Some ritualistic, some pure, the action without attachment. ||6||

Some for physical organs, some originates in mind;
Originate some actions with conscience, fair. ||7||

Some work self oriented, some for welfare of family;
Some work for village people, in the form of service religion. ||8||

Which religion this is to work for our body?
Mundane work it is, happens with ease. ||9||

Likewise eventually performance of festive activities;
Not significant in it, the occasional work. ||10||

Everyday work easy, an indispensable to perform;
Disrupts society if not performed but mega religion it isn't. ||11||

Only to work for belly, not pious labour;
An act of service in time left, religion it is. ||12||

The act of humanity it is, meant labour for others;
Do their works even birds, beasts. ||13||

Work, good and evil, likewise keeping aside one's ego;
Labour to perform for the world with devotion to God. ||14||

Learning of *Geeta* this, time to time with firmness;
Worship of Almighty inclusive, the act acceptable to *Geeta.* ||15||

No one without work, understand me without doubt;
But, not to treat it as work which doesn't increase product. ||16||

Where service real is, not of people godly;
No degree we render to it of *Geeta* suggested action. ||17||

Today ample production, medium it of mass service;
Whoever will struggle for it, experienced he *Geeta.* ||18||

Instead of immersing nose in temple, better to pick up thorns on road;
To provide water to sufferer, the best pilgrim place. ||19||

To dig a land of hand length, worship better than others;
Effect its, more than hundred lectures. ||20||

What makes food available to labourer, work, the best than *yagnya;*
Otherwise something else not to support by mentioning *Geeta.* ||21||

A youth slept lazily, said this needful for life;
Slept longer consequently, woke up for meal. ||22||

Slept again after meal, how will it like to family members;
Made fun of him, said this too work is. ||23||

Some account having money, some seek interest in quarrel;
Some create nuisance by every mean. ||24||

Though this work stopped, to me no obstacle will be;
But, if ceases production for needs, how life will survive? ||25||

All have to work, village's wealth to increase;
Here poor-rich not to observe for work. ||26||

Sri saint Gora[1] laboured physically, God too helped him;
Rich acts lazily, mega sin it is. ||27||

An audience asked, "no work is apparently for labourer";
Unemployed increased; how can be work for rich? ||28||

An audience's thought line, nourishment for the illusion;
Entire nation, poor, illiterate, there no work seen. ||29||

To take birth again and again to make happy motherland;
Speak great persons from core, work there not visible to them. ||30||

In nation, hill of work, flows flood of poverty, sorrow;
People, half naked, half empty belly, why not to see their sorrow? ||31||

No time for rest here, workers ever powerful;
Need step to step, work before our nation. ||32||

But, those who want to be officer to dominate others,
Expects laxity without work, unemployed they remain. ||33||

Utility of education by propaganda and experiment;
But, diseased they themselves become in social life. ||34||

On one side of educated rich, the same of workers, poor;
Laxity, laziness of both reside with pride at home, visible. ||35||

When hunger of belly demands work house to house;
Otherwise, with laziness they lie carelessly in cottage. ||36||

Work at eight in morning, leaves at ten from home;
No involvement in work, disrupts work. ||37||

Said, what happened to rich? Are they compelled to beggary?
What loss ours if we don't work? ||38||

No eagerness to work, on tongue relentless speech;
Not giving money for labour, piques with people. ||39||

This, wrong to do; money apt to be taken for work;
But, to run away from work, not our motto ever. ||40||

Workers to wake up in morning, after routine morning work;
Soon to leave for work after house work. ||41||

When bell of work will ring, workers walk from all ways;
Speeded up industry, this to happen. ||42||

Relies production on labour; production, village's prime wealth;
To search excuse in it, madness it is. ||43||

Doesn't know labourer's trust in work, become lazy rich one;
So tedious has turned the life of nation. ||44||

Speed of production hindered, increased tendency to enjoy;
What the mother earth will do if no tilling of land? ||45||

For this, all responsible, power, wealth, thought, propaganda;
Nothing is on right track, so village desolated. ||46||

No affinity with work for rich, no affinity with production to poor;
Deems labour low educated, paves way for laxity. ||47||

This not to occur, all to improve mentally;
As thus, my request to all earnestly. ||48||

Whatever one performs in work, treat it as service;
Welfare ours to aim, ornamental it for village. ||49||

One who doesn't work for belly, not improves production;
He to oppose thoughtfully by village man. ||50||

Propagation of dignity of labour to be, sympathy to all;
System this to be beautiful, increasing village production. ||51||

To increase village production, to create new in village;
What to do? Listen questions time to time. ||52||

Remedy for it at priority, labour which workers perform;
Whatever a strength is left, to be assisted by others. ||53||

And wasted others much time uselessly at village, home;
If channelise with determination, the scenario of village will change. ||54||

Raw material in village to be utilised completely;
By experimentation in research, soil to turn precious. ||55||

Fascination of youth in other nations, relentless new research much;
Spell of it to experience by educated village youth. ||56||

Artisans experts in village to be encouraged;
New items to be created in village, useful for life. ||57||

In industries machines to be manufactured, not succumbing to foreign nations;
By creating, we to experience glory all. ||58||

Work from spinning wheel, rod; experiment on food, grains;
Houses all suitable to create by us. ||59||

In every house subsidiary business, hobby to all men, women;
Efforts to eliminate obstacles in life. ||60||

Some make bags and strips, some weave *khadi* at home;
Some footwear from leather of dead animals. ||61||

Some mattress, some seats, some chairs, some playthings;
Some bucket, cot, coarse carpet, soap in house. ||62||

Some shape beautiful earthen pot, container, vase fine;
Some show skills by making tiles strong. ||63||

Some make bricks proportionate, some break stone slab;
All this operable house to house in their ways. ||64||

Some decorate oxen; some search colours in possible modes;
Everyone is doing something, somewhere. ||65||

Such is village well equipped with subsidiary business;
No lacuna left by anyone, anywhere. ||66||

Such skilled jobs to perform, cottage industries;
Anywhere unemployment will not be seen growing. ||67||

Beautiful art it to call, otherwise shelter house of dissolution;
Hiring ornaments decorate our bridegroom. ||68||

Whatever in village, work it to motivate;
But, it to be proved suitable for village. ||69||

Backward our village industry, enlightened by education;
Our village to be improved this way. ||70||

Commodities to produce, to be learnt if not known;
In houses, those village commodities to be visible. ||71||

Whatever produced in village, to be utilised by us;
In village remains village wealth, increases village power. ||72||

Cobbler dies with hunger in village, educated wander in city for shoes;
What intellectuals to respect village these are! ||73||

In village, weaver empty handed, needs him silk *dhoti;*
Kills village for luxury, what patriotism it is. ||74||

Some say our money we will expense as we like;
Village destroyer he deems to be, selfish-man. ||75||

Village artisans, backward, not to die with hungry belly;
We, embedded with outer things, no ornament, stigma it is. ||76||

Taj Mahal, single in nation, determines it not nation's situation;
Bankrupt people in home to home, how can it be evaluated? ||77||

Wrester, giant in village, others frail and thin;
Can't be deemed village physically well built. ||78||

Few, great persons born, others don't elevate;
How can it be treated social elevation by conscious one. ||79||

For it needs every element, knowledgeable, well hygiene, industrious;
Then only eligible it for ornament of ideal village. ||80||

So, everyone to boost up rural articles in village;
Improvement is to be to elevate artisans. ||81||

Such all industries to be run in villages with joy;
All people to live freely with happiness, contentment. ||82||

In village, exhibition of products to be, created in village;
Seeds, farm industry equipments to be placed in it. ||83||

Playthings, ornaments, business, wooden, smithy, construction items;
Pottery, weaving, leather works to be there. ||84||

Beautiful house to be, in it diverse, beautiful objects;
Emphasis to be on whatever created by us. ||85||

Wealth of products in village to be seen by people;
By providing apt cost, they are to be purchased. ||86||

In village, business committee to be for continuous progress;
Will channelise rural economic life by taking rein. ||87||

By acquiring share of wealth from village's rich persons;
For welfare of all in day and night, it to be utilised. ||88||

Some are landlords, rural economic store they are;
Their all work to be handed over to workers. ||89||

Or, if rich persons not turned by strength of farmers, workers;
Drop by drop to accumulate of their small savings. ||90||

Out of it, collection of objects to create, useful storehouse for all;
Without doubt, shop of all items to run collectively. ||91||

In it ownership of all, control of wise farmers;
With consent of all, unity in business to be in village. ||92||

Single grain store to be to run village transaction;
In it share of all people, as per convenience. ||93||

Occasionally grains to take, taxes to decide collectively;
Occasionally all to share in the best way. ||94||

From it, village to serve for a person who toils;
Village improvement, its benefit to use. ||95||

In village, prevails competition, this will check it;
Village bank will paralyse business man, money lender. ||96||

In village oil mill necessary, the sign of pure oil products;
Village works to perform in village usefully. ||97||

Work to give to workless, to make them happy by work;
Like ours they to be made well, happy. ||98||

Work to perform by everyone, to eat fully with right;
Whatever needs to demand, an honest he is. ||99||

A person without work, his name to be suggested to committee;
Village service officer will provide work to him. ||100||

His duty to provide work, out of deposited fund in village;
Remuneration to give to him for work useful. ||101||

Full labour charges to give for happy family life;
Likewise production to increase in village. ||102||

All will be happy, quench the thirst of life;
Village state will be fine, wealthy of finance. ||103||

For this rich, an educated, a power holder, an artist, a farmer, a worker;
All to elevate village by village industries. ||104||

Flow towards cities to cease without doubt;
Such plan to meet two ends at village. ||105||

Village, creator of city—city consumer, village producer;
Instead of migrating to city, people to turn to village. ||106||

Such village service to be, such work to like by God;
No doubt to linger in mind, Tukadya says. ||107||

Such *Sri Gramgeeta* book, *Guru*-discipline-self experience-accepted;
Narrated principles of village industries; the Eighteenth Canto completed. ||108||

Note

1. Gora—A saint in *warkari* cult in Maharashtra, who was a potter.

Canto XIX

Life Education

An audience asked, city larger than village;
People we speak this, but a sign not to forget. ||1||

In city, higher education, how can it reach to village?
Whosoever educated came, rustic he became here. ||2||

'In city, urban one becomes', for it students from city require;
In village, 'one has to plough', this happens. ||3||

Listen, those who believe in this, concentrate on words;
Here, our basic conception of education not right. ||4||

Decorative clothes, hollow dignity, glamour in bureaucracy;
This, not motto of education, pay heed to this clearly on priority. ||5||

Surprising educational system where not operable father's wish;
A father plans for farming, a son strives for job. ||6||

To become officer, less work, money ample;
Advanced degree, mere decorum, not this a higher level. ||7||

Forgetting past all, education to give to boys and girls;
Will enhance dignity of village in all senses. ||8||

Not mere higher education, gone by in the past era;
Now, able the son of India to be laborious, powerful. ||9||

In education, life and work, both to merge well;
No worry to be for food, no need to beg for money. ||10||

In offspring, single quality to be to fill belly;
No obstacle will create in family in any way. ||11||

All needs of life, every means to earn;
Total knowledge of related subjects to be included. ||12||

To swim differently in river, lake and well;
Saves when calamity impends, such education to be. ||13||

In village, the occasion for meal, one has to cook well;
Such art to be taught with experiments to boys and girls. ||14||

Such education seems simple, but of priority in life;
Otherwise living like animals, not knowing cooking. ||15||

Learnt a girl in school, but can't cook at home;
What to do of knowledge skill? Lame she without work. ||16||

Uneducated eats after cooking, educated without food;
Can't cross strands of rope, dependent everywhere. ||17||

Offspring can't serve food, fetch water at home;
Remains immersed in one's decor, futile knowledge it is. ||18||

Whatever lacuna at home to be filled by an offspring;
Work to be done with courage, education applied it is. ||19||

Provides knowledge politeness, free, dauntless makes it;
Determination to enhance by education for victory in life. ||20||

Education to seek to live life beautifully;
Fatal which makes, education not it is. ||21||

Attacked village by dacoits, students swiftly locked doors;
Dignity of parents to test, what is use of education? ||22||

So, needs boys with strength, knowing wrestling, *mallakhamb*[1];
Resistance with valour, then education useful. ||23||

In era of sages, education's applicability to life was;
For it, system of *ashrama* prevailed before. ||24||

Knowledge of archery, *mallavidya*, Ayurveda, and weaponry;
The best fourteen disciplines were taught by *Acharya*. ||25||

Painting, leather art, *rangoli*, the best arts;
Building work, pottery, others, sixty-four arts myriad. ||26||

Music, cookery, fine techniques of home management;
Horse test, emerald test, all, life knowledge in education. ||27||

Such was method before, now seek higher education;
But, don't improve village farming with available sources. ||28||

Reached education at glory point, no thought for village education;
Not know how to bring higher education in simple life. ||29||

To be brought schools of higher education in village certainly;
With tactics, village life they will beautify, teaching people. ||30||

Diverse arts to teach to students, agility, trust in goal;
To look after our village, education to be given. ||31||

Education core to be to make village, an ideal;
With active involvement, knowledge to be grasped. ||32||

Strong notion of cooperation, the focal formula of education;
No importance to education without cooperation. ||33||

To be complimentary to each other, this appreciation of education;
Horrible sorrow of individual orientation in human life. ||34||

Everywhere importance to be attributed to certificate of people service;
Today's offspring to elevate for tomorrow's nation. ||35||

Character wealth, village's prime wealth to secure;
Enhance it will village glory, bright like character. ||36||

Children to teach so as to mould village as we will;
By learning all people to make wise. ||37||

Percolates education in childhood, difficult when grown up;
Senses don't mould even when attempted to do so. ||38||

Remains he illiterate, anyone can deceive him;
Trouble, an anger experience he, like blind in life forever. ||39||

Doors closed of progress, life burden to pull;
But, a farmer doesn't understand new knowledge of farming. ||40||

No improvement in equipment in different crops;
Chaos as ox of oil mill, of his life. ||41||

Son, not taught by father, sharer of sin he is;
As to give birth is duty, to provide education indispensable. ||42||

If we can't manage, handover to nation upliftment institution;
But, not to deprive him with an illiteracy ever. ||43||

Not to keep children attached to themselves only;
To be handed over to schools, protector of them. ||44||

Parents' duty to give birth, teacher's to educate;
Nation's wealth of son not to disturb by the attachment. ||45||

Parents love children to fulfill their insistence;
Turned boy dull, deficient, workless by an excessive favour. ||46||

At any cost teachers will not tolerate it;
Know them psychology how to mould them. ||47||

So, the entire village has to open children care home;
Male, female are to be appointed by providing them education. ||48||

School, children garden, children home to be in village;
Keeping kids there, they to mould. ||49||

No time to parents, an obstacle in going to work;
Inconvenience to children to end by labour in the education. ||50||

Education of this to be how to look after children?
How to allot our work to boys and girls? ||51||

Children in childhood not to succumb to an addiction anywhere;
Otherwise teacher, parents to take to task. ||52||

One sided tendency developed by seeking education;
Others to be deceived by deceiving self, not to happen. ||53||

Says, I inclined to education, turned holy teacher of children;
Though made incarnation of addiction, mind not disdained. ||54||

Says to children, behave well, smokes *bidi*[2] up to ten;
See how he speaks with finesse with hot words as train. ||55||

Knowing responsibility of village, teacher works with sympathy;
Then becomes village as heavenly abode, no need of others. ||56||

The best learning at home and outside, understands whatever needs;
Fructify the blessings of teachers for progress of work. ||57||

Education of life elevation, the enrichment in village only;
Planning of our rural structure to teach to enhance. ||58||

Beautiful to be school where boys and girls literate;
Ready to work, where practical teaching is. ||59||

Melodious song, speech, and conduct to live at home with aptness;
They to teach to do work by self. ||60||

Such will lead to progress, offspring to the best students;
In future they learn industrial enterprise. ||61||

Students begin with work, inclusive of Maths and Sciences;
Otherwise reading, recitation time to time, no physical work. ||62||

So, besides education, preparation to be with active work;
Of his life, boy performs all work. ||63||

Knowledge in which, he excels, let him seek that;
Let him immerse in study and research. ||64||

Each aspect of life, important works to teach;
Liking to be to do work, no shame to work for students. ||66||

Boys educated seems literate, well versed in work;
No shame to do work, inbuilt in him. ||67||

Does he cutting, rooting out, unloading, ploughing;
Eager his mind seems to remove cow dung too. ||68||

All types of work he performs as hobbies;
Enhanced village pride, thinking he trained. ||69||

Such village care to be in the ignorance of children;
Then, it will elevate village with the ease. ||70||

Though the span of eighteen years, salvage it will thousand generation;
Education sought will provide model of the best village. ||71||

Bright aspect of life children will learn with passion;
Glory of village will enhance, whatever we dream for. ||72||

Our little offspring will be young activists of tomorrow;
Service they will render for village, with exquisite qualities. ||73||

So, villagers restore the wealth of kids;
Who will tell, in how many village gems will surge up? ||74||

To give birth by God, occasion for mother, father;
Knowledge, teaching of *guru*, moulds fortune of village. ||75||

In tender buds, Jnaneshwar, Ravindra, Shivaji hidden;
Blossoming they, hundred great persons will emerge. ||76||

Many will be service oriented, many skilled artists;
Village they will enrich with industries, business. ||77||

Many will create machines, many will be historian;
Some will be skilled advisers in our village. ||78||

Many will be judges, many creator of poetic world;
Many will increase yields in farm by new researches. ||79||

Many will be politicians, many philosophers;
Many will bring laurels in sports for village. ||80||

Many saint adviser, many brave, protector;
Many expert in commerce, serviceman, in every work. ||81||

Such will village group, the ideal high of all qualities;
No living being will down in our village by *sanskar*. ||82||

Village rules village state, no over indulgence of anyone;
In village, we will live by all means. ||83||

With love all will serve to benefit village well;
Then what treasure will left, of which village will deprive of? ||84||

What lacuna of strength though Jnaneshwar born in village?
Operated reins in village by Shri Krishna and Mahatma Gandhi. ||85||

Listen friends, surely I look for education of children in village only;
Debt will be clear, all people will be happy. ||86||

Some say, caste is an idiot; how children will be bright?
Some are brilliant from beginning in education. ||87||

Idea this an incorrect, discrimination not in birth;
Appears it with the roles of tradition, environment. ||88||

One's father Justice, an uncle Professor;
Performs *katha, kirtan,* then why he not intelligent? ||89||

In vicinity group of intellectuals, nutrient and sweet to eat;
Company good at home, outside, his progress with ease. ||90||

Father, shepherd, brings wooden sticks, uncle sells bengals, clothes;
Another uncle, job holder, but he, security guard, an attendant. ||91||

Staple food to eat, herd of cattle in company;
Why not to appreciate if he proceeds in study? ||92||

To him, the best company to provide to upgrade his status;
New society of intellectuals will emerge out of it. ||93||

Needs education for it, worthless speech without it;
Educated people will be when people will realise. ||94||

Foolishness ancestors did, children to suffer;
Not swiftly to rectify it, demerits continue in family. ||95||

In family one committed sin, in future generation to be victim;
As a consequence continues this among people. ||96||

To wipe out blot, pious work to be done;
Then feasible to escape from stigma which chases one. ||97||

One practiced good virtues, his fame crossed boundaries;
Though offspring's miscreants in future, continues his fame. ||98||

Rescues past name, says to look at father's fame;
Become famous ancestors well in family tradition. ||99||

But, more sin committed, came into light name;
Then, no one asks, what admirable is in past? ||100||

Tradition same continues if outstanding doesn't happen;
On the earth, such is travel of name. ||101||

Elevates one twenty-one generations, other defames double;
In nutshell, new change if something significant happens. ||102||

Ravan from holy lineage of *brahma,* but his race of demon;
Became Vishvamitra[3] *brahmarshi* from *Rajarshi* with speciality. ||103||

Such glory of conspicuous deeds, realising one to labour;
Our family, village to elevate by imparting education persistently. ||104||

Children of poor parents, no strength of education to them;
They to be educated by government or public. ||105||

By providing education, beggar's children to mould good;
Piousness village will experience by returning debt. ||106||

Different educative modes to teach, though poor or rich;
By this mode, village to supply more wealth. ||107||

More wealth to invest by donation on an ancestor's name;
Heavenly village will be if school, pious, well equipped. ||108||

Ideal students will be, village life will change;
No where will be rustiness, lasting change will be. ||109||

When raised value of education, fortune of village in hand;
Not to forget basic hymn principally, Tukadya says. ||110||

Such *Sri Gramgeeta* book, *Guru*-discipline-self experience-accepted;
Narrated progressive of learning; the Nineteenth Canto completed. ||111||

Notes

1. *Mallakhamb*—Short wooden pillar to exercise.
2. *Bidi*—Leaf rolled circularly to smoke.
3. Vishwamitra—An ancient sage from royal family background.

Canto XX

Woman Elevation

The education's base, village's uplift, tomorrow's nation, to do;
Need for this ideal teachers, creators of nation. ||1||

Knowledge, greater than *guru*, favour of an ideal mother;
Her *sanskar* on children from embryo formation. ||2||

Hand that rocks a cradle, upgrades the world;
Narrated such greatness of mother, more than hundred teachers. ||3||

Son's mould as per mother's nature, enlightens him her conduct;
Relies male's greatness on luminance of woman. ||4||

Says, 'son as father', but mother's importance more;
Develop children in character by mother's power. ||5||

Male does work, but confines himself to out of home;
Experiences he peace by practicing all thought constructive. ||6||

The best mother does it, looks after her home with mission;
An ideal she makes children, besides the warmth of love for all. ||7||

"Welcome mother God", honoured by *Vedas* in beginning;
Treated her as mine of gems, unparalleled. ||8||

Kayadhu, Prahad's mother, Chhatrapati's, Jijabai;
Kaushalya, Devaki, all, respected in books. ||9||

In some legend initiatives to disdain woman;
By all means, it was punishment of mean. ||10||

Renunciation to firm by separation, mind to retrieve from sensual;
So, in it admiration for erotic tendencies disdained. ||11||

Not narrated fault, conflict in renunciation, no obstacle in penance;
No adverse comment in fame, the mean, not complete. ||12||

So, pointing to senses, erotic drive, mortality of body, uncleanness;
Narrated for renunciation, it not personal distain. ||13||

Wherever mind lures, it to be brought back;
Saying "no, no", to insist like small kid. ||14||

Told this to male for female, same approach of female to male;
There whose meanness more? Away, away, calls discipline. ||15||

But, though disdained, disrupts it care, nutrition;
Ceases cycle of life, branches it out low ways. ||16||

So, apt it is said, no world without female;
What has male done? Impure house has become. ||17||

The best work at home, often woman's sign it is;
When visitors come and go, no difficulty when woman at home. ||18||

Servers, she bearing sufferings, lovely minute work;
Knows the best spouse without exhaustion, carefully. ||19||

Not realises male heart which understands female deeply;
The ballads of her pious emotions, difficult for me to narrate. ||20||

Total uniformity, brings it unity;
Whatever plans, implements she completely. ||21||

In world, many animals, open to all their tendencies;
But, no honour of love like mother. ||22||

God created the earth, how many mines in her womb?
But, nowhere finds light of love like mother. ||23||

Natural action of mother, human religion it calls in the world;
Love from core of mother, so dear to God loving people. ||24||

In sainthood, the form of mother, so attains godly level;
Diverse means followed but not realised the form of God. ||25||

Self realised motherhood, natural mould of woman;
To blossom if fully, the best education must. ||26||

Surprising is woman's alertness, not noticed by male;
If children seek that education, facilitation to family. ||27||

Male is pragmatic, female conscious, sympathetic;
If both attitudes merge, the earth turns paradise. ||28||

With the best male, the best female, their family heavenly;
To little extent, more qualities female has. ||29||

When male succumbs to anxiety, woman at home reflects;
When occasion to visit, many times I noticed. ||30||

Whatever homes I observed, experienced additional;
Signs of skills more visible in women. ||31||

Guess of human nature, alertness viewing an occasion;
Persists the planning of future in woman's nature. ||32||

Devotion, knowledge to woman, restrain, wisdom to her;
Seems it, operates she the wheel of world. ||33||

It doesn't mean male has nothing of that sort;
Setup this of human nature, naturally explained. ||34||

Though told, colours of emotions are infused in it;
For not experienced I, pleasure, pain of family. ||35||

My family is the world, all male-female, father-mother;
Whatever necessary I spoke from practical standpoint. ||36||

But, one to learn from this, where to keep away woman;
Where to bow down treating mother, to realise with conscience. ||37||

Where to behave like friend, where to worship like Goddess;
Where to look like rival, envisaging place, time, character, difference. ||38||

Ran to forest those males who haven't understood this;
Why has he painted his face superficially? ||39||

Wherever they will go, she is before and after;
Inside-outside, nature coils around of living being. ||40||

Only for our tendency, woman disdained principally;
Sinful it is to criticise adversely the place of motherhood. ||41||

So, kept aside woman in renunciation, with conscience they practiced;
Then they addressed, honoured calling her mother. ||42||

But, dishonour her knowing her one side;
Culminated it into terrible downfall of social life. ||43||

Made woman society low, feeble, subjects grow like it;
Says, treat woman as beast, all cruel the world became. ||44||

Assumed some object to enjoy, decked up some as doll;
Entered *kali*[1] in every home, strengthless motherland turned. ||45||

Says, woman is slave, she has no right to elevate;
Verdict this, blind, selfish doesn't suit to wise. ||46||

Says woman is an obstacle in work, so her progress to hinder;
Knowing this consciously increases barrier on a road. ||47||

Actually both born in *sanskar,* elevate by self efforts;
At last, in her hands, her elevation is. ||48||

Are God, Goddess differentiated? Haven't sages looked after wives?
Haven't women renounced a born? Glance at ancient scripts God's nature? ||49||

Hadn't women penned *Veda*? Thought of God's nature?
Well acquainted they in different disciplines of learning. ||50||

Hadn't women fought war? Hadn't inspire husband, son?
Hadn't women sacrifice their lives for mission? ||51||

Hadn't women tender than flower, turned to ash for mission;
Less is our admiration for their deeds, marvelous. ||52||

Fascinating unlike woman, renounced unlike woman;
Soft unlike woman and iron-hearted *Ranchandika*[2]. ||53||

But, where to direct her attention? What to instill in her mind?
By which education she to prepare? This depends on company. ||54||

If association with sensual pleasure, turns she vagabond;
If influenced by renunciation, not possible to grapple by dacoit. ||55||

On her own she will embrace death, but not spoil for greed, fear;
Such thought to ingrain by balanced male. ||56||

For it, she to place like this, good company and education;
Relations are to be such intact for woman. ||57||

From childhood, the living of good conduct;
An agility in work, alertness in life, to be taught by education. ||58||

Seek some girls physical education, brave they than boys;
No courage to dacoits to attack them. ||59||

Why curtain to be there? Calamity of dependence on other;
With self power, women kill evil forces ever. ||60||

But, neglecting this, retaining one's upper hand;
Barren they make women's lives with selfishness. ||61||

Some entrapped her after wedding, no freedom to speak;
'Cooking and child' only work assigned to her, tells her. ||62||

Some imprisoned at home, no world of her own;
When spotted outside, beat her to mould. ||63||

Girls to be hidden, boys to wander in village;
Such heinous ritual not to continue, think we. ||64||

Oh! she behaves well, speaks well in society than male;
Knows she how to teach thou wisdom; how does she lag behind? ||65||

To suppress her through this, not honourable in the present age;
Where equal rights, good are for bride, bridegroom. ||66||

God created principle this to keep both equal, holy;
What have boys done everywhere to live in the world? ||67||

Different rules for status, ban on widow marriage;
No opportunity to meet both ends; why such discrimination? ||68||

Some women turned widow, ugly they look with tonsured head;
How does it attain, renunciation? I don't know. ||69||

Hiding one's weakness, other to defame;
Wickedness this is, inhuman as if. ||70||

If widow intends to renounce, better to keep her at *ashram* in forest;
With self will she to study in service camp. ||71||

We to eat, wear beautiful; she with overburden of sorrow;
Better was her death near funeral pyre of husband. ||72||

Detached she to be in attitude for study of transcendental;
Not understood, what benefit is by making oneself ugly? ||73||

To assume widow as evil, girl as sign of poverty?
Mean when grows in age, this deception of society. ||74||

As a male can be celibate, a woman be spinster;
Lacuna of rights all to be eliminated. ||75||

Shackle of family planning to woman, not for male;
Words these not thoughtless but mischief it is. ||76||

Regulation to be for all, training to be given to both;
Thought power to be spacious, knowing pains of nation. ||77||

Respect which for male in society, same to be for female;
More though to be given to her in society. ||78||

Here society wrong, one lifted up, and another suppressed;
Bitter fruits of this tasted in many places. ||79||

But, not attention at it, no best lessons for girls;
As pasture to grow for cattle, same in the society. ||80||

This to be changed, education to be given everywhere;
Women's lives to be enlightened to survive village state. ||81||

Wise persons not to be forgotten, arrangement in village for all;
Which will cause elevation of male as well as female. ||82||

Village will beautify on both sides of male and female;
Heaven will descend with the progress of work. ||83||

Inner qualities of woman will flourish by education special;
When given to her to change the world in future. ||84||

Higher education for woman, place of life in education to be;
In life, significance of peace, kindness to be. ||85||

Lessons to girls to provide by those who prefer social progress;
Education atleast necessary for writing, reading. ||86||

Cleanliness, singing, speaking, behaviour apt to be taught;
Woman to guess naturally by looking at home. ||87||

To maintain girls, the prime duty of parents;
Children of our home will render national service. ||88||

I saw, boys more educated, become mechanic, skilled worker;
But, planning for girls' education more dull. ||89||

This not to happen in society, girls to educate as boys;
Their status, respect to be in cooperative spirit. ||90||

Girls to be taught as different higher education for boys;
No negligence, to be understood by society. ||91||

But, independent girls' education to be, different works for male and female;
When both merge, an invitation for difficult situation. ||92||

Whatever happens with thought, planning prevails there;
When lured by thoughtless act, danger creeps up. ||93||

Educate consciously, to make like two wheels of a chariot;
Village to be infused with power, tact. ||94||

Always in control, both to operate at different places;
Then how nature to mould when in contact? ||95||

Neurotic ideas of male, female allude to each other's mind;
For this, brother-sisterhood to nourish by suitable relation. ||96||

Planning in education not to disrespect each other;
Educating to all in this way to shape morally. ||97||

When both realise mission, all mishaps at bay;
Though separate in cage, their tendency confused. ||98||

Education cooperative not deficient if moral values alive;
By all means enlightenment in education, the work of parent, guide. ||99||

Balancing body and mind in education, girl to be intellectual;
Valorous qualities to infuse to secure our mission. ||100||

When male dwindles, can't tolerate woman's nature;
To improve him, organisation of women ought to be. ||101||

As organised army of boys, organisation of women to be;
To express our happiness, sorrows in meeting, conference. ||102||

As place of inspiration for males, improvement home for women;
In it, activities of women, meeting, prayer, *katha*[3], *kirtan*[4]. ||103||

Keeping aside caste discrimination, collecting all women;
Til-gul[5], *haladi-kumku*[6], festival of Sharada[7], meal together. ||104||

Celebration of holy women, their birth-death anniversaries;
Libraries for women, necessary everywhere. ||105||

Independent seminar, conferences of women for their honour;
Indispensable for them consciousness for resistance. ||106||

My urge for audiences, whatever happiness for males;
Means of freedom, happiness for women without differentiation. ||107||

All benefits for males, all sorrows for women;
Which discipline does it speak? It to deny. ||108||

Male upgraded but nothing understood by female;
Village it one sided; deterioration, sufferings to follow. ||109||

So, both wheels of chariot to strengthen by carving;
Then family cart of village life will be pleasant with pleasure. ||110||

An ideal such parent will give birth to ideal offspring;
Heavenly abode they will make India, Tukadya says. ||111||

Such *Sri Gramgeeta* book, *Guru*-discipline-self experience-accepted;
Narrated woman elevation; the Twentieth Canto completed. ||112||

Notes

1. *Kali*—The evil force.
2. *Ranchandika*—The Goddess for valour on battlefield.
3. *Katha*—Narration of scriptures.
4. *Kirtan*—Musical presentation of religious script.
5. *Til-gul*—Sesame mixed jaggery distributed at the time of *makarsankranti* when sunrays become more intense.
6. *Haldi-kumku*—The celebration of *makarsankranti* among women.
7. *Sharada*—The Goddess of knowledge.

Sanskar Search Quinate

Canto XXI

Wedded Life

Complementary to God's will, only two elements of society;
Operate male and female, the cycle of world. ||1||

To continue the flow of world, to restore qualities of nature;
For this arranged wedding by knowledge seeker of religion. ||2||

Male, female, two wheels when complementary to each other;
The chariot of world moves, an ideal becomes village. ||3||

But, this kept aside, changed the custom of wedding;
Then emerged thousand sorrows of society. ||4||

For *purushartha* wedded life, the mean for stability of society;
But, increasing ignorance, greed, disrupted society. ||5||

Many girls beautiful but remain spinster due to dowry;
Boy's conduct like it in many castes. ||6||

Such evil practices led to misconduct everywhere;
This sin more attached to society. ||7||

Arranged parents wedding considering family, wealth, status;
Before wedding none asks to both a boy and a girl. ||8||

Beings of different nature, brought together by others;
How life can run of both smoothly? ||9||

To respect parents, why to spoil family?
Why this motive to retain by elders? ||10||

Before wedding, both to see with determination;
Freedom of thought to give, an indispensable. ||11||

Parents to see a sign, is decision of wedding blind?
It, not to be cause for remorse to both. ||12||

With the consent of both, wedding to arrange with good minds;
Both to live in harmony to make family happy. ||13||

Tuning of both thoughts will flourish work;
The enthusiasm more of both will render service. ||14||

The best living, the best speech, the best beauty, holy carvings;
With equal thought they beautify home as godly figures. ||15||

Shameful become all whatever done without thoughts;
Listen we such complaints in the past. ||16||

Wedding for sensual pleasure, runs family with blindness;
After lapse of a year, confused both animals. ||17||

Both not on talking terms, suspects one another;
What family? Hellish pains for husband, wife. ||18||

Married for sensual joy, not recognised each other;
Wasted it the entire lives of both. ||19||

Wedding only for physical enjoyment, strange it seems;
What happen when beasts gather together? ||20||

When unity of men, dwarf heaven's pleasure is;
With their union, the attainment of progress marvelous. ||21||

Animal instincts of dogs give birth to beings;
Once born, puppies are left over by all means. ||22||

It, not of human beings, their living of responsibility;
Single offspring, of great work in time span. ||23||

In nation, all wealth, forest wealth, carvings in caves;
Money, mines, and cow wealth, all we need. ||24||

In all wealth, treasure of offspring, increases nation's honour;
Hence, bride, bridegroom to marry after search, with thought.
||25||

Otherwise, frail offspring to drawn family;
To blot nation too, not to happen this. ||26||

The best land for the best seed, rapidly tree grows;
Offspring to be like this as Balbhim[1] strong. ||27||

Such offspring beautifies an ancestry, makes respectable generations;
With self work glitters nation ours. ||28||

But, limit to be for offspring, no calamity to be for nation;
Treasure of body conservation not to lost in family. ||29||

Blood not inflected, the best qualities, well natured offspring;
This not totally relied on caste-generation, *gotra*[2]. ||30||

Both beings marriageable, intend to marry in different castes;
With thought consent to be given necessarily. ||31||

Quality attracts quality, listen we in the ancient scripts too;
Vain it is to view, cross wedding causes disorder. ||32||

Cross wedding not to victimise against will;
Space to give to think with cheerful mind. ||33||

'In a battle of life we must marry' with thought;
When lovers with conscience view, not to interrupt them. ||34||

In the past, quality based marriage many of Shri Krishna[3], Arjuna[4];
In society, many experimentation of diverse marriages. ||35||

Cross wedding of similar qualities, marriage of test for valour;
Marriage to eliminate differences among nations, in different tribes. ||36||

Such many principle based weddings, some satanic marriages;
With compulsion, bodies are bound for many reasons. ||37||

Such actions to prevent, marriage not to be in childhood;
With the sense of conscience marriage to perform. ||38||

Fascination for some parents, at the age of three years;
Or, three months, girls marriage arrange. ||39||

Adolescent became bride, bridegroom, not known human transaction;
Succumb to rituals, both animals poor. ||40||

In future no match for each other as snake-mongoose;
Then events of litigation-notices, spoils life in it. ||41||

Became some girls widow, husband demised in childhood;
Creeps up trouble tomorrow without marriage. ||42||

Tells ritual not to marry, mind disturbed, how to control?
Secretly inclination towards sin, sorrowful it is. ||43||

Such evil customs whatever are to be discarded;
Again new creation of social rules ought to be. ||44||

Widow who intends to marry, has to speak with elders;
With kind heart marriage to arrange treating it nature of life; ||45||

Widow who doesn't will, not to disturb her;
Assuming she as *sati*,[5] detached, society to retain. ||46||

Let such to happen as per human nature;
Then justifiable it is to call human being. ||47||

Some arrange marriage, takes dowry as one desires;
Not see whether matched or mismatched for sake of money. ||48||

Though bridegroom old or diseased, nice bride given;
Evil transactions of different types for wealth. ||49||

Accepting wealth of boy and girl, despair they nourish;
Does trap of love with cost operate for anyone? ||50||

Children have no speech, don't utter words though beaten;
But, they as butchers arrange marriage mismatched. ||51||

Such modes fanatic to be eradicated out;
Love from core for life, treasure to deem. ||52||

A person who took money from boy and girl to disdain;
Then only insistence incorrect will crumble. ||53||

Otherwise, dowry will lead life to doom;
At the end, many boys and girls incline to suicide. ||54||

Many run away with someone, infects social life;
But, greed not left by so called wise for money. ||55||

If this not rectified by village, hills of sin will increase;
Entire village is sharer, to be understood. ||56||

In some home, girls marriageable, boys ready for wedding;
There some make transaction in family relations. ||57||

Boy and girl not paired, openly for their convenience;
Burden parents impose on their necks. ||58||

Then pique there, girl not sent to mother's home;
Or, leaving her spoils her life. ||59||

Some for their honour bring sorrows to her destiny;
Increased such evil rituals in many villages. ||60||

In some caste, veil on face, as the work of confinement;
Creeps up trouble after marriage sometime. ||61||

Not seen girl due to veil, now realised she was squint eyed;
Some say, by breakage one has to revert. ||62||

Pertaining to veil system, wise turns fool too;
Husband if misplaced in crowd, she falls pray to miscreants. ||63||

Hides miscreant behind veil, many women carried away;
In spite of it, the eyes of society don't open. ||64|

Misleads veil system in many ways, not to come before elders;
But, deprived of service many girls due to this. ||65||

Such strange customs to demolish in society;
No single person to stigmatise for it. ||66||

Misdirect some parents, male can behave in anyway;
Tortures girl and beats her, an attitude such satanic. ||67||

Some parents protector of girls, attack others on petty issue;
Such education, misdirected, cultivates sorrows many. ||68||

Somewhere husband and wife organised, but hindrance for elder's respect;
Breakage, opposition, or quarrel make their lives barren. ||69||

Some hide, girl not sent in the post-married life;
Some snatch girl, open show they make of life. ||70||

Some hide lacuna before marriage, when realises it;
Turbulence to experience throughout life for all. ||71||

Some show fake decorum, some adamant for gifts;
Not understanding reality, they prove troublesome. ||72||

Greed for ornaments to some, no realisation for virtues;
Trap them artificial glory, destruction of girl's life. ||73||

Marriage market for boys, girls for education, beauty, job;
Cost they decide, not envisaging life values. ||74||

Express joy some brokers of marriage, with pink powder;
Victimise they boys, girls for their selfishness. ||75||

Intend some to sell girls, not considering moral, amoral;
Situation such deteriorated by various customs. ||76||

Bargaining with an astrologer, manipulates numerical;
Telling alternative name increases unreality, seriously. ||77||

Observe planets in the sky, here in nature, different insistences;
Revulsion which rises in life, not seen by them; ||78||

Says, the best of bride and bridegroom, matched thirty-six virtues;
Here, rivalry or polarity full, spoils life. ||79||

The virtues of bride and bridegroom, ornamental for each other;
Though marriage performed gloriously without them, unholy. ||80||

Somewhere marriage performed, lunatically money poured;
Not useful this mode, why to implement it? ||81||

Rituals many of wedding, mother-in-law, father-in-law, uncle all;
Whims many of participants, not to call this wedding. ||82||

Bustle disorderly, investment unwanted, and hectic work;
This work to call unholy, an expense useless of money. ||83||

Debt for marriage, interest to deposit throughout life;
For marriage to be penniless, which God has told? ||84||

Marriage for four-five days, various obstacles in marriage;
Why to make mimicry of richness? ||85||

Why to stress for date though many hindrances there?
Why to nourish such tendency custom bound? ||86||

Fresh air, water, season, this apt time for wedding;
Interferences other, we treat as meaningless. ||87||

Day pleasant to search, air and water convenient;
Hoping joyful it will be for all. ||88||

No expense for massive *pandal*, scenario to be of nature;
Or, assembly place of temple to be planned for this work. ||89||

Time, money, and labour to save, planning well;
Supreme importance to qualities leaving the illusion, caste, wealth. ||90||

Assembly place to beautify, suitable people to invite;
Bride and bridegroom in front, intimations to be given by an informer. ||91||

Introduction of bride and bridegroom, determination for good work;
Holy work to perform by uttering *mangalashtake*[6]. ||92||

Mangalashtake, the wedding's motto, proper advise by a person virtuous;
Not to indulge a fragment of decorum, unholy in it. ||93||

Meeting to be with honour, not to smoke;
Wedding, religion *sanskar,* remembering fire God. ||94||

Blessing of elders to receive, to behave with love for all;
The event of marriage to be performed with pleasant talk. ||95||

Rural *khadi* for bride, bridegroom, old or new, simple;
With such attire auspicious rice granules to fall on both heads. ||96||

Clothes to wear whatever available, if not, to be washed;
No gifts, marriage to be attended by people with respect. ||97||

Visit on the occasion of marriage to initiate their family;
Or, planning to fulfill deficiencies in village. ||98||

In retrospect, marriage event to perform with thought;
Understanding situation, time, everything. ||99||

Such holy event honours national facet;
Social life will unify, village's fame will boost up. ||100||

Sanskar of marriage, its importance the greatest;
On its base social temple, so make it beautiful. ||101||

For this, spoke with bride and bridegroom, marched with new creation;
Free I became, telling pleasure and pain of society. ||102||

Female and male, two wheels, complementary to each other, really;
With heavenly joy, village will flourish, Tukadya says. ||103||

Such *Sri Gramgeeta* book, *Guru*-discipline-self experience-accepted;
Narrated the wedding *sanskar*; the Twenty-first Canto completed. ||104||

Notes

1. Balbhim—The character, one of Pandavas, with mighty physical power in Mahabharata.
2. *Gotra*—Ancestry.
3. Shri Krishna—The narrator of *Sri Bhagavadgeeta.*
4. Arjuna—One of Pandavas, who was in dilemma on the battlefield to be or not to be. Shri Krishna motivated him to fight as duty against injustice by narrating *Sri Bhagavadgeeta.*
5. *Sati*—A tradition in *Rajput* in which a wife sacrifices her life after the death of her husband.
6. *Mangalashtake*—The eight stanzas to utter at wedding ceremony for pious, good happenings.

Canto XXII

Funeral Sanskar

Marriage *sanskar* necessary, but expense not to be more;
Knowing its nature, principally to be practiced fully. ||1||

Offering fruits, thread ceremony, tonsuring at pilgrim place;
Exaggeration not to be in house worship, naming ceremony, birthday. ||2||

Like it, decorum not to be in death *sanskar*, funeral rites;
Becomes life of living beings sorrowful due to dead one. ||3||

Listen for death *sanskar*, treat people death differently;
I say no one, the best like death. ||4||

As river merges into sea leaving all differences;
So, the work to be performed to meet with sea. ||5||

Flows it in self style, experience people peace with ease;
Pouring water on body, contentment they experience in life. ||6||

But, the importance of sea to her, likewise man is;
Breaking bondages of attachment turns to self-nature. ||7||

Whatever passion he has to work, supports life;
Manifests it again in life to come. ||8||

Body destroyed but passion infused in life;
When birth new surfaces again, happens this. ||9||

Greed in this life perished, received the best *sanskar;*
Travelled beyond the cycle of birth and death. ||10||

But, happens this seldom, attains ultimate goal;
Because of attachment, animals come and go. ||11||

Chained to senses by attachment, acted as his will randomly;
Favoured by people too, they have selfishness too. ||12||

Born, grew, and matured, many phases of body;
Flowers and fruits in six seasons, an old turned as a tree. ||13||

Reached neurosis to peak, body organs defunct;
Then look for his original home. ||14||

Intend to bind with shackles of attachment, give medicines;
'Save, Save' speak earnestly with hope to work. ||15||

To provide life when on verge of death, to make him active;
This man's duty good, understand we. ||16||

But, not saved after efforts, left corporal frame;
Deemed our being merged with God's nature. ||17||

Then pray for God, peace in God's abode;
Not to infect our joys and sorrows to him. ||18||

No cause to weep, same course ours is;
Bind to see the same Home when body ceases to work. ||19||

Crying after death, expression of ignorance it is;
Why to pose when understood, experiencing depression? ||20||

Attains what one deserves, why to weep?
Something substantial to be done for fame. ||21||

Whatever left to be done, to honour his name;
Honourable to become in one's family, proud for elders. ||22||

When demised such being, he to be carried by all;
Not to see his caste, creed; who he was? ||23||

Respect for departed to give, not anything evil;
To be accompanied with responsibility with inner urge. ||24||

Situation to balance by associating each other;
Our *sanskar* to remember for welfare. ||25||

Death to treat good, cooperation for funeral procession;
With *dindi*[1], rhythmic verbal rendering avenue to improve. ||26||

Evil, ugly, and nauseous, not to be any custom;
At condolence speech, one's participation to be. ||27||

At graveyard, an arrangement to be to protect from rain;
Sanskar mandap for all, holiness in surrounding. ||28||

Burning corpse, surrounding to be holy;
Requirements at suitable place in village to be. ||29||

Pitamber for corpse, to sell house for it;
Experience of sorrows, not to be practiced by any one. ||30||

Conduct as per availability, clean to be old cloth;
Carry corpse wrapped in it with contentment by poor. ||31||

Need of new cloth though suggested by *shastra;*
Not known to *shastra* how we run our home. ||32||

No meal without butter; who follows this dictum?
Why to stress *shastra* for butter to massage corpse? ||33||

Death in one's home, no grain to eat at home;
For what aloofness to maintain by him? ||34||

Starvation for poor if no work in a day;
Tell you, how can he be on fast for ten days? ||35||

So, work finished after burning, bath at home after return;
Death place to make holy, completion of funeral *sanskar.* ||36||

Then with free mind he has to go for work to earn;
The meditation of good thoughts to be in solitude. ||37||

Implementation of ritual to be aloof, tendency to grief it reveals;
Whatever bondages, interfere to be eradicated. ||38||

Basic purpose of it this, when contacted with corpse;
Infect germs while serving, so aloofness to be. ||39||

But, father demised at hundred miles, son aloofness at Mumbai;
This reversal to be eliminated, focusing on the base. ||40||

Sprinkling of cow urine, to eat lemon, *agnisanskar* for corpse;
Aloofness, not to touch, all for hygiene. ||41||

So, bathing with pure water, clean cloth to wear;
Whatever clothes and utensils, to be washed of patients. ||42||

This, indispensable to do, deem it as aloofness;
But, to grieve for ten days, unacceptable to mind. ||43||

To convey sad news to all, letters to send;
Improvement in this way of society. ||44||

For maturity of thoughts, righteous books to read;
But, what is a cause of weeping for six months with guests? ||45||

Emotion to control with conscience, prayer on the thirteenth day;
Amid people, the joy of *bhajan* to experience. ||46||

Story to tell as memory, giving gift to other if possible;
Service to render on occasion; if not, no sorrow. ||47||

Freely to kneel down, 'I will behave well' to plan;
Work of service to continue for sake of spirit lost. ||48||

Look for our situation, not to make fun of living one;
Turn bankrupt providing gift and donation; not to happen this. ||49||

Trapped some in rituals, draw debt for corpse;
Series of meals gathering relatives, familiar. ||50||

To *sadhu*, referee or *brahmin,* money given as fine;
To offer some sweet meal, troublesome for poor. ||51||

Some are wealthy, but fear for hell, without offspring;
Adapt someone at death door, difficulty for family members. ||52||

Adapted one, luxurious or invite quarrels;
Money wasted; how can escape from hell? ||53||

Experiences living being fruit of self deed; who can save him?
Attains heaven due to good fame, not because of offspring. ||54||

Heaven or liberty, not different from righteous motion;
Mind tilt towards truth, elevates motion of life. ||55||

Work for village welfare if one has own money;
Well, school, and hostel for village with righteous intention. ||56||

Or, road to build to avoid troubles for people;
Non-attachment paves for heavenly route. ||57||

Or, his relatives have to search for constructive work;
For the best work, money to utilise. ||58||

Which renders fame, righteous people call it heaven;
Qualities appreciated by people hearts, no heaven different. ||59||

Whose spreads defame, how can he attain freedom?
After death admire people, life such to be. ||60||

For this, the best education, the best living, the best behaviour;
All to be moulded into best for fame. ||61||

Fame, heaven indeed; defame, hellish terrain;
In this world, its repercussion, animals see. ||62||

Though gone to heavenly place, bad work, sorrow for Devendra[2];
Performing ninety *yagnya*, serpent egoistic unnecessarily. ||63||

In work, heaven and hell, appreciation futile of blind faith in book;
People misplaced in illusionary fiction for selfishness. ||64||

Says crow has taken *pind*[3], then to heaven gone;
Otherwise soul entangled somewhere. ||65||

This saying irrelevant, no importance to *pind* here;
What important one has done in human life. ||66||

After death, spirit wanders; goes to heaven after offering *pind;*
Otherwise, falls in hell, meaningless such words are. ||67||

If the best work done, the best abode he will have;
Otherwise, again to enter in base course, natural. ||68||

Experience animals fruits the best, the worst due to one's work nature;
This to change by *pind*, not possible. ||69||

Though lifted many *pind*, who hasn't done constructive work;
How can we say elevated his life is? ||70||

What will happen, clutching tail of cow given to *bhikshuk*[4]?
Can lost spirit crossing river, *vaitarani*[5]? ||71||

This, orthodox ritual, entertainment of relatives;
Fascination of new generation, alternative for contentment. ||72||

Not to condemn the book on death, its practice of contentment;
But, this, salvation of life, don't believe we. ||73||

To retain name of dead, something to give for social service;
His virtues to appreciate to become like him. ||74||

Real *pind* to lift by us, life to adore by work;
Attribute, it will fame glorious to life. ||75||

Otherwise, weeping after death, no caring when alive;
Why to pretend like this by society? ||76||

Meal not given when alive, playing on instruments after death;
Pind for crow, gifts for other; what return by it? ||77||

Spending lavishly on *shraddha*[6]; dying for public shame;
Why to practice this foolishly? ||78||

Don't stay living spirit to eat after twelve months;
Carrying sin, virtuous deed, birth repeatedly to taste fruits. ||79||

Living spirit to come again in righteous company;
To eradicate fault in past, constructive planning to be. ||80||

Or, glory of qualities to remember fully with trust;
This *shraddha* unparallel in the form of condolence. ||81||

To retain his fame in public, work of donation, virtues;
For memory in our village with appreciation. ||82||

Whosoever demised of disease, not to infect others;
So, on the occasion, help to be for village hospital. ||83||

Unknown to people religion's essence, proceed for pilgrimage with debt;
Facilitates it business at pilgrim place. ||84||

Some righteous people go to pilgrimage with bone-ash;
Says, perishment of sin with the water of Ganges[7]. ||85||

At Kashi one attains salvation, increases illusion in people;
Do insects emancipate when they die in the water of Ganges? ||86||

Selects devotee Kabir, the resident of Kashi[8], Magahar[9] for *samadhi*[10];
Door to hell, people call it, turned into holy land. ||87||

Weaving thread and thought, life visualised God in people;
How can stones in Ganges know the glory of devotee Kabir? ||88||

Did evil deeds throughout life, not decided in Ganges' water;
Dropped down now bones, says right motion of life spirit. ||89||

Those who say and follow this, think for their bellies;
So, performs after death, not told when alive. ||90||

Listen! futile it is where mind not involved;
What to happen where body and mind don't work. ||91||

Tell with honour *panda*[11], worshipper to send thou father to heaven;
So, asks what contribution will thou give? ||92||

Poor simple, plain farmer, labourer or devotee;
Says, contribution will be paid by taking debt. ||93||

But, when thou will send our father to heaven?
Weeps he bowing down before *panda*. ||94||

Increasing superstition such, nourishes deceptive selfish motive;
Massive sin this in people, of no labourers. ||95||

At such time he waits to tap an opportunity;
Tricks beneficial to be told by *panda, bhikshuk*. ||96||

Though, thou have thought, thy parents to go to heaven;
For it, determination to practice in Ganges. ||97||

To send my parent to heaven, I determine cordially;
Not I will touch liquor, opium, *bhang*, etc. ||98||

No wrong transaction, no deception of poor people;
Cooperate I will with all for righteous service. ||99||

Though *panda* thought this, their bellies fill;
And welfare of people too will be by this mode. ||100||

But, *panda*, addicted, misbehaved, strive to engulf without effort;
Then how can he elevate society? ||101||

So, blind orthodoxy not to nourish by anyone;
Village to treat as Ganges, everything to offer to her. ||102||

Searching lake or river beautiful, well, etc.;
Attain purification by bathing, remembering Lord. ||103||

On occasion righteous work to do; why to see pilgrimage outer?
Permeates Lord in everyone for all time ever. ||104||

So, mode this to change, everything to perform at village;
Whatever possible with right intention, all to mould. ||105||

Turn some corpse in *samadhi*, invest land;
By doing this way, the entire land will be covered. ||106||

Samadhi for corpse, crowd of person related;
Then how can land be left for living ones? ||107||

No home for living man, no land for labourers;
Therefore, what exaggeration of *samadhi* for death? ||108||

So, simple to perform, not to succumb to greed of corpse;
By fire, ritual corpse to merge with five elements. ||109||

As remembrance at home or village, apt photograph to display;
Time to time, as virtuous person to remember. ||110||

Construction of *samadhi* by anyone, thy sign of attachment;
Tell me, what will happen constructing *samadhi*? ||111||

Constructing *samadhi* one visualises, clicks picture in mind;
Significance of entering in mind, core in all. ||112||

The best place to create, where people seek education well;
As a memorial, it to dedicate to villagers. ||113||

This, natural situation; why to make unnatural?
Whatever set society in order, its significance to enhance. ||114||

Human beings or animals, their *samadhi* not to witness;
Keeping society alive, motive to be of right order. ||115||

For it, various *sanskar*, the immense importance to different times;
Focusing beautiful to make, suitable to village state. ||116||

Though, death or birth celebration, not merely adoration;
By saving, village glory to increase, Tukadya says. ||117||

Such *Sri Gramgeeta* book, *Guru*-discipline-self experience-accepted;
Narrated funeral *sanskar* apt; the Twenty-second Canto completed. ||118||

Notes

1. *Dindi*—The procession in which devotees sing with religious fervor, accompanied by musical instruments like *veena, tal,* and *dholaki,* accompanied by palanquin.
2. *Devendra*—The king of gods in heaven in Indian mythology.
3. *Pind*—Rice ball in Indian funeral ritual.
4. *Bhikshuk*—A person who demands *madhukari*, wandering door to door.
5. *Vaitarani*—The river with turbulences.
6. *Shraddha*—Funeral ritual to remember dead one.
7. *Ganges*—The holy river in India.
8. Kashi—The pious pilgrim place. It is believed that after funeral ritual at Kashi, a man becomes free and the soul reaches to heaven.
9. Magahar—The place on the boarder of UP and Bihar, which was preferred by Kabir for his funeral, which was believed to be unholy.
10. *Samadhi*—A place for burial of corpse.
11. *Panda*—Ritual practitioner.

Canto XXIII

Festival Celebration

An audience queried, thou narrated wedding and funeral *sanskar;*
The best we felt it to our mind. ||1||

But, birth celebration good, experiences joy by festive celebration;
Enliven it will rural life, hobby this to all. ||2||

Treated you little it, its cause to unfold;
Now answer to be listened by audiences. ||3||

No date left in a year when celebrate we festivals;
Birth death anniversaries numerous, birthdays additional. ||4||

For celebration of all these, work, business all gone;
How can this only revive all motives? ||5||

So, minor, major to select with conscience;
Considering situation one has to behave all time. ||6||

Understanding whatever one performs, reason to tell;
Merely to eat *ladu-pethe,* birth celebration not to be. ||7||

Purpose ancestors conceived, it to understand;
Festival celebration to be as the objective planned. ||8||

Custom, tradition of India, scrupulously planned it was;
Smoothly it controls the order of society. ||9||

It to enlighten again, so spoke naturally;
Principally, no secondary place to festival. ||10||

Celebration love, man's nature, his honour for festival, occasion;
For special work, he runs for ever. ||11||
Rooted in the mind to do some special work;
No hesitation, with inner urge, expense recklessly. ||12||
For sake of festival, not to spend money lavishly;
As then told to save for utility in righteous cause. ||13||
Otherwise, celebration of *Diwali*, avenue for bankruptcy;
Laugh people in village saying amateur Nataraj[1]. ||14||
Not to succumb to fiasco, company for meal with all;
But, never to turn our life to dust. ||15||
Festival celebration on a day, its repercussion for another day;
None has told such family religion. ||16||
Understanding festive days in future, one has to think;
Occasion in succession to come, cooperation to be given. ||17||
Money to save for celebration on some occasion;
When arrives festival, all energy not to invest. ||18||
For celebration by anyone, lacuna to observe;
Then step to take for joy, fascinating. ||19||
More to include, to live with joy time to time;
For behaviour, regular lesson to learn. ||20||
Knowledge of life to increase, not to increase bad qualities;
Then mind to be fearless for occasion. ||21||
Some festival at home, some at public place to celebrate;
Collectively, load to share some. ||22||
On occasion of festival, meal to take together;
Behaviour in practice to nourish brotherhood. ||23||
Bringing food from home or cooking collectively;
Eating together love and joy surge up. ||24||
Whatever *prasad*[2] one has to be distributed;
But, in eating only, time of society not to be consumed. ||25||
Katha[3], *kirtan*[4], *dindi*, game, entertainment fine;

But, in the best way, society to channelise. ||26||

Real festival and routine work, with thought religion to follow;
But, behaviour to know the core of occasional festival. ||27||

Datta[5], *Ramanavami*[6], Hanuman[7] birth anniversaries, *Gokulashtami*[8];
Shivratri[9], *Ashadi*[10], *Kshrushipanchami*[11], to practice with varied works. ||28||

Vatsavitri[12], Sharada[13] festival, *Rakshabandhan*[14], *Sankrantiparva*[15];
Worship of Gauri[16], festival of women to celebrate collectively. ||29||

Day of industry, get together, progress of strength, day of prayer;
Day of mind progress to *Geetajayanti*[17], penta-celebration necessary ||30||

Including all castes and tribes, *haladi, tilgul,* gift of gold;
Competition, village purification, incantation of Rama, speech to arrange. ||31||

Important is *Pola*[18], the festival of oxen;
In it exhibition of oxen, with equipment of farms. ||32||

In row, disciplined ox to arrange, body to deck up;
One who excels in service to felicitate. ||33||

Pair of oxen healthy, some feed nutrients to oxen;
Prizes to be given to them by villagers. ||34||

Some maintained farm, some kept servants joyful;
Positions their to elevate on holy day. ||35||

Pair to visit homes in village, to return home at end;
Gift to be taken by caretaker, pleasant tendency to retain. ||36||

Play cards in day after, degradation of society this is;
Some win in game, some lose clothes too. ||37||

Such custom to cease, if needs wrestling to arrange;
Labourers to give prizes, naming sturdy, agile. ||38||

Such is *Dashera, Vijayadashami*[19], enthusiastic;
Increases it love bond in village best. ||39||

All to celebrate together, sing song of great persons;
Sages to admire, nation to honour. ||40||

The best determination on that day, 'what is ours of all' to learn;
Differences to forget giving the leaves of *apate*, the gold leaves. ||41||

No grudge after, all to pay, respect to all;
Well wishes to accept of each other, deeming others companions. ||42||

Respecting saint and God, one has return home dignified;
Blessings of parents, grand-parents to receive with admiration. ||43||

New work project to formulate to retain for a year;
Such celebration to practice by all with unity. ||44||

After arrival of *Diwali*[20], all to celebrate;
But, one has to see who is left hungry? ||45||

He to be invited, sweet meal to be provided;
Cooperating each other glory of all to retain. ||46||

In village, single *Laxmipujan*[21] to be, erecting in massive pandal;
All to be given refreshment, meal by all. ||47||

Joy to surge up in every home; happy cows, calves, man, woman;
Such to happen to enhance brother, sister relation. ||48||

Brotherhood, sisterhood dwindled in society;
To boost it up, plan of *Bhaubij*[22] in new generation. ||49||

Exhibition of cows to arrange, cows with more milk;
Bull enriched with qualities, with height to observe. ||50||

To be honoured by all, to be prized by all;
Significance of cattle to instill on all people' minds. ||51||

Cow of each one to be improved in future;
Next *gudhi*[23] to be erected, assuring to give prizes. ||52||

Likewise significance of manure to increase, centering on *Narkasur*[24];
Operation of cow-dug manure to be illustrated. ||53||

With compose of manure and urine, farm gives more yield;
As thus, they to preserve by digging land. ||54||

Cow dung to go to farm for the blessings of the earth-mother;
To be told at every home, this real *Diwali* festival. ||55||

In village, people will live in joy if wealth retains;
By such efforts, we celebrate real *Diwali.* ||56||

After twelve month *Diwali* arrives, all houses clean;
Wall, front shed with smearing of cow dung, colours. ||57||

Next day no sprinkling of cow dug water, no sweeping;
Spreads dirt of all types hither and thither. ||58||

In such celebration of *Diwali, Dashera,* desolation creeps up;
Better to wake-up in morning, this real *Diwali.* ||59||

Being festival, holy bath to take, otherwise smear face;
With black crude oil, which wisdom we have learnt? ||60||

Few to be done daily, bath, meditation, recitation;
Labouring beauty to enhance in home and outside. ||61||

On the pretext of *Diwali*, cleanliness, holiness to learn;
Garbage to clean, lighting lamp of cleanliness. ||62||

Always home to keep clean, more labour;
Real festival this, daily fine conduct. ||63||

One who cleans always, practices festival from all angles;
The best to eat vegetable, *bhakari*[25], offering to gods. ||64||

Real *Dashera, Diwali* to those who follow this discipline;
Otherwise, burning of our lives entire. ||65||

Festival of *Holi* arrives, more conflicts in it;
Keeping aside dignity, respect, people wander like lunatic. ||66||

Strangeness such increased, not this festival;
In it too principle to receive by society. ||67||

On this day, Pralhad[26] tortured by *Holi;*
But, being devotee of God, sorrow not experienced by Pralhad. ||68||

At the end, torturers burnt, appreciation for villagers;
As thus, people cried disdaining them. ||69||

On that day, Shankar burnt Kam[27] with third eye;
As thus, army of ghosts retaliated Kam raising sounds, hubbub. ||70||

On that day, planned righteous people annual *yajna*;
Cleaning entire village, waste to burn. ||71||

In its light, all to assemble, evil deeds to narrate;
To plan not to do in future, with remorse. ||72||

Lacked in self will, so other people cried;
In this way, village's sin washed away. ||73||

In future, distorted it, abuses each other;
Scripts say, "speak abusive", not knowing core. ||74||

Say some, only a day in a year for abuse;
But, what cause for righteous people? Impetus for evil person. ||75||

For this festival, colour play, the ancient sign of village cleanliness;
On that day, told in scripts, untouchables to touch. ||76||

First public worship of fire, in it burning of evil tendency;
Then ash to take at garbage place, bath to take collectively. ||77||

Such joy of village service, imparts fragrance to others;
To create pleasantness, plan for entertainment. ||78||

At places, singing, music play, smearing of colours, powder;
To keep mind pleasant, plan for *Holi* festival. ||79||

In king's kingdom, places, sensual form to it;
In the name of Shri Krishna, operation of colour pipe. ||80||

In village, reversed situation, lost purpose of village purification;
Throwing waste in drainage, give troubles to people. ||81||

Some steal woods and items from home, dump in fire;
Burn accessories of vehicles, houses, cot too. ||82||

Festival this creates tension, desolate village becomes;
Attack people of conscience, treating situation this evil. ||83||

But, this to change, such madness not to happen;
In it, beauty, holiness to infuse by singing, music. ||84||

On the pretext of *Holi*, exercise of male, female to arrange;
Plan of entertainment by short play for village improvement. ||85||

Holi, village purification, likewise mother day, children day;
Labour day, Humanity day, Independence day, and others. ||86||

Likewise many small festivals, in them principle to be;
Decorative mean of belly filling, futile it is. ||87||

Festival celebration for progress, some festivals for unity;
All to conduct it, collectively with cooperation. ||88||

Ganesh festival at homes before, nuisance of various customs;
National importance attributed by Lokmanya. ||89||

Single Ganesh of village, programmes for all;
National attitude it will nourish, this intention to be. ||90||

The best festival, festive day, fulfilled with national tendency;
This to practice massively, addressed saints in society. ||91||

Festivity people like, search for remedy in that way;
Awakening of national spirit dauntlessly, festival it to follow. ||92||

On auspicious occasion all to work organised;
Burden it will not place on anyone. ||93||

Otherwise for our entertainment, disturbance to other;
Celebration, festival like it, degradation of people. ||94||

Others happy, we happy, ready for each other admiration;
Conduct of all for all same to be. ||95||

To create such mental mould, festivity in villages to change;
Lesson it will provide to people for conduct ever. ||96||

Festivals in all religions, some big, some small;
Which will honour man to man for ever. ||97||

Increase of collectivity everywhere, main crux of festivity;
Variation of collectivity, real festival it is. ||98||

Festive day, ethereal when village has become one;
No discrimination between rich and poor in festival. ||99||

To give who has nothing, to channelise who misdirected;
To lift who fallen down, treating as close one. ||100||

This real magnanimity, sees festivity in village happiness;
Retains it festivity in village for ever. ||101||

In early time, twelve regions, group of eighteen castes;
Relied on each other cooperative life. ||102||

Brings fisherman net, sticks goldsmith sticker;
Take barber, washerman, milkman, grains to their homes. ||103||

But, law it not now, no gain to festival coming;
To tell about festivity, not business of any one. ||104||

Service pure this to enlighten inner lamp;
Question of belly fulfillment not to enter in festivity. ||105||

All have to work, festivals in time left;
Pandals to be erected with sense of service by all. ||106||

Verdict this different but misleads it simpleton;
Being confused, speak people like atheists. ||107||

In past labour-division was, increased it selfishness;
Motivated it beggars, *gosavi* to disgrace ancestors. ||108||

Work to be given to people who work by village;
Arrangement complete to fill belly by labour for all time. ||109||

No unemployment in village, no extravagantly spending;
Whatever motivates in right direction by festivals to perform. ||110||

Righteous motion, festival it, otherwise call for trouble;
To avert it, village to be organised and functional. ||111||

Enthusiasm in work, festival it without doubt;
Let flow current of peace, happiness, Tukadya says. ||112||

Such *Sri Gramgeeta* book, *Guru*-discipline-self experience-accepted;
Narrated kernel of festivals; the Twenty-third Canto completed. ||113||

Notes

1. *Natraj*—Here, an actor.
2. *Prasad*—Pious food to distribute among devotee after worship, prayer.
3. *Katha*—Discourses on religions script.
4. *Kirtan*—The traditional folk performance with musical accomplishments, in which anecdotes from religious texts; legends are presented.
5. *Datta*—Three-headed deity.
6. *Ramanavami*—The auspicious day of Rama's birth.
7. *Hanuman*—The ardent disciple of Rama.
8. *Gokulastami*—The birth celebration of Shri Krishna.
9. *Shivratri*—The festive celebration of Shiva.
10. *Ashadi*—The auspicious day for the devotees of varkari cult in Maharashtra.
11. *Kshrushipanchmi*—The day for reverence to sages.
12. *Vatsavitri*—In this festival a married woman worships baniyan tree ritually praying for longer life of her husband. It also relates to the mythological story of Satyawan and Savitri.
13. Sharada—The goddess of knowledge.
14. *Rakshabandhan*—In this festival of brother and sister, brother assures for security to sister and she ties *rakhi* on the brother's hand as a sign of love and respect.
15. *Sankrantiparva*—Geographically the Sun transits in new phase in January and its celebration.
16. Gauri—Parvati, the wife of Lord Shiva.
17. *Geetajayanti*—The birth celebration of *Geeta*.
18. *Pola*—The festival of oxen.
19. *Dashera, Vijayadashami*—The auspicious day to pay respect to elders by offering the leaves of *apate*, the plant.
20. *Diwali*—The festival of light. The earthen lamps are lighted and placed in row in night.
21. *Laxmipujan*—The worship of the goddess of wealth.
22. *Bhaubij*—The auspicious day on which a sister expresses love and reverence for a brother and wishes for his property.
23. *Gudhi*—The ritual in Maharasthra to celebrate new year.
24. Narkasur—The demon.
25. *Bhakari*—A thick chapati of maize grain powder.
26. Prahald—The son of Hiranyakapshu who was the devottee of Vishnu.
27. Kam—The demon who was killed by Shiva.

Canto XXIV

Pilgrimage Assembly

Queried an audience, in village sects different;
Different gods, religions, celebrations they have. ||1||

Though in public celebration, treat they themselves different;
Assuming their cultures different, continue they. ||2||

Their tents differ, in different temples they celebrate;
Somewhere worship of images, some idol opponents. ||3||

Some long for pilgrimage, motivate they other;
No care though here desolate village turns. ||4||

Different their opinions, different their saints;
In their group, they make fun of others. ||5||

Various branches of disciples, various *guru* too;
Don't come they closer, conduct their celebrations. ||6||

Knowledge some, real-unreal; blind rituals they attempt to teach;
Groups of different devotees, blow their trumpets. ||7||

Fiasco of organisation until they unite;
Tell us how to search remedy for this? ||8||

Hits nail audience's query, necessary to listen answer;
Indispensable to view panorama from village to the world. ||9||

Formed different groups, walls of differences among them;
To diseased society, narrow opinions teach. ||10||

Providing impetus to superstition, wrong conduct people implement;
Kinds of their celebration strange are. ||11||

Waste of ample money, sowing of evil customs;
Deeds of many to increase cleavages in people. ||12||

Many *buwa*[1] in garb live on such groups;
No real knowledge impart they, selfish, to people. ||13||

Immersed village in illusion until such trend continues;
Hindrances creep up in the way of improvement. ||14||

Remedy for this, not to keep oneself aloof;
Fearlessly one has to unite with them for collectivity. ||15||

Let sect be of anyone, let *buwa*, sage be any;
Treating all as ours, we have to merge. ||16||

Five celebrations ours, failed deeming them inferior;
How can we gain integrity if separated? ||17||

So, tell remedy, let anniversary of saint, holy day;
At public place, it to celebrate unitedly. ||18||

No separate language though of any sect;
Saying saint, virtuous, friend of the world. ||19||

Honour of truth in the celebration of all sects;
Through it, knowledge to infuse. ||20||

Not to be aloof, not to celebrate at home only;
Cooperation of all to seek, the crux of organisation. ||21||

Influential programmes to arrange for the effect of celebration;
Discourses by great one, the best *bhajan* to organise. ||22||

Admiring saints, not to tell fascinating miracles;
Influence of the best conduct to be on society. ||23||

Sant Jnaneshwar, Tukaram, Namdev, Sawata, Chokha, unparalleled;
Eknath, Damaji, Bhagwatottam to narrate to people. ||24||

Sajan Kasai, Ravidas cobbler, Sena, Santaji, Gora potter;
Krishnadayarnav, Vaman, Sridhar, Saint poets too. ||25||

Ramdas, Tulsidas, Keshavdas, Kabirdas;
Sundardas, Vishnudas, Surdas etc. ||26||

Shankaracharya, Ramanujacharya, Madhvacharya, Vallabhacharya;
Radhaswami, Basawacharya, Raman Maharshi, Sri Chakradhar. ||27||

Shahadatta, Gorakhnath, Govindnath, Dayalnath;
Narsi Mehta, Ramtirtha, Sri Samarth Adkoji. ||28||

Great soul Mansoor, Muhammad, Kawarram, Sheikh Farid;
Zartustra and Gautam Buddha, Vivekananda influential. ||29||

Guru Govindsingh, Nanakdeo, Chaitanya, Gaurangdeo;
Ramakrishna Paramahansa, Jain Mahavir Swami. ||30||

Great soul Yeshu, Tolstoy, Marx, Socretes, dauntless;
Great soul Gandhi, Raja Ram Mohan Roy, Dayanand, knowledge seeker. ||31||

Devotee Meerabai, Muktabai, Kanhopatra, Janabai;
Ranganaiki, Bahinabai, Annie Besant, Nivedita. ||32||

Those who were influential, their biographies to explain;
What they did for society to channelise. ||33||

Birth anniversaries of such people to celebrate, prayer by all;
Life sketches their by competent speakers to mould people. ||34||

Their vastness to explain, emotion of equity to follow;
Society to follow same for its progress. ||35||

Though saints differ in bodies, their motto, strategy unifying;
Though means different, theoretical mind same. ||36||

Convincing this with study, unity of various sects will be;
In all means, the abolishment of superstitious practices. ||37||

Otherwise, cleavages among sects, breakage in cooperation;
Selfish, hypocrite fill their bellies on it. ||38||

Lured they their devotees in celebrations many;
Disorders superstitious village life. ||39||

Narrowness to bring on open ground keeping aside differences;
Then all tongues will speak truth holy. ||40||

Let saints come to village to advise in prayer;
Or, at public places, celebrations for all. ||41||

No unreliable story to tell, no evil custom;
Search people consequently, avenue to real knowledge. ||42||

Not much discrimination on the stance of knowledge;
Views parallel to each other by all. ||43||

End it with differentiation, principle people will realise;
Remedy this valuable to eradicate walls of sects. ||44||

Where people sit with equity, facilities real discussion;
Slowly leads to unity of gods, saints, religions. ||45||

As thus, such occasion fine to bring in village time to time;
Sadhu, righteous person to be bring closer of sects various. ||46||

In villages, celebration of saints to be with sense of unity;
Honour of pilgrim place, village will receive. ||47||

In pilgrim place, pure assembly of *sadhu,* their philosophic discourse;
Principles people to learn, significance of pilgrim place. ||48||

Otherwise stones at pilgrim place, God in virtuous person;
Clarion call saints have given like this. ||49||

If direction, people don't receive at pilgrim place;
What gain to people running after there? ||50||

Pilgrimage for service, to inspire thoughts;
By these means, village to be pilgrim oriented. ||51||

Pilgrimage for directions, demands people without work;
No holy work to take place, only illusion, ego. ||52||

Why to go *Kunbhamela*[2], starving kid at village?
God, in village less, at pilgrim place different, not this. ||53||

But, people succumb to trap, entangle in the web of *panda*;
Die as lamb running after rituals. ||54||

At twelve miles from Pandharpur[3] Sawata lived;
Experienced Lord at village, though not on pilgrimage. ||55||

With honesty if did service of public deeming them gods;
Consequently, good of Pandhari will run to village. ||56||

Village, pilgrim place beautiful, where such saints, servicemen reside;
Receive people inspiration to turn village into paradise. ||57||

Where love and holiness prevail, its name pilgrim area;
Why to visit pilgrim place to witness confusion? ||58||

Village's public place to treat as pilgrim place great;
Their body, mind, wealth to invest of magnanimous persons. ||59||

At pilgrim place no expense to be, village avenue to improve;
Worthy treasure of pilgrim place village will receive by service. ||60||

Saving village wealth, holy idol to carve of village;
Then not visiting to pilgrim place, gain of good by village upliftment. ||61||

Whatever contribution we collect for week programme, *yagnya*, celebration;
For some year, it to invest for improvement of village. ||62||

Birth or death, anniversary, week programme *yagnya*, meal;
Good work to perform considering situation of village, nation. ||63||

All sects to unite for constructive work of all;
Not to insist adamantly on the issues sterile. ||64||

Experienced one runs to forest, devotee of goddess ready to sacrifice;
Some spend money exuberantly in isolation. ||65||

Collecting contribution some sacrifice animals to goddess;
But, by such celebration, disease not to cease without village cleanliness. ||66||

In village pilgrimage, many evil operations;
As pouring of poison in society, spending money. ||67||

For it, pilgrimage committee to organise assembly, celebration, market;
With national spirit, improvement to bring hand to hand. ||68||

Organisation for village upliftment to infuse national spirit;
With physical, mental energy for fame too far as pilgrim place. ||69||

When pilgrimage assembly at village or near village;
There service to render becoming self volunteer. ||70||

Likewise, to put forth clear identity of our village;
Better to open exhibition, conference, pilgrimage in village. ||71||

For road, straight; pure, clean, hygienic water;
All ideals in village construction to follow there. ||72||

Toilet, urinal on four sides; gradation of many items;
Elevate they nation to higher height of glory. ||73||

Many entertainment to continue, but not to permit addiction, *tamasha;*
Slowly interest to cultivate of nationality in people. ||74||

Beautiful arts of industries, performing arts like music;
Behavioural art of humanity to plan there. ||75||

How to walk on road? How to sit? How to speak?
How we to behave in home and community? ||76||

Fine lesson to give, unity of all to teach in village;
New luminance in all to infuse by pilgrimage, celebration. ||77||

Servicemen to labour more to close down evil rituals;
Various remedies to implement for pilgrimage purity. ||78||

As Swami Dayananda *Maharaj,* his *Arya Samaj*;
For improvement of pilgrims, he worked tirelessly. ||79||

As Gadge *Baba,* an idol of renunciation, his service committee;
Attempted always in the best way for village purity. ||80||

Pilgrimage planning to be, assembling virtuous people in village;
Pilgrimage means 'come nearer' to instill on people's minds. ||81||

Massive mob to gather, good advice to give;
Dignity of people lives to raise by saint-leader. ||82||

Though came thousand people, no disorder in hygienic condition;
Arrangement to facilitate in and out of people. ||83||

Constituents of life to gain by *katha, kirtan*;
The best rapport after meeting with others respectfully. ||84||

Format to prepare, various committees to form;
In people, improvement consequently to bring. ||85||

Many exhibitions useful, many competitions in it;
Likewise, all programmes of people education to arrange. ||86||

On occasion of pilgrimage, conferences of different sects to organise;
Discourses by saints intellectuals, of unbiased thoughts. ||87||

Not hurting anyone, virtuous principle to honour;
Concluding session, focusing on unity, core truth. ||88||

Melts differentiation there, no operation of hypocrisy;
If remains aloof strangely, sweep away by current. ||89||

Real and false, diamond and synthetic glass structure will know;
When thoughts will be tested in public. ||90||

Who saint? Who not saint? What unreal? What real?
Realising this, acceptance of sect for coordination by people. ||91||

When an elephant visible, complete, then no blind, one sided;
Willn't deceive others, saying different parts as an elephant. ||92||

Though sects increased in the names of saints, gods;
Attain everything when message of truth reaches everywhere. ||93||

As *Granth Sahib* penned by *Guru* Govind Singh for people;
Collected words of various saints, nutrients for organisation. ||94||

With right intention, Mahipati wrote the biographies of saints;
Collectively, binding all people with fabric of oneness. ||95||

At Pandharpur, saint like Jnaneshwar did *Gopalkala*;
Garland of all sects woven by that way. ||96||

Likewise conference of saints, remembrance of all saints;
Attainment of mass, unity easily in village if practiced. ||97||

As rivers merge in sea, experience holiness;
Make village holy unifying all sects. ||98||

Celebration of all saints but no honour to miracles;
Duty orientation to be remembering their lives. ||99||

Deem the earth, Pandhari continuing such work celebration;
None will be unhappy; where male, female pleasant. ||100||

If not this happens in village, though pilgrimage more;
No salvation to life, Tukadya says. ||101||

Such *Sri Gramgeeta* book, *Guru*-discipline-self experience-accepted;
Narrated pure signal of festival celebration; the Twenty-fourth Canto completed. ||102||

Notes

1. *Buwa*—Fake saint.
2. *Kumbhamela*—Ritualistic fair at pilgrim places—Haridwar, Prayagraj, Nashik, Ujjain.
3. Pandharpur—The pilgrim place in Solapur district of the Western Maharashtra.

Canto XXV

God Temples

Sadhu, saint, great beings, magnanimous in thoughts;
No interference of discrimination there by any means. ||1||

Though public celebrations, their followers treat different;
Different their gods, no resonance. ||2||

Different God, different religion, their penances differ;
How can be union of their emotions? ||3||

Conference of saints held, meeting for short span;
But, widens cleavage in people by practices. ||4||

Where fame prevails, where wealth ample;
Worship people those deities, some to others. ||5||

Tell remedy for this feasible for ever;
By *sanskar* they will be united with the inner urge. ||6||

An audience's query hits nail, indispensable for village welfare;
As saints, unity of gods to achieve. ||7||

Treat men differently their religion-action-God;
Though village one, their approaches differ. ||8||

Signs their different to identify sects;
Opened their shops, attractive of sects. ||9||

One says Rama great, to another Krishna great;
Third says Shankar great ours of all. ||10||

Some say goddess great, some worship women devilish;
Some *mhasoba-bahiram-sole malhaara*,[1a] quarrel deeming them great. ||11||

Some utter Hari, some salute Nalyahaidar[1b];
Worship some serpent, tiger, sacrificing hen and sheep. ||12||

Some make gods of gold, sell them at time needy;
Such is mockery of God by devotees. ||13||

Sacrifice some for God, eat meal in the name of Goddess;
Drinks lunatic liquor treating it holy water. ||14||

In temple, God of stone, its platform of gold;
Threat of burglar, so vigilance at temple. ||15||

Embed God as per one's choices;
As thus, eyes on decorum, God invisible. ||16||

One says beautiful necklace, another says crown jeweled glorious;
One says fine glare of gold outshines devotion to God. ||17||

One says gold-throne, another says raiment silky;
One says smearing of saffron, musk sandal, nine jewels in neck of God. ||18||

Some say, God awakened, now sat, now took food;
Now, rested after chewing betel leaf. ||19||

God to sleep on velvet cloth, close doors from outside;
Sleep they don't without pressing their legs with tender hands. ||20||

In retrospect, what one likes gods too like;
Then becomes God pleasant, believe some. ||21||

Who thinks whether it is vice or virtue?
Succumbing to superstitions continue they onward. ||22||

Touch of feet, worship, salutation, bondage, love, self-expression;
Understanding they outerly, pose decorum of devotion. ||23||

Some immerse to devotion in separation, some in company;
Some praise self-devotion in any way. ||24||

Some pique whether Allah great or Rama;
Break recklessly idols picking in hands. ||25||

Abuse the devotee of Jesus, says misbehaved Hindu's God;
Sixteen thousand his wives, how God he is? ||26||

Pique at every home, not done what to do;
Oh! Have they realised the crux of the idol worship? ||27||

Quarreling for gods, proceed to litigation;
Vows he of gods, saying, "I speak truth". ||28||

Became people atheistic due to the untrue deed;
What will happen though worshipped God more. ||29||

Lost understanding; utter what dignity of God?
Urinated mouse, sitting on him. ||30||

On contrary say some, God awakened, blesses when one trusts;
Say I, trust is deity, why not to say? ||31||

In a place, God awakened, in other whether ghost?
How do thou presume reversely? ||32||

Cleavages among people, created by so called worshippers;
Supporting it by disciplines, dragged down society. ||33||

Deem this God worship, whatever narrates worshipper;
Believes devotee without conscience, how to know God? ||34||

One conceives God as one's faith;
There faith as prime level naturally enters. ||35||

One more prime sign, saint who erected temple;
On his greatness deemed people the stature of God. ||36||

Worshipped stone righteous person, others turned it into God great;
Fame his increased, fare boosted up. ||37||

Jnandeo not visiting Pandhari, no assemblance of saints;
Who worship God there, tell me? ||38||

God same everywhere but appears different as one conceives;
Though good, turns alien, due to greedy deceptive worshippers.
||39||

Happened this with us, so increased presumptions various;
Missed urge for devotion to God, inclination more to wealth.
||40||

Importance now to God place which is wealthy;
Money to expense for worship, God pleases by it, says. ||41||

But, God not great by decorum, God not great by huge temple;
God not great by ringing bells day and night. ||42||

God not great by lamp, God not great by fire rituals;
God not great by *myna*[2] as mountain. ||43||

God not great by nature's beauty, God not great by massive pilgrimage;
God not great by dignified glory of devotee. ||44||

God great by faith, sublimity of faith;
Equal for all by the inner devotion. ||45||

Let any God, no discrimination there;
Ornaments they moulded of same spirit. ||46||

Though one became infinites, manifested in diverse forms;
But, when searched, One is in operation? ||47||

No discrimination between Hari, Hara, same in everyone;
Visualised Rama, Rahim one, God-Goddess unified. ||48||

Bow holder Rama, *Meghshyam*[3], flute player;
Hands on waist, with attributes Vitthal He. ||49||

All gods one, remembered by different name;
Though diverse forms, the principle same under flow. ||50||

One expense, one luminance, myriad forms on occasion;
Sacrifice gods all their lives for the single motto. ||51||

No pain to righteous person, no one to be poor, empty bellied;
For that life to sacrifice when time demands. ||52||

Those who did this, sacrificed their lives;
In mortal world, God and Goddess they became. ||53||

Protection of righteous person, eradication of anti life elements;
Guarding of faith, justice, virtues, the work of all gods. ||54||

If this, why to create quarrels among God-Goddess;
Why to immerse the character of deities for our fun? ||55||

Righteous one to avoid this tendency, respect for all;
None to be different in sect, treating them one. ||56||

To all the core principles of temple, the significance of worship;
Divinity to understand, what functions they have? ||57||

Differentiation it will end, comprehension of practical worship;
In temple, practice will be of the core principle apt. ||58||

Asked one query, what is core principle of God's abode?
Temples these different due to diversity in sects. ||59||

Tractor to drive to make all structures same;
What difference it will make in devotion without temple? ||60||

Listen to clarification, no unity by hurting others;
As thus, apt it is to provide momentum to the philosophy of temple. ||61||

At beautiful and serene place, simple *bhajan* of God;
Without *math*, temple, looks mind too at God. ||62||

But, tomb, monastery, temple, shrine;
Inspire good impact on minds of all, the influence of place. ||63||

As thus, laid saints foundation to increase character ethic in people;
For studious, one peaceful place due to temple. ||64||

Confuse calculative men, somewhere quarrel among offspring;
No peace to reflect for short duration. ||65||

At this time, to go worship place to remember great men;
With their courage to experience contentment. ||66||

Attitude to forget time to time, temple to revive thoughts;
Awake conscience of right duty such places. ||67||

Annual festivals, birth and death anniversaries, monthly practices;
In places like temple are performed collectively. ||68||

The mean of collectivity, the source of village's joy;
In such place, the origin of sanctity full. ||69||

Temple means school, the celebration of education;
Accumulated amount total to be utilised for this work. ||70||

Village culture to awake, love, ethic to nourish;
Monastery, temple, all were centres there. ||71||

Love for all beings, honour of virtues to increase;
Created temples for this in village to village. ||72||

Assuming such highest motto, temple founded;
But, seem to reverse their nature today. ||73||

Turned temples, places into shops, worship started earning;
Came forward donation boxes for belly. ||74||

Tied buffalos, cows in temples, waste here and there;
What worship, fragrance of powder, oil, lamp? Tobacco's smoke all. ||75||

Play worshipers chess, songs of harlots in temples;
Tamasha, dandhar time to time in temple. ||76||

Spacious mansion of temple, the working place of dacoits;
Fear to resist them for righteous one. ||77||

Go illiterate women to temple to listen scripture blindly;
All concentration for entertainment, no one hear with tranquility. ||78||

Pique frequently, trapping of innocent devotees;
Conflict prevails for money among *panda*, worshipers. ||79||

To rein such situation, all people to resolve;
Accumulated amount in temple meant for social work. ||80||

Worshippers deceptive, no right behaviour though instructed;
Uniting villagers all they change by organisation. ||81||

Temple plan to revive, people-education to begin;
Seriousness to implement there to motivate righteous thought. ||82||

Not to construct new temple, old to clean, to beautify;
Whatever exists to operate for right work. ||83||

Removing waste, garbage, campus to make clean;
Fresh flowers, plants, wind for peace to devotees. ||84||

Libraries, pharmacies, *yoga*-school to open in vicinity;
Arrangement for worship to maintain for all. ||85||

To go to our temple only, others to view from distance;
To speak whimsically to spoil God, lunatic it is. ||86||

Increases sin deeply if one's God touches another's;
As thus, one's God to worship, not to accept this by others. ||87||

Words these of sectarians, less knowledgeable merchants;
The strategy of progress this not to me. ||88||

This to leave, temple to be kept clean;
For all people, place it to be opened for the obeisance to deity. ||89||

God, saviour of downtrodden, never runs away from fallen;
To him, his all children equal, no discrimination. ||90||

No caste for God; God, true to core to devotee;
At temple, no sect of non-devotees to be. ||91||

God, *mahar*[4], many, cobbler; God, sweeper, *labhani*[5], *wadar*[6];
God, *mali*[7], *brahmin*[8], potter, in all castes. ||92||

God, *kshatriya, vaisya, gawali*, pervades God in nature;
Permeates God's presence on the earth. ||93||

As thus, temple to be of all, though *brahmin* or *mahar;*
Right of temple to him whose conduct pure. ||94||

Village, referee of five villages of temple, every man of village;
Enhance honour of human beings, propagation this to be. ||95||

Collective prayer by all to be on stipulated time;
In festival, prayer, discourses to deliver. ||96||

All to speak, it to be studied by all;
In discourses, our happiness, sorrows to express. ||97||

Discourse to be arranged to increase national spirit;
To be complimentary by men for men. ||98||

From history, the recall of sages with support;
Same base to continue further by discourses. ||99||

Not entertainment only by *kirtan*, festival, discourse;
Programme to be arranged to enlighten villagers lives. ||100||

Temple to embed to expel nuisance elements;
It to infuse with good fame, right mind. ||101||

Humanity, the centre of progress, the abode of pure wealth;
Temple to maintain village to retain rural-culture. ||102||

To increase pure love, devotion to temple;
Villagers to be involved to activate devotional spirit. ||103||

Not to see sect-difference, not to unearth conflict;
Motto of temple this, to bridge man and man. ||104||

As thus, God as mediator although His earth is;
But, reap people benefit with consciousness otherwise in loss. ||105||

Creation of temple, *sadhu*, saint to impart consciousness;
'God in man' to learn, this principle at core. ||106||

Look at our object of devotion wherever we move in any temple;
Single principle, this trust to observe in all forms. ||107||

All gods to respect, where songs of pure worship;
Godliness to experience by an individual with divine virtuous work. ||108||

Why to discriminate? Let anyone worship any God;
All to experience same 'realisation is God'. ||109||

Brought Shankaracharya five deities together for organisation of devotees;
Where is controversy when worship of other gods with our deity? ||110||

No tolerance here for opposition of gods but for living beings too;
Give love to them for God is in all living beings. ||111||

Planning of contribution to temple to make village happy and wealthy;
Service this liked by God, of our beings. ||112||

Principle of beings' service, as importance of work;
And divinity of nature, equal of all gods. ||113||

Conduct of all with same trust in mind;
Math, temple, discrimination of sects, no hindrance for progress. ||114||

Cause will be each temple to enhance unity;
As thus, revival of pure principle, Tukadya says. ||115||

Such *Sri Gramgeeta* book, *Guru*-discipline-self experience-accepted;
Crux of temple narrated here; the Twenty-fifth Canto completed. ||116||

Notes

1. (a, b) *Mhasoba, Baliram, Sole Malhaara, Nalyahaidar*—The folk deities.

   Meghshyam—The bluish complexion as cloud.
2. *Myna*—Hill *mynas* are renowned for their ability to mimic the human voice; the best taking bird and the best mimic in the world.
3. *Meghshyam*—The bluish complexion as the cloud.

4,5,6,7,8. *Mahar, Labhani, Wadar, Mali, Brahmin*—All castes based on professions.

Foundation of Love Religion Quinate

Canto XXVI

An Idol Worship

Permeated Lord everywhere, not divided in sects;
Then, why to say less or more to anyone? ||1||

Listening this explanation, an audience asked the question;
Why to support an idol, when Lord, vast, comprehensive, perfect? ||2||

Let be sign of any religion, created an idol by man;
Where is godliness there? Why to worship it? ||3||

Doesn't accept God anyone's worship, not necessary such ritual;
Spoke with devotee, "I require pure love". ||4||

Listen answer to this, create love for an idol;
Cosmic it to make, this only motto of worship. ||5||

Viewing an idol of God, considering life work;
Enters energy in mind, principally by psychic resonance. ||6||

To reflect mind, to cultivate fascination for road;
Planning of an image worship by sage, saint. ||7||

Needs mind some support, as thus, initially assumption of form;
Permits God everywhere, an idol there in trance. ||8||

People deemed God, who supported conception;
Blindly started worshipping respective image. ||9||

Though worshipped an individual, an idol, never say, I am incorrect;
But, sets aside conception, an ignorance it is. ||10||

Planned for happiness, designed map for home;
But, despair at the end, focusing on map only. ||11||

No house to reside, remained on map only;
Becoming conscious further, happiness it fragments. ||12||

Happened same in an idol worship, whatever sects we see today;
Devotees they before an idols, nothing important more. ||13||

Focused only on an idol, treat others fool;
Prevailed corruption without an idol worship, says he. ||14||

Not realised religion, the essence of an idol worship;
Unnecessarily increased illusion in mind poor. ||15||

At home, an ardent worshipper, an untruthful outside;
Rival he has become of everyone. ||16||

Hold ears in temple, practice *pranayam*[1] closing nose;
Abuse others inhumanly when came out of it. ||17||

Perform fire ritual of fire in temple, beat beggars outside;
Never provide penny to those empty bellied. ||18||

Truth speaks our God but speak we lie;
Devotee we become in spite of it. ||19||

Called himself devotee of Rama but not trustful to one's wife;
Worship Hanuman daily, succumbed to addiction like corpse. ||20||

God destroys evil one, works at devotee's home;
See devotee unfaithful, sleeps at home lazily. ||21||

God says, "I everywhere; poor, beggar, my sons";
Devotee squeezing them day and night experiences pleasure. ||22||

"Lord, ours savior of downtrodden", uttering this sings;
Treating man, an untouchable, wretched, finds pride in. ||23||

For an idol of lord, fix gold, diamond in crown;
A cloth's strip not given to labourer though died in building temple. ||24||

What a worship of lord? Mockery of an idol worship?
What an ignorance percolated in our mind. ||25||

Bhajan in temple, false speech outside;
Who will ask to such worshiper? tell me. ||26||

As thus, wrong to forget, holy to recognise by worship;
Steps to take onward and onward by study. ||27||

As one's feeling is, one to trust deity in mind;
But, devotion not to miss of righteous work. ||28||

A meaning of an idol worship to become oneself an idol alike;
Thus, one has to conduct likewise by study. ||29||

Biography to read whose idol we are to worship;
In future, work to continue on that line. ||30||

What my lord has done? Nothing I know;
Fanatic it is to embrace an idol only. ||31||

Worship is to increase qualities of duty;
Greatness to procure by fulfilling duty. ||32||

When impends calamity, character to reflect inside;
Luminance of study to enhance on attitude. ||33||

Ask to saint when misled, dare to work more;
Happiness to give in one's way to living being. ||34||

For this, installation of an idol step to step;
To remind devotee time to time. ||35||

For holy attitude ever, installation of an idol place to place;
Deemed tree, animals, birds as virtues concretised. ||36||

Innerly an idol to worship; listening, narration, recall to be;
Righteous work to perform by self as an idol. ||37||

Keeping aside diverse emotions, devotion to embrace;
Treat the best wherever mind experiences freshness. ||38||

Luminance of power to take where contentment mind seeks;
Mind to engross in work of righteous virtues. ||39||

Making lean body, mind, worship with the right intention;
Pure surrounding to meditate God. ||40||

Significance of psychic worship, strength of thought, principle core;
Godliness one attains in life by efforts. ||41||

To know core principle, to experience self in all beings;
Narrated saints worth of worship this way. ||42||

Spoke saint to chant *Harinam*, medium good it is;
But, fulfillment of life when chant with understanding. ||43||

Nam, verbal idol of Lord; '*Nam* on tongue, salvation in hand' says;
Significance to retain than *yagnya*, known to all. ||44||

But, why to chant *nam*? What to attain by it?
Whether all works futile without knowledge of motto. ||45||

Chant *nam* many persons, roll chain, beads;
But, not for a while involves mind in Ram. ||46||

Utter *nam* on tongue but practically downward work;
Takes the oath of God, religion committing sin. ||47||

What is this chanting? Only to deceive selfishly;
No leaving of hope, desires of sensual passions. ||48||

Conscience to be, single mindedness to be in *nam*, chant;
Then in life, place of happiness one attains. ||49||

On tongue, reflection on *nam*, in hand social work;
But, maintains character, a devotee real is. ||50||

Brings chanting of *nam* power to face catastrophe;
But, fruitful it is when *purusharth* operates. ||51||

Obstacles due to mis-conduct, resistance to righteous person;
Fruitful it is when kept aside crime by body-speech-mind. ||52||

Though chanting of *nam* in temple or farm;
Yagya it is though sung while walking, speaking. ||53||

Foundation of core *nam* to orient towards duty;
To attain this, tell saints' utterance, chanting of nam. ||54||

How they can be relived when chanting without *purusharth*?
Blind work it is at the doors of Lord. ||55||

Rama our works, we demand food to others;
How devotion it is to wander becoming beggar? ||56||

Kills Rama to demons, we to adapt worship utensils;
How devotion it is to surrender turning feeble? ||57||

Devotee means not separation, to merge in one;
Alleviates Lord people's pain, Why we to harp on Lord, Lord? ||58||

At last, an idiot he is who chanted like this;
What happens when blames Lord? ||59||

Utterance of *nam* to destroy sin but to commit sin in future;
Who has spoken this in reality? Tell me. ||60||

To such occurrence, chanting of *nam* those who assign;
Stigma he is for chanting of *nam*, I say. ||61||

Better it is to live well though no chanting;
Sorrow, not given to anyone on any occasion. ||62||

Perfom work with labour, accumulate wealth by industry;
Always experiences pleasure with playful spirit, love. ||63||

To provide to needy, not to say good and bad;
Experiences pleasure, pain of others as ours, the righteous person. ||64||

Chanting of *nam* time to time told to learn this;
Living always beautiful with love among all. ||65||

First *nam*, then meditation, mind to focus with certainty;
Then social service being motivated for right work. ||66||

No performance of right work, chanting of *nam* without virtues;
For fulfillment of self elevation, it will not lead to. ||67||

As thus, trust to keep in saint's words with alertness;
In books, narrated signs of the return of chanting. ||68||

Lord said, "Perform work, travel in nation without fear";
Turn towards service, prevails Lord everywhere. ||69||

Devotion fulfilled when realised Lord in masses;
Towards cosmic tendency oriented in realisation. ||70||

Uttered *nam* to attain it, relief for life;
To end ignorance, illusion, root of sorrow. ||71||

World to save saving oneself, it to infuse with power, tact;
People to awaken with *nam*, pointer of saint. ||72||

Composed *abhanga*[2], understandable with ease, by saint Tukaram;
Opened road practical for people, innocent. ||73||

Roared speech, simple most, piercing vedic thought;
Cleared illusion at that juncture, of ignorant, material people. ||74||

Expressed from thousand tongues, "realised we Vedanta";
Understood deep knowledge who saluted Lord of Pandhari. ||75||

Says, no need of knowledge of *Brahma*, glorification of self;
Moulds us to experience, we devotee, "Thou Lord everywhere". ||76||

From where to bring intellect? Service in our hands;
Nam to utter while labouring to worship Lord of Pandhari. ||77||

Listened Lord to their service, came to rescue in calamity;
To salvage people with words, miraculous it is. ||78||

Numerous saints were, devotees of idol, with various names;
Idol they had become though serviceman as Hanumanta. ||79||

Kinds of devotion in all cults, the essence in adhering to the principle;
Showed coordination fair in practice by Ramakrishna Paramahansa. ||80||

Became Lord, chanting *nam*, worshiping idol, devoting Lord;
Started worshiping entire world forgetting gender discrimination. ||81||

Idol worship, chant, penance, no harm when the principle attained;
Verified it when peeped into experience by saint people. ||82||

To make *bhakari* of clay to prepare the best *bhakari* in practice;
As showed an idol worship, a road to abstract Lord. ||83||

At core, Lord is inside, its devotional practice outside;
Prevails no distinction when realisation with conscience. ||84||

The righteous knowledge to do the righteous work;
Mode of an idol worship over a seeker. ||85||

Left only to behave like it, to become Lord, worshiping Him;
Experiencing causes to become Lord. ||86||

My Lord, kind hearted, fulfill urge of downtrodden, repressed;
Expected I to be trustful, made me so. ||87||

Continuous chanting in heart, service of system in hands;
Percolated colour like it in body day and night. ||88||

Remained now in service to others, infused Lord out;
Not to see anyone in any form. ||89||

Forgotten personal form, merged in work form;
As thus, entered lordliness in corporal frame. ||90||

Faced diverse rivals, tolerated many troubles;
At last, determined all, real this is. ||91||

Embedment to man as embedment to idol before;
Being "no least trouble in my village". ||92||

Real Lord worship this, no alternative avenue;
Spoke saint, lord peeping into my heart. ||93||

Melted corporal ego as realised Lord consequently;
Merged salt in sea water, uniform sea has become. ||94||

After this, next step, climb up adhering to tendency;
As experiences, being becoming cosmic inside. ||95||

Says, manifests me in all, became cosmic in cosmos;
Began to perform all work for inner reality. ||96||

Nothing left without me, permeated in atoms, molecules;
Perfect *yogi* when experiences this. ||97||

Saw in beginning idol in temple, then in beings, masses;
Manifestation of self in all forms, when perfection. ||98||

To realise treasure of joy, installed Lord for worship;
To see invisible and visible visions in one principle. ||99||

Determining on this line, myriad kinds of worship;
To know the essence of the best of devotion to Lord. ||100||

Otherwise, increase illusion though idol worship more;
No peace at any time in mass psyche. ||101||

Impetus to ego unnecessarily, "Our image more great";
No end to hatred for cults without knowing ever pervading Lord. ||102||

As thus, not to stick to image, ascend stepwise;
With dynamicity, Lord to see in the world. ||103||

All people, our lords, all villages, our temples;
To render service relentlessly, worship ours. ||104||

Work with honesty, chanting Lord's *nam* ours;
Unified love for all beings, religion ours. ||105||

Transcendental not greater than this when deeply determined;
Essence this transcendental of those who experienced. ||106||

Practicing principle this, unify all devotees;
To worship village-temple, Tukadya says. ||107||

Such *Sri Gramgeeta* book, *Guru*-discipline-self experience-accepted;
Narrated worship, remembrance; the Twenty-sixth Canto completed. ||108||

Notes

1. *Pranayam*—Yogic practice.
2. *Abhanga*—The couplet form in Marathi devotional poetry.

Canto XXVII

Collective Prayer

An idol worship, *nam,* chanting, its principles, glorious;
But, occurred its deterioration more in people. ||1||

God and Goddess visible here and there, stones, pebbles from lanes;
With urge sees no one at them. ||2||

Influential idol apt, inspires others when viewed;
Fulfillment of philosophical thirst, rare visible it. ||3||

Exaggeration of faith there, becomes an intellectual, an atheist;
Says, harmful this chaos in the name of devotion. ||4||

An idol, their memorial, no hunger for virtuous work;
Deeming idol as God, behaves more lunatically. ||5||

Prayers at dawn, night, five hymns, worship, reading of holy script;
No discipline, seriousness, peace; no stimulus for righteous attitude. ||6||

Leaves one, enters another, stands someone in between;
Throws flowers, coloured rice randomly in chanting, flower offering. ||7||

Beating of drum in one way, sound of *manjira*, bells in another;
What clapping? As if hail storming it is, feels one. ||8||

Never attains the principle of devotion by such disorder;
Benefit to all when discipline, peace, piousness prevail. ||9||

For this, pointed to people the road of mass prayer;
Today's devotion this for welfare of all. ||10||

Asked an audience, which remedy for eradication of sect differences?
How can village life be with spirit of unity? ||11||

Many sects in villages, many God worshipers, *vaishnava, gosavi;*
How can various castes, tribes to behave in unison? ||12||

For it, the solution of mass prayer to comprehend;
Where religion-sect-saint-God on single platform. ||13||

When continues this stream pure, village will be conscious ever;
And enrichment in all means by collectively. ||14||

Then asked an audience, how to perform mass prayer?
Collectivity, village will attain by it. ||15||

With righteous trust, villagers with the united mind;
How can fulfill the work of mass prayer? ||16||

In prayer which God to plan, acceptable well to all?
Which content to read to coordinate in village? ||17||

Listened the questions, spoke thou with thought;
Hindrance of differences in villages all. ||18||

Keeping aside God-temples small on stipulated time;
In single temple, peaceful all to collect with trust. ||19||

Forgetting our difference there, worship to be;
But, not understood by many, ours great, say they. ||20||

Many temple, many Goddess, unity not understand they;
Question remains, which one to select? ||21||

In the past, the same question for saints when sects combated;
As thus, placed before all *Vitthal*, the idol of *Brahma*. ||22||

There united all sects of the righteous saints;
In the mansion of Maharashtra, lighted the flame of knowledge, love. ||23||

To improve devotional rituals in Bengal, the stories of Krishna retold;
United different sects of trustees, *pundits* by Chaitanya Prabhu[1]. ||24||

Witnessed period tense, changed the means of worship;
Directed Tulsidas and Ramdas at Rama, the bow man. ||25||

Likewise, as per nation, time, the organising centre to select;
Which form to choose to link nuances with the present. ||26||

Thought I before, experienced more and more;
At last, selected *Gurudeo* mine with determination. ||27||

Though called *Gurudeo* mine, non only mine is;
Welfare oriented one has become for all beings. ||28||

No sect, party to him, witness one in all nations;
The President of all gods, the righteous *Guru* King. ||29||

All human beings here and abroad;
No religion different their indeed, some truth in all. ||30||

As spirit, not differentiated, *Gurudeo* infused;
The sky is fragmented, not this. ||31||

For all, truth same and untruth is untruth;
Likewise, for all *Gurudeo* is same in totality. ||32||

Be it in Vedic or others, respect for *Gurudeo* in all sects;
Devotion to *Gurudeo* immense in Islam, Christianity. ||33||

Propagator of sect, *Guru* different, prevails dualism there;
Free, experienced *Guru* different, sublime by knowledge. ||34||

Guru, not of bones, flesh; *Guru* not of caste, cults;
Guru, pure knowledge principle of experienced. ||35||

One who receives this knowledge, cosmic his mind becomes;
Cease sect-party-religion, all merge there. ||36||

Dear one has become to all, supporter of human beings;
Though languages differ, one feasible to experience by all. ||37||

Creates the righteous emotion, care of poor sufferers;
End all impure roads by body-speech-mind. ||38||

So, narrated great ones, *Guru* becomes *Brahma*, Vishnu;
Maheshwar[2] spoke to *Guru* with this strength. ||39||

Guru as *Brahma* in reality, remained *Guru* encompassing all;
So, prayed God this, *Gurudeo* mine. ||40||

Great ones various but became *Guru* with gravity;
Ceased individuality, religiousness in the form of *Guru*. ||41||

His worship not with *tilak*[3]; His temple vast;
Limit to vastness but *Guru* infinite than it. ||42||

Cosmos his area complete, all earth his seat;
Deem the Moon, the Sun, the lamps bright of *Gurudeo*. ||43||

Engrossed religion sects in it, encircled everywhere;
No space empty without Him. ||44||

When knowledge of Him, where are jealousy, conflicts, hate?
Avails presence of happiness, peace in all. ||45||

So, to experience this knowledge, constructed the mean with vast mind;
The place of collective prayer for collectiveness. ||46||

There collective God to imagine, then to experience in work later;
The *Gurudeo* mine in cosmic form to be seen. ||47||

This description of *Gurudeo*, now listen the means of prayer;
Place to search to elevate village complete. ||48||

Vast temple or *Gurudeo* square, where all people can sit;
Female, male, children, devotees with righteous intent in evening. ||49||

At first, the lead serviceman to sweep with broom;
Quickly ground to make clean for prayer. ||50||

On every Thursday, visiting house to house;
All people to call at prayer place soon. ||51||

Mother, women, all righteous people, children, old, young;
Inviting them to call for prayer. ||52||

Intimation to all in village, society entire to coordinate;
Blanket, *gonpat*[4] to bring while coming. ||53||

Sitting arrangement for all, all to sit in row peacefully;
Increases it the righteous emotion in all minds of prayer. ||54||

Pure to be atmosphere, the extreme peace and seriousness;
All to stop conversation at that place. ||55||

Platform to set at front with fine carpet it to cover;
Prepared in our village skillfully of *khadi.* ||56||

Pillow beautiful to keep as if someone sits there;
Such fascinating scenario of purity to appear. ||57||

Suggester, singer near, devotee third to speak;
On other side, worshipper, reader to chant *Namdhun.* ||58||

Such group for prayer, servicemen sit on four sides;
Security person on backside stands there. ||59||

Duty his to maintain peace, to stop disorder in vicinity;
To sit all in discipline with gentleness. ||60||

Whoever will come late, to be sat in sequence;
Then bell to ring with two strokes only. ||61||

Stands a worshipper before platform, light incense sticks, lamp;
Then stands an informer in front to intimate about prayer. ||62||

All to recite in single tune with peace;
Develop such prayer, taste to fascinate mind. ||63||

With ease mind will turn there, singing in prayer such;
Chanting of name, *Gurudeo* will be in time to come. ||64||

Any name there keeping aside differences, illusion;
To retain same faith in all religions. ||65||

When this ends, intimate an informer to speak;
Then in the end, a speaker expert speaks with the righteous motto. ||66||

We all are one, then why to see differences?
All to be cooperated as family. ||67||

Right conduct deeming man, the component of world family;
To infuse energy, prayer to be powerful. ||68||

All saints are same, all gods, same motto;
Listening all messages, knows one principle in all. ||69||

As thus, all to cooperate as possible by one;
Family to make heavenly at our level. ||70||

This to tell in prayer, service godly in it;
Not different than this, the road to transcendental. ||71||

Completing speech, the text of peace to utter;
With single mindedness, salutation with single method. ||72||

An informer to intimate to stand all persons;
With slogans of victory, the earth to reverberate. ||73||

Acclamation of *Gurudeo*, inclusive of salutation to all gods;
The principle of prayer beautiful, spoke to you. ||74||

After completion of prayer at square, one's blanket, belongings;
To take back to one's home, rendering service fully. ||75||

Prayer content not spoken here, in other book it appears;
As thus, not elaborated; see in *sakriyapathi*[5]. ||76||

Friends! listen my words, though desire for village welfare;
Never leave the mean of prayer for mass prayer. ||77||

Tell this with experience, prayer treat I as village wealth;
Procures society our by this means heaven, salvation. ||78||

God ours resides in society, works all for society;
Encompasses all on the seat of prayer. ||79||

Meets One in public work, as prayed we;
Infused trust pouring spirit in prayer this. ||80||

Asked you question, so expanded such;
Realised One in vast nature, becoming one with prayer. ||81||

Experience of core principle, knowledge perceived, cosmic God;
Presumed we in the prayer *Gurudeo*, One. ||82||

One the seat of *Gurudeo*, though require we an idol;
As per desire one can imagine of any God. ||83||

Embodied gods in *Gurudeo*, became devotees one in prayer;
Opened the temple of humanity in the world in such form. ||84||

One's prayer to merge in many prayers of many to know infinite;
To attain unity in principle, infinite prayer is. ||85||

Walked on road understanding it to respect religion, sects varied;
To treat pious all saints in the prayer. ||86||

For this planned prayer vast, creepers woven of devotees;
To know the depth of all religions in core form. ||87||

The prayer of *Veda, Upanishad,* "happiness to all beings";
Proposition for elevation of all beings in the prayer of sages. ||88||

Prayed Jesus Christ for peace of all beings;
Blessed him the deity of tolerance. ||89||

Prayed Muhammad to make wise scattered Islam;
Organised he people his at that time. ||90||

Piousness taught by Zarathustra[6], control by Mahavira;
Developed Buddha non-violent *Sangh* by the prayer. ||91||

Kirtan, chanting of name by saints, deem it as mass prayer;
Organised remembering all gods to impart knowledge to all. ||92||

In *Kaliyug*, significance of devotion, *bhajan,* and *kirtan;*
In *yagnya,* the best name, chanting, in prayer all include. ||93||

An idol worship and meditation, the crux of nine modes of worship;
For all people, in prayer the simple means there. ||94||

Discipline, peace, seriousness, knowledge of conduct;
In prayer, avails one the education of humanity. ||95||

Prayer, the school of humanities, the core feel of rural culture;
In the mould of prayer, ends conception of difference. ||96||

'Companions we all are', thought such to increase;
On this, rests the heavenliness of village. ||97||

At the end of prayer, sermon to give to know culture to all;
Tradition this to continue in our village. ||98||

Prayer this to sustain in village, then survival of rural culture;
All time, the lamp of collectivity will light. ||99||

Peace can be in the world, how impossible it for village?
Forever unity by collective prayer, Tukadya says. ||100||

Such *Sri Gramgeeta* book, *Guru*-discipline-self experience-accepted;
Narrated prayer; the Twenty-seventh Canto completed. ||101||

Notes

1. Chaitanya Prabhu—A worshipper of Krishna in Bengal.
2. Maheswar—The name of Shiva.
3. *Tilak*—Pious mark with sandal paste, *kumkum*.
4. *Gonpat*—Rough hand woven material to sit.
5. *Sakriyapath*—The text of prayer to recite.
6. Zarathustra—The ancient persian prophet, spiritual leader, and ethical philosopher who taught a spiritual philosophy of self-realisation and realisation of divine.

Canto XXVIII

Prayer and World Religion

Coordination of all religions, remedy for world peace;
School of people's reform, mass prayer. ||1||

Elaboration such, but pay heed to our question;
How can they be one when in all religions prayer systems differ? ||2||

How will single text interest? Different everyone's road;
How will devotees of deities various sit together? ||3||

Feel corruption of religion when sits with religion, seeks another;
Tell, which remedy does operable for collectivity? ||4||

Listening to the query of an audience, precise narration of therapy;
Philosophy of the right religion to convince people myriadly. ||5||

Though religions many appear, single crux of all;
For the world consciousness, the best, the right religion it is. ||6||

To build the world consciousness best, peace for all people;
Attempted religion propagators for this single motto variously. ||7||

"To make all world Aryan", joy for people of three worlds;
Brotherhood vast of saints, sages, not for selfishness. ||8||

People not to be image worshipper, prayer for single God;
The advice of Muhammad not for single nation. ||9||

Directed Jesus Christ the lesson of love, sacrificed life too;
There no man omitted from the assembly of gods. ||10||

Buddha and Mahavira, Shri Krishna and Zarathustra;
Care for them to make the world happy. ||11||

Adhering to tendency inclusive, in respective nation, religion;
Rendered saints' service for vast human society. ||12||

Moulds in past and possible in other nations and languages;
Honoured the great persons in their words in books. ||13||

Not acceptable to religion, preacher the concept of corrupt religion;
Equal care for them of the entire world. ||14||

One God of the entire world, living beings His offsprings;
Trust this only though names different. ||15||

God of Hindu for Hinduism, of Muslim for Muslim people;
Of Christian saves Christians, narrow such words are. ||16||

Sublime consciousness, the conception of the world mover;
How differences are there? Who is our and other? ||17||

Roads may vary, but God not in differentiation;
Motto of the core religions is not in differences. ||18||

Says all, created our God the entire world;
Gave the message of religion to us by elders. ||19||

Are Lords of the world hundred in world?
God, single, the mover of the world, of all. ||20||

Allah, God, Arhat, Ahurmajda, Nirvana, Shiv;
Though names different of Supreme, *Gurudeo* one mine. ||21||

To make the world happy, elevated, acceptable to Supreme;
Then how can the nature of religion different than this? ||22||

Happiness, sorrow of others ours too, beneficial knowing this;
Message this in all religious reverberates. ||23||

When thought about it, all sects, religion, devotion, kinds;
Why to differentiate by devotees when single principle prevails. ||24||

Home they make narrow whose mind has feeble strength;
But, the world this is single, the army of human beings. ||25||

Same land for all, same air, water, pleasure, pain;
Bodies all composed of five elements. ||26||

Origin of life one, the last destination one;
Service religion pure one, in myriad forms. ||27||

Flame one in all eyes, power one in all bodies;
Expansion one in all, who other has come? ||28||

Not from the sky Muslim, Christian;
Before that the earth was embedded with human beings. ||29||

The world one created by God, life by five elements;
Trusting this, the world not different of sects, religions. ||30||

Hindu, Muslim not in religion; Parsi, Christian not in religion;
No *Sikh*, *Jain* in religion at core when looked into. ||31||

People's amnesia for the crux of religion, turned Hindu, Muslim;
Lost they humanity located at core. ||32||

Wore masks of nation and language, changed customs due to weather;
To exterior religion they call, less knowledgeable. ||33||

Living as per nation, speciality due to whether;
Diet system initiated by production. ||34||

Did human essence change? Is difference in the principle of truth?
On contrary, appropriate feel some sin, sorrow too. ||35||

This verdict I dislike, treat I all same;
Priority to the stance of humanity, place for sect-difference latter. ||36||

Is alien to humanness though living different, devotion vary;
What happens though prayed by diverse modes? ||37||

Transformed the sea's vapour in the form of water;
Merged in single place at the end though separated in drops. ||38||

Likewise of man, though man of any religion;
But, his significance equal for social structure. ||39||

All one at beginning and end, in between appreciation of social service;
From the view of human religion, their value same too. ||40||

Says religion to be worshipper, says religion to be sweeper;
Says religion to sing, dance for all. ||41||

Though deed performed myriadly, no otherness there;
Became one uniting all, religion it is. ||42||

All in religion but conscience to be there;
Not to perform which rebels against humanity, religion says. ||43||

Humanity, the planning of religion, management for humanity;
To attend call whenever mismanagement is. ||44||

When management this incomplete, created groupism;
Increased fascination for individual principles by means varied. ||45||

Fragmentation of the world, scattered all anywhere;
Assuming name, form randomly, broke religion. ||46||

Created means considering nation, time;
Deeming twigs as religion-tree, groups formed. ||47||

As thus, names different, Hindu-Muslim-Christian religion;
Jain-Sikh-Mahanubhav, external names in religion. ||48||

Numbers not dwindled in present, based on sect, cult;
Approaches to the religions' names operate. ||49||

Religions vary of homes; religion, each action in practice;
'Our living' the crux of truth, illusion prevails this. ||50||

When such custom increased, culminated into sorrow;
As thus, rival religion, sects are to punish. ||51||

To control this created power, money, punishment, differences;
Implementation of this kingdom's religion, the duty of man. ||52||

Initiated they judicial session who organised by the means of religion;
Established they kingdom as per their convenience. ||53||

Rules for religion but extracts benefit for it;
Because of an attachment, an entanglement with an ego. ||54||

Then omitted religion, politics became religion;
Created chaos for it in all nations. ||55||

Forgetting the base of social service, pride in ruling;
Man to operate man completely, happened this. ||56||

Then for man's happiness, in calamity sacrifice of man;
Among people, routine it has become. ||57||

Lost convincing with love, sharpening the edge of sword;
Victorious, religious he is who committed violence more. ||58||

Religion strong on the strength of power, number;
When power determined religion, truth fragmented. ||59||

Then religion turned into weapon; war, destruction for religion;
Rebel for religion, war increased among people. ||60||

None asks for truth, sacrifice, and service, insist people on their views many;
Prevailed such chaos on the earth. ||61||

Disordered the mode of religion, less power to rectify it;
As thus, compelled God-Goddess to hold weapons. ||62||

Religious war for justice it was, no impulsiveness there;
There 'powerful rules the world', non-religious it is. ||63||

No jealousy, sin in religious war but when attachment to nation;
That time, man's intellect directs to doom. ||64||

Then arrogance of nation in war, activities with wickedness;
Though non-religious it is, operable in unjustful war. ||65||

Kills man to man, suppresses without crime;
In discipline of religion, vicious it is though war. ||66||

When understood this justice, ceases the winds of war;
Before the Goddess of justice, human society to meet with humanity. ||67||

Whatever in war, in small quarrel too, in family differences also;
Display of ignorance, this all in myriad forms. ||68||

When over intoxication of religion, sect, party, nation;
Turning man an insane, not allow on the righteous road. ||69||

When rules Muslim, erects mosque demolishing temple;
Beats drum to acclaim, he is wise in the world. ||70||

When ceased their power, collapsed Hindus their mosque;
Intimacy they develop with other sects. ||71||

When rebelled Christian, increased their churches;
Network they spread as per their whim. ||72||

Contentment of anger, hate, the mean of wish fulfillment;
So, with revengeful mind, outbreak of war, repression. ||73||

This, not the thought of religion, use of power it is;
Destruction of human beings, innocent, not acceptable to religion. ||74||

In religion, order, peace, mind, love for justice are;
Convinces non-violence, the excellent religion it is. ||75||

Labours man for man, seeks happiness in others;
But, what non religion can be than destruction of man by man. ||76||

Treated as great persons who realised this;
Though confined to any sect, religion, good they for us. ||77||

All religions, gods of sects, the promoter of religions, the great persons;
Consciousness they have to make human beings happy. ||78||

To prevail happiness and peace, to follow brotherhood;
Worked tirelessly the great persons without differentiation. ||79||

Presuming this motto vast, created sects as the need of time;
Preached they, penned books, time to time by them. ||80||

For this till today, *Koran*, legends, views of religion good;
But, all have not understood depth of it still too. ||81||

Efforts from beginning, resisted who haven't understood;
On that road, efforts still continue. ||82||

We, effort oriented, communicators, vast with divine;
Let good wisdom be prevailed, so began prayer. ||83||

Nothing new interwoven, the apt import of religions before;
Arranged it together in different forms. ||84||

Sublime thoughts of great persons, essence of all methods;
Put forth the form of plethora before society. ||85||

Where contentment of each other, beautiful life of all;
To facilitate rapport, prayer initiated. ||86||

The prayer text to coordinate, not iron frame it;
Opportunity there for everyone to enter. ||87||

Principle to receive from anywhere, no one sidedness to be;
Tolerant mind to be for contentment of all. ||88||

Such prayer influential for peace, needs vastness for peace;
For vastness, arrangement to be of each other. ||89||

Brings intimacy, the touch of each other's heart;
Winning the world by it, attainment of happiness, peace will be. ||90||

Quarrel of religion-sect-nation, not possible to end without love;
To attain that love, no level best than prayer. ||91||

Principle of prayer in every religion, equality perpetual in good;
Understanding importance of it, all to bring at one place. ||92||

No relation in each other, so change in system;
How can be sin now when brought together? ||93||

One prayer for whole world, one stance for whole world;
Why not to bring unison in whole world? ||94||

Single reason not to come nearer, our narrowness;
As thus, religions interpreted from one's approach. ||95||

Vast minded they become when one concept of God;
Fiasco of human religion to ill knowledgeable. ||96||

Treat they others corrupted and mean, great themselves;
Though religion not understood they themselves. ||97||

At prayer all to come, then quarrel after prayer;
They not prayer seeker; diplomat, selfish, they. ||98||

Deviated people due to selfishness, combated among themselves;
By devotion they will come nearer. ||99||

For it, knowledge to impart, the principle of religion equality to teach;
Prayer for respective religion till no comprehension of this. ||100||

Prayers by different religions, proposed to the principle of religion;
Respect will increase everywhere by this means. ||101||

View it will create, every religion like ours;
Happy and peaceful world will be, becoming one. ||102||

As thus, this practice, simple collective prayer;
Intention to be collective began virtuously. ||103||

Inner will of God, many from One;
By this means to experience Oneness in multiple. ||104||

Efforts from all corners by all to come nearer;
Appreciation of the principle, not to delay. ||105||

Without the germination of theoretical philosophy among masses;
Not possible for ever to eradicate hate among sects. ||106||

Feasible it is to germinate this principle by collective prayer;
As thus, efforts to be for this work in village to village. ||107||

Equality of religions in village to village, then world happy;
Honour of heaven for the earth, Tukadya says. ||108||

Such *Sri Gramgeeta* book, *Guru*-discipline-self experience-accepted;
Narrated coordination; the Twenty-eighth Canto completed. ||109||

Canto XXIX

Service to Downtrodden

Asked an audience doubt, reiterated thou equality in all religions;
But, the speech 'terrible of alien religion', roared *Geeta*. ||1||

Fulfilment in death in self religion, but fear in alien religion;
Then, how can be coordination among religions? ||2||

Listen to support of the book, though alien religion terrible;
But, its meaning to search by audiences. ||3||

Hindu, Buddhist, Muslim, Christian, Parsi or Jain;
At that time no nomenclature was in religion. ||4||

No birth of different religions, then why did *Geeta* tell alien religion?
There variations in duties at centre of it. ||5||

One's nature for work, one's nature for qualities;
How can one attain quality of work of others? ||6||

In some power, some tact, some knowledge, service;
Adopting means convenient, devotion for God in masses. ||7||

As per one's nature, one to serve for nation;
Carrying another's work on head, destruction bound to be. ||8||

As thus, alien religion terrible, narrated this without doubt;
In butter no survival of fish though better than water. ||9||

Self religion is religion of spirit; spirit's nature, truth, knowledge, love;
For this, burning of life purposeful for all. ||10||

Falsity, ignorance, difference, rivalry, injustice, misconduct;
Sorrowful religion this without spirit, alien religion terrible. ||11||

Whatever in self control, happiness it; in other's control, sorrow it;
Narrated this by great persons in many religious books. ||12||

Alien religion, blindness of desires; self religion, validity of justice;
Principle of understanding this given in hands by them. ||13||

To embrace being ours, repulsion being another;
Such reverberation not anywhere of sages. ||14||

To kill when uttered Muslim, to drive away when Christian;
To favour though sinful, not meaning of self religion. ||15||

Say some, we are Hindu, stern rival of Muslim;
Never respect for Christian, treating him brother. ||16||

Say I, honour for qualities irrespective of caste, religion;
Why to respect Hindu if Hindu commits sin openly. ||17||

Though good conduct of Muslim, hateful he is;
Audiences tell me, who has given this justice? ||18||

Came Christian from distant land, demised serving;
Though not spoiled thy religion any way. ||19||

Not acceptable this to dispel him;
Treating him ours, he to retain as brother, dear. ||20||

Follower of truth, whose love, mind cosmic;
Though confined to any religion, tribe, deem him ours. ||21||

Religion is humanity, relies humanity on justice;
Remains justice same to anyone for ever. ||22||

But, faded this vision, strengthened selfishness;
Caused cleavage in religions, sects; not visible closeness. ||23||

Melted down basic principles, increased orthodox practices;
Pertaining to ignorance, emerged sectarian tendency. ||24||

Doomed real religion as continued such happenings;
For that religion, difficult it has become to lift up. ||25||

Declined quality work, how to know self religion, alien religion?
Society confused due to differences, illusion. ||26||

'Vishnu oriented world' is self religion, narrated this crux by saints;
But, no end to our differences, illusions, evil such. ||27||

'Man' only our name, then self religion is 'human religion';
Pay attention to this, essence of truth in simple words. ||28||

Human beings we are to enhance honour of humanity;
All children, elders to be happy, this our work only. ||29||

Anticipate I, religion, justice, moral, pure character, urge for love;
Which treats social ideology, situation with equal sense. ||30||

Whosoever says religion without this crux;
Understand we, these signs of religion incomplete. ||31||

Then, take saying from any book but core not different;
Humanity, sign only for coordination of all religions. ||32||

All religions same principally, where humanity in religions;
Geeta not against this, of socialist Krishna. ||33||

Says Krishna, 'all is *Brahma*', equality is divine religion;
Visionary with equality, an intellectual best; equality, essence of *yoga*. ||34||

Vasudev everywhere, such belief, not experience;
Rare great soul, God spoke in *Geeta*. ||35||

Leaving all religions surrender to one God;
Realising him all pervading, core it of elevation. ||36||

Equal trust for all, Vasudev in all beings;
Real man is he who understands this; truth, his religion. ||37||

Whatever is done with this approach, worship of all mighty;
Where no difference, self-other, mind in coordination. ||38||

Then, let he of any caste, creed or religion, tribe;
Self religious friend, real our, deem we. ||39||

Asked an audience, narrated you equality in all religions;
But, benefits availed up till now by crafty men. ||40||

Some won people by war, pulled with force to our religion;
Some lured by greed, do you feel it proper? ||41||

Came some people from places far, enter by rendering service;
Converting religion, deceive they innocent people. ||42||

Increasing our strength, movement for power to be;
Such game to gain all from service, non-religious this. ||43||

Opportunity for religion conversion, saying equal trust in all religions;
Boat of nation it will sink, tell some remedy for this. ||44||

Listen answer to this, equal trust for religion and its conversion;
Much distance in this, in real sense not one this is. ||45||

Thought of religion conversion, apt it for knowledgeable;
But, why religion conversion who understood crux? ||46||

No significance of external differences who realised equality in religion;
Then, it will follow principle in self religion, whatever needs. ||47||

No aggression on anyone, no confinement to anyone;
Acceptance of alien religion with greed, fear, degradation it is. ||48||

Torture by war, religion service name to it;
Great sin it is, uttered it before with determination. ||49||

Cast spell religion mismatched on society, ignorant;
How can elevation by it? Disguise it of multi-masquerade. ||50||

Man's nature hungry for love, lured due to some needs;
But, its benefit not to be reaped by others. ||51||

Anyone came forward for service, but religion conversion by fascination;
Increment of our people count, cunning politics it is. ||52||

Religion at core one, but interferes politics in it;
Rivalry for each other increasing strength of numbers. ||53||

Under the garb of religion propagation, craving for power;
In religion, assume his attitude corrupted. ||54||

Not confined he to any religion, religion his selfish;
Keep aside though close to heart. ||55||

Likewise, not knowing self essence, imparting importance to others;
Run unreliably to alien religion, no place for him anywhere. ||56||

Mixing in all understanding principle, but not to leave religion for belly;
Why to do all, not understanding self-road. ||57||

Stigmatised it is wherever this has happened;
When peeped, visible it is now to experience. ||58||

We are also cause here, this to remember;
Who do give active knowledge of real religion to downtrodden? ||59||

Applaud people, religion-religion, but not helpful when time demands;
Though they possess all, test our mind. ||60||

Proud of religion, but no place for religion brothers;
Don't respect as dog and cat; to him, these religion test is. ||61||

Impart sorrow to them assuming man's touch sinful;
Treat him father when moves to another religion. ||62||

Thrust, hunger of downtrodden; happiness, sorrow of downtrodden;
Not understand egoist, idiots harping a self religion. ||63||

Says, *brahma* in all but works as an illusioned;
Essence of religion not this, spoke saints anywhere. ||64||

But, where are advisers to this? Who will convince people better?
Entangled all in fulfilling belly in the name of religion. ||65||

Propagated by belly worshipper, transaction for our benefit;
Distance between man and man for self happiness. ||66||

Untill wiping out ignorance, all this in men;
Assume difficult it is to progress world fully. ||67||

For it, one to follow, improve our area of religion;
Understanding all to interpret philosophy of all. ||68||

Ceremony of happiness to see by religion, caste which anticipate;
Many efforts to be made for this by conscious people. ||69||

Some to do tribal development visiting forest, village;
To see cottages of poor people, how they are. ||70||

Wear leaves and bark tribes poor, tribal in forest;
Below trees resides many people. ||71||

Not understand how to speak and walk, run away with fear when looked;
With love those families to bring nearer. ||72||

To them medicine to be supplied, writing and reading to be taught;
Workers to mix in festivals, collective meal. ||73||

Untouchability not to remain in people, meal, temple;
Place, respect, all means to be same for all. ||74||

Simple living without addiction to be taught mingling in them;
They not to be deemed pointing lacuna outside. ||75||

Obstacles to be avoided, good thoughts to implant;
By various means, entire society to be of equal qualities. ||76||

Service to be given as punishment to those who neglected;
Their range to increase providing an opportunity with good will. ||77||

Those who are in trouble, wretched and diseased;
For them abode to be created of happiness, peace, and hygiene. ||78||

Not assuming tuberculosis or leprosy as curse of fate;
Remedial experiments to be in village to village. ||79||

Human idols cracked, devotion to God in their service;
How can one experience liberation without providing peace? ||80||

With right heart they to be visited who deprived of life;
Liked by God and religion, those who worked for happiness for orphans. ||81||

Blind, lame, dumb, insensitive, weak, handicapped, orphan;
Of religious character they are, who paint pictures of God. ||82||

Perform this work people of another religion, so affinity people have;
Nausea, laziness in our mind, degradation ours. ||83||

Leaving this nature, our life to sacrifice for service;
Deeming downtrodden society as God to serve is religion. ||84||

Followed this religion by saints, realised Lord in people;
Decorated garden of world with love detached. ||85||

Rama, Krishna, incarnation of religion, sweep front yard of untouchables;
Took meal Ekanath, carrying child in lap. ||86||

Embraced, downtrodden, and diseased, by Chaitanya Mahaprabhu;
Satisfied leprosy patients by Gandhi, Jesus rendering service. ||87||

Deemed widow, orphan-handicapped service, pious treasure by Paigambar;
Rejected false pretension of discrimination by Gautam Buddha. ||88||

Jujube of Shabari eaten by Shri Rama, embraced Gruhaka with love;
Cultivated friendship with tribal monkeys, uplifted Ahilya. ||89||

Brought up Krishna in milk-men, turned espouser of females;
Wedded with Jambvanti of a tribal community. ||90||

The father of Bhisma favoured a girl of fisherman;
Hundred examples such in earlier scripts. ||91||

Sita, Shakuntala, Karna, Kabir, orphan girls and boys;
Became great after caring by society, likewise sages more. ||92||

Jnandev and Namdev, saints, embraced downtrodden society;
How many idol of devotion emerged in backward community at that time? ||93||

Became entire home of saint Chokhoba, temple of devotion;
Manifests godliness in marginalised society by imparting *sanskar*. ||94||

Sajan butcher, Ravidas cobbler, Dadu cotton comber, Gora potter;
Kanhopatra, Jani, Banka *mahar*, come up like this. ||95||

Likewise, emerged today famous male-female in home to home;
For it, improvement to be of exploited society. ||96||

Understood the essence by Mahatma Gandhi, Jyotiba Phule;
Did work of upliftment of downtrodden, our work it is. ||97||

To treat equal man by man, to elevate others;
To infuse joy in society, real service of religion it is. ||98||

Not to trouble others, not to deceive others;
Not to repulse anyone, all to deem ours. ||99||

Facilities their to care for, conduct will all justifiable;
Discrimination will eradicate out, life to create like this. ||100||

Then they trust, our nature they like;
Mind their turn as you mould in any direction. ||101||

Religion service this is, it to perform with right trust;
All downtrodden persons to teach, treating as brothers. ||102||

Barren land to be fertile, to be blossomed with flowers and fruits;
To anyone no one to be addicted. ||103||

Not to hate other's religion, not to point out other's lacunas;
Wild-fire of selfish mind not to be lit by servicemen. ||104||

Though our father respectable, other's not hateful;
Principle of religion ancient this in all religions with equity of trust. ||105||

This vision to be imparted to all; in society, humanity to be increased;
Then in village, illusion of discrimination in religion will not remain. ||106||

The best means in all means to mould mind by *sanskar;*
Inroading in minds of all people by the mode of service. ||107||

Art group, discourse, *kirtan, tumbadya,* powada, legend;
Plays, every means to plan for this work. ||108||

Whatever one knows, it to be taught to society;
Benefit to be given to people, deeming human religion. ||109||

Real religion people will realise, visualise One in many;
Then selfish tactics of other willn't interfere. ||110||

For this, *bhajan, kirtran,* mode of the best mass education;
Family-beyond, religion-knowledge to be taught fully through it. ||111||

No being in our village to be ignorant;
This, real work of village; fulfil it servicemen by labouring. ||112||

When shakes the sea of the right religion, become rivers of religion one;
Then, where are religion and religion conversion? Give *sanskar* to all. ||113||

Let diagnosis of religion be through images of illusionary rituals;
For it, plan mode of *bhajan* enlightening people, Tukadya says. ||114||

Such *Sri Gramgeeta* book, *Guru*-discipline-self experience-accepted;
Service of downtrodden narrated; the Twenty-ninth Canto completed. ||115||

Canto XXX

Bhajan's Influence

An audience asked, is *bhajan* adoration of God?
Means of propagation it is; how can sanctity be there? ||1||

To mould *bhajan* like this, misdirect thou;
Simple things taught through it, not acceptable to religious one. ||2||

Listen the answer of this, religion means trust beautiful;
In it, thought of all aspects of life. ||3||

In *Kaliyug*[1], in *bhajan, kirtan*, devotion, more special power;
Verdict of saint, not one sided, only to experience freedom. ||4||

Possible for *kirtan, bhajan* to change entire life;
Veda, discipline, *Smruti* born for this cause. ||5||

Social structure, village structure, marriage *sanskar*, state plan;
Medicine, farming, arts, various narrated in *Veda, Smruti.* ||6||

Ancient Sanskrit Vedic time gave birth to legend time;
To know *Prakrit* to masses easily, saints practiced *bhajan.* ||7||

Penned sages and saints *bhajan* of name with trust in devotion;
To know people, the message entire with ease. ||8||

Narrated some metaphors in *Vedanta*, some spoke with renunciation;
Wrote sage and saint, some *bhajan* with closeness with humour. ||9||

Penned *bhajan, bharud*[2]; multifaceter, *gondhalee*[3], johar[4], snake charmer;
A petty officer, *matan*[5], village bully, metaphors of social life. ||10||

Composed songs of miracles, dairy women, cowherd boys, Godess and God;
Honour of social improvement described some. ||11||

As occasion demanded, rendered *bhajan* variedly;
To know this essence, incomplete intellect of people. ||12||

To end evil tendency, to implement dutifulness;
To retain healthy state of society, performed saints *bhajan.* ||13||

Singing *abhang*[6], *virani*[7], spell they cast on people;
Creating affinity with misdirected people, enlightened them. ||14||

Singing and dancing in many modes, infusing devotion in songs;
Enlightened masses through it, wise they made by saints. ||15||

Saint Tukaram, Namdev, Sheikh Muhammad, Jnandev;
Chaitanya Prabhu, Nanakdev, Jana, Meera, Muktabai. ||16||

Kabir, Tulsidas, Ramanand, Surdas, Dadu, Brahmanand;
Narsi, Deonath, Parmanand, saints many. ||17||

Came many saints, narrated *abhang, bhajan;*
Elevated they many people by *bhajan* of names. ||18||

Pierces the space system listening words in *bhajan;*
Came, will come too, saints, the righteous people like these. ||19||

As thus, spoke to all people, "not to leave *bhajan-mode*";
But, learn conscience in *bhajan*, this to assert. ||20||

Rama existed, Krishna existed; saint, leader lived;
But, what to do in present, narrated this they. ||21||

Changes the motion of the world, today and tomorrow different;
What to speak with whom, how can one know? ||22||

What to do of romantic *rasa* when corpse on the way to graveyard?
Tempo of renunciation to develop by mode of *bhajan.* ||23||

Called *bhajan* singer for marriage, narrated he tragic *rasa* of death;
Said people, "remove him, what he speaking at this place?" ||24||

Performed *bhajan* in temple, sang about woman's beauty romantically;
Look people mockingly deeming lunatic. ||25||

Went *bhajan* singer to battlefield, uttered, "leave rivals";
What to do of illusionary chaos? Who will listen to this? ||26||

Bhajan to perform who realises this all;
Innocent people all to make wise. ||27||

Ritualistic society has become, principle pure to tell there;
Social work to elaborate whenever time demands. ||28||

Viewing the occasion, the message to give, not to leave principle truthful;
Truth to tell with sweetness envisaging time. ||29||

Understanding this, created saints books, songs, *bhajan;*
Likewise, all to interpret today newly. ||30||

Coordination of all sects, harmony of all castes;
Bhajan such will find solution to our village. ||31||

Though, this road pointed by saints, onward we have to follow;
Those who describe are in illusion, so breathed last they. ||32||

Sing some *bhajan* of knowledge of *Brahma*, read and utter without content;
Deeming one knowledgeable, creeps in ego unnecessarily. ||33||

Memorising from saints, turn they in *Mahatma fine;*
To meet two ends throughout life. ||34||

Dance some in *gaulani*, perform in *dandhar*[8] changing clothes;
With sensual drive, extract they joy without content. ||35||

Listening these miracles of Krishna, different approaches of masses;
As if fun they made of gods many. ||36||

Sing some in classical favour, breaking words end of meaning;
Mould they words as their whim in *bhajan.* ||37||

Memorise some more, sing without harmony;
Furious one became when listened, meaning misplaced entirely. ||38||

Sing some more melodiously, rhythm skilful, stress sweet;
No sprouting of meaning, no import of *bhajan.* ||39||

Before performing *bhajan,* search opportunity for opium, tobacco;
Without tea and *prasad,* no crowd of *bhajan* performers. ||40||

Say some, their *bhajan* different, how can thou understand?
Requires it lotus by the hands of *Gurudeo* on head. ||41||

Sectarian some, performers of *bhajan*, blow their trumpets;
Quarrel for beads in necklace, *tamburi*[9], enemies from long. ||42||

Angry some for *khanjiri*[10], some come forward by competition;
But, no contentment in mind to least extent. ||43||

Say some, not to sing *bhajan* of other saint in our *pandal;*
Our *bhajan* of sect for ours only. ||44||

Friends! now this to leave from core of being;
The righteous speech of any saints to be uttered with love. ||45||

Bhajan, not comprehensive, not to say with our strength;
Repercussion, reverse of it occurs in society. ||46||

Enlightenment of village, heart, work by *bhajan* to be;
Orientation towards the righteous work by all to tell people. ||47||

Performer of *bhajan* lazy, what he will tell people?
Make fun of oneself, not to practice this by anyone. ||48||

Work to be performed with understanding, no step without thought;
Leads thought to salvation, witness such of great ones. ||49||

Worship of God without thought, there too seems to be fiasco;
Say people, with greed, worship of God spread by deceptive. ||50||

Performed *bhajan* throughout night, succumbed to illness;
Then, which chanting of names? 'Oh! Father!' cries. ||51||

Fasting without study, acidity and gout for two days;
Then, medicines and citric fruits for six months. ||52||

Why to do this? Conscience to keep aside;
Then, throughout life, consequences to experience. ||53||

Intellect to operate by man, advice of experienced to be taken;
Excessiveness to omit, self elevation by study. ||54||

To change the means which cause harm to society;
Drums of saints' thoughts to beat with thoughts. ||55||

Its many types, knowing differences in taste;
But, core theory great, not to keep aside. ||56||

Tunes to set modern to attract towards words;
But, will show, in present, saints spoke the same. ||57||

Let many kinds of *bhajan*, thoughts of past and future;
But, springs out saints' poetry sublime with impact. ||58||

But, the shop of saints' *bhajan* massive, their items invaluable;
Will give as per container, selecting apt one from them. ||59||

In *bhajan* of saints, not only worship of God, anecdote from life too;
Occasionally, convinced with abusive words too. ||60||

Bhajan of love by Meerabai, song of miraculous deeds by Surdas;
Likewise, philosophy of life by Goswami and message song of Kabir. ||61||

All dear to God which causes service for life;
Understanding this, society to enlighten by *bhajan* this time. ||62||

Told some chanting of Rama to awaken society;
Told some chanting of Dutta, moulded people to service. ||63||

Dyed Meera in the colours of Krishna, waste to her royal glory;
Fascination in home to home of devotion by her influence. ||64||

Evil rituals run away due to the roar of Chaitanya's speech;
Holy became the land of Bengal in *bhajan* of Shri Krishna. ||65||

Performed *bhajan* in abroad by Kabir and Nanakdev;
As Vivekananda, Ramtirtha influenced the world. ||66||

Many courses taken, but incomplete they are;
Not covered nation too, to channelise society on the right road. ||67||

Deficiency of it now, people backward are;
To compensate, require still propagators, are service oriented. ||68||

The best propagator, he, who knows time and situation completely;
Reliable road he directs, giving call to people. ||69||

Says, nothing ours is, narrated saints well;
It to elaborate, religion this of *bhajan* performers. ||70||

Sit on a seat for *bhajan*, in the notice of masses;
View him people in right spirit, serious he to be seen. ||71||

Simple living and pious carved cave, lenient gesture and sign;
Pure words, loving, and speech to be of masses in *bhajan*. ||72||

Lines on the forehead, rolled eyeballs in zig-zag;
Tilted mouth, expression distorted, not to happen this. ||73||

In mind deep respect, in attitude emotional warmth;
Expression of wonder to be in performers of *bhajan*. ||74||

Speech to be tender, utterance penetrating heart;
To enlighten by speech, to focus on people right. ||75||

Bhajan to be sung simple, pure, melodiously, with taste bright;
Rhythmical, harmonious without doubt, meaningfully, dauntlessly. ||76||

For this pious propagation, worked saints tirelessly;
To know their language to people lip to lip. ||77||

Trustful devotee of our nation, faith his *bhajan* oriented;
On the utterance of God and religion, energetic he becomes. ||78||

Disgust of name for *Hiranyakapashu*[11] but Narad *bhajan* oriented;
Mystery of *bhajan* such is, silent becomes serpent too there. ||79||

As thus, significance of *bhajan*, secondary speech is;
Understanding this principle of saints, performed *bhajan* with love. ||80||

In speech, social approach, religious approach, politics;
Public issue, scientific approach, seem dry to all. ||81||

Understand people *bhajan's* importance, gold's aroma when told content;
With miracle the world changes, happens this by *bhajan.* ||82||

Sounded *khanjiri* in *bhajan*, play on *mrudunga*[12];
Obsessed and passioned became people to listen *bhajan.* ||83||

Like *chataka* wait people, when will be another speech utterance?
Enlightened village will be when society lured. ||84||

In our village, *bhajan* to be to enlighten old-young;
Women, girls, all righteous people work for village. ||85||

On every tongue, songs to improve our village;
This only told by God in books, says all. ||86||

Shepherd, farm-labourer, shopkeeper, tailor, carpenter, blacksmith;
Grinding and pounding home to home, sing *bhajan* with pleasure. ||87||

Say, come all! come, let take work in one's hand;
Let village to be improved at our level. ||88||

To inspire this, progressed *bhajan* by saints;
To experience contentment in people with service, right *sanskar.* ||89||

Did job for service, transaction of life on *bhajan;*
Imparted no value to this means, religion for belly it is. ||90||

Veena and *chipalya* turned into beggars, wandered door to door for belly;
Vanished, seems to be penance of saint behind it. ||91||

This to change again, people to infuse with *sanskar;*
In home to home sapling of plant, of service attitude. ||92||

One serviceman, service oriented to show road to thousand people;
With determination, welfare of human beings to attain. ||93||

When Hanumant, spirited, proceeded with the chanting of Rama;
Completed the work assigned with the pleasure of Shri Rama. ||94||

Likewise, we have to do today, the mean of *bhajan* to improve;
Brotherhood to infuse in people in village to village. ||95||

Love for all, in it emergence of service;
Increases honour of character after *sanskar* of *bhajan*. ||96||

Continuity of *bhajan* tradition, spring of righteous attitude to people;
No remedy pious of mass education than this. ||97||

So, urged villagers! Youths! Old people!
All to sing loving songs, such propagation to be. ||98||

Let speech be dyed with Harinam, let passion of right work be;
Let disgust be of bad addiction to all people by this. ||99||

Retain rural culture, let *bhajan* be for people enlightenment;
University of people, sure it is, Tukadya says. ||100||

Such *Sri Gramgeeta* book, *Guru*-discipline-self experience-accepted;
Narrated the means of *bhajan* for village welfare; the Thirtieth Canto completed. ||101||

Notes

1. *Kaliyug*—The time phase in which evil forces operate more.
2. *Bharud*—Folk form of song.
3. *Gondhalee*—Performers of festivity of Goddess like Amba.
4. *Johar*—Salutations offered in song by low caste singers.
5. *Matang*—A singer of low caste.

6,7 *Abhang, Virani*—Traditional forms of devotional poem.

8. *Dandhar*—Musical folk form of dramatic presentation.
9. *Tamburi*—Indian string instrument.
10. *Khanjiri*—Circular shaped musical instrument with thin disc structures in periphery.
11. Hiranyakaposhu—The father of Prahlada, the devotee of Vishnu.
12. *Mrudunga*—Drum instrument.

Mean for Divinity Quinate

Canto XXXI

Saint's Miracle

Propagation of God-*bhajan*, our elevation will be;
But, to save world, strength within to be. ||1||

Understand saints that work, who become like God inside out;
What happen if anyone performs *bhajan*? ||2||

With *Ramnam* floated stones, but its writers, complete;
Now, if anyone throws a pebble, it will drown. ||3||

Moved non-living wall, made mountain of gold;
Made poison ambrosia, powerful real they are. ||4||

Uttered *Veda* through bull's mouth, kept papers dry in whirpool;
Such saints, famous, great, the saviour of world. ||5||

Their *bhajan*, speech, will elevate the world with kindness;
Tuntune[1] of our *bhajan*, seems to be fiasco. ||6||

Saint, mother-father benevolent, immediately make like them;
No time consumes to salvage for distressed when blessed. ||7||

When listened to their chanting, loss of sinner to be;
Beings are elevated, not possible by any *bhajan*. ||8||

Such thought of audiences, says, saint will do miracle;
Then, the world will be saved, the means it proper. ||9||

Audiences! Listen to this, though saints salvage with miracles;
Then, no one would have left in people with inertia. ||10||

Came many saints whose power operate in nation;
Those saints with all theirs; why not were they saved with kindness? ||11||

"All to be happy", this feels from core to all saints;
But, powerful they become who perform their duties. ||12||

Benefit not by saints if no performance of work by person;
Not to say, when his words chanted, salvation takes place. ||13||

Make saints like themselves, turn iron into gold by alchemic stone;
But, clay piece, not gold, indeed, to understand with conscience. ||14||

Elevation, saint's work, but in it prevails different essence;
Which religion of discipline ours to understand. ||15||

If people behave as per direction of saints;
Elevate they in the world, such is. ||16||

Elevate not saints, point at road to masses;
Progress to attain by their message, speech by devotee. ||17||

Feels thief tactful to be, says luxurious passionate to be;
Likewise, feels *sadhu* to our people to be righteous. ||18||

Propagate all, as it transactions of *sadhu;*
Devotee to know, which is the best? Which has no sanctity? ||19||

Which road did people follow? Whose propagation did benefit them?
Who had enriched life with fame? ||20||

Deteriorated one due to gambling, died one due to sensual passion;
Became one thief injustifiable, village dacoit. ||21||

One who approached to saint, salvaged by the righteous way;
In all people, the best propagation facilitated. ||22||

Company of saints such, impetus we receive by listening their words;
But, elevation visible by work only. ||23||

Say saints, speak truth, we to speak lie;
Which justice, words to assign at end to saints? ||24||

Insist saints to keep aside vices, our container to fill with sin;
Why to sing the ballad of saint for elevation sake? ||25||

One to control vices, follows saints' verdict;
He to become receiving pot for blessing of saints. ||26||

Blessing, nature of saints, no other treasure of blessing;
Exchange to take place without efforts. ||27||

Special sign one, in the words of saints' infusion of love;
Attraction to mind of the righteous work. ||28||

Looking at his conduct, experiences mind freshness;
That work to be done by us, feel people. ||29||

But, attitude more outer oriented whose *sanskar* evil;
Much difficult for them to experience awareness. ||30||

Orients attitude to the best work, receives the message of saints;
Smiles destiny with greatness once determined. ||31||

Pained man with sorrow, turned to renunciation with thought;
Illumined the message of *Guru*, realised the road of destiny. ||32||

Stepped some with conscience, understanding worth in the righteous work;
Bowed down to saint's feet, salvaged with fortune. ||33||

Those who made the means, followed the speech of saint;
Incomplete, it is admiration though praised lot. ||34||

Determination pure of saint he realised, manifested lamp;
With the valour of determination, elevated the righteous disciple. ||35||

Farm land turned the best, seed apt fell on it;
Enhanced love of family when yield of crops increased. ||36||

Happens likewise of seeker, the first pure conduct, pure mind;
When conscious of saint's words, increases crop of devotion. ||37||

When irrigated like this, seed sprouted, grew up;
The fruit of experience ripened with the grace of saint. ||38||

But, in the customary mode, bow down to saint's feet unnecessarily;
Assume people inside, happen all due to it. ||39||

Why to work if everything happens by bowing down;
Without toil food for belly, salvation by orthodox practitioners. ||40||

Not right notion this more, not this mode of it;
Polite to be for all, such theory of it. ||41||

All to be polite for all, about welfare to ask;
Elders to tell youngers as a part of duty. ||42||

But, lakh people to bow down, not to follow what great one suggests;
Strangely, this accepted by the nature of devotees. ||43||

Custom this to cease; in listening, taste to increase;
Reflecting the words of saints, great ones to practice. ||44||

Boosts up sainthood this, becomes saint in the company of saints;
But, being saint, home to leave, not to happen. ||45||

Remains saint though in family, an ideal in transactions;
Though, not saint holds power of the righteous *guru*. ||46||

Sainthood like this, attains it by the mode of the righteous company;
No strangeness in them of any type. ||47||

While putting foot to mount horse, was asked to show Supreme Power;
By penning the book at last, emancipated Jayatpal[2]. ||48||

Performing miracle, saint doesn't elevate;
Determination this to be in mind, their essence of message. ||49||

Succumbing to miracles, many culminated into dust;
Not to narrate saint's miracle in future, the righteous people. ||50||

Asks an audience question, weren't saint miraculous?
Why not to tell people though we saw face to face? ||51||

Fragrance in vicinity though threw dirt from drainage;
Taken out one sugar-candy from the closed palm. ||52||

Supplied food from small container, filled audience's eyes with joy;
Stopped watches all by one, in village entire. ||53||

Friend! Have seen you but virtual, unreal it is;
Not signs of saints these, never, at any time. ||54||

Insignificant play at saint's home, deem some they powerful;
But, to mission of service they will deprive of. ||55||

By trick to bring invisible, to feed some people;
And why to surprise to see where from it has brought? ||56||

Sacrifice some for fame, procuring money from black market;
Bring they object invisible from other places. ||57||

One to pick pocket, says to others to accept gift;
Miraculous and tactfulness this entire to deem. ||58||

Serve some for *Guru*, continue life with miracle;
Leave jewel of life practicing the means of money. ||59||

With penance to walk on water, where boating can be by payment;
What greatness in this, at last to corrupt with ego? ||60||

But, this don't understand by masses, desires various from saints;
Expect they giving gift, donation for greed. ||61||

Knowing intent of people, come many deceivers to village;
Plunder people deceptive *buwa* chasing them. ||62||

Practices these, misguide people and corrupt rural life;
Deceiving innocent rustics succumb them to addictions. ||63||

Give some farm, money, then look back;
This, madness thine of our blind selfishness. ||64||

Collecting money some perform celebration of devotion;
Drive some women and children to beggary. ||65||

Leaving mode of efforts, desire benefit by short route;
Fall pray to miraculous tricks of enchanter. ||66||

Lure people to miracles, then regret they;
Say some experience their hypnotic spell. ||67||

In reality, saint isn't magician to perform magic;
Transaction this which continues of belly fillers. ||68||

Salutation where miracle is, receives magical tricks impetus;
Doesn't recognise man, real saint without miracle. ||69||

Luring to illusion this, to village, home, came saint;
But, sin not washed, say people. ||70||

Say some, disease not eradicated though met him;
Say some, no child given to us by saint. ||71||

Say some, chanted words but no elevation caused;
Spreads net of sorrow over mind ours day and night. ||72||

Say some, though met not received any money;
Say some, employment to give us by saints. ||73||

Say some, grown up girl, but no engagement feasible;
Say some, though taken pious water, temperature not subsided. ||74||

Say some, though met, but starving from eight days;
No saint has given chance to smile fortune in betting. ||75||

Say some, though met, but thieves not escaped from prison;
What happened though stolen? Free to be after thy sight. ||76||

Say some, our fortune to smile when saints came home;
Without work, intend we to rule state. ||77||

Why sight of saint when everything happens without work;
Without toil, saint has to give readily to workless. ||78||

Say thou saint kind, lunatic our child has become;
He to cure immediately by his blessing. ||79||

Thou we sinful, he to determine for welfare;
Without our knowledge, he to solve troubles. ||80||

After chanting *mantra,* saint to elevate us;
Not he to crosscheck our right. ||81||

Then, he to call saint otherwise to treat him deceptive;
On what ground to deem, what we speak is wrong? ||82||

Tell, where this has happened, though people speak like this?
Which saint has made all happy, prosperous? ||83||

Not thinking for this, look for time to time for miracles;
Has saint's sense of discrimination not to give peace to others? ||84||

Why does infertility prevail though *sadhu*, saint give child?
Why are beggars though saint attributes money, glory? ||85||

Why does *buwa* breath last though saint cures disease?
Why not to happen, no one has to die in the world? ||86||

Open doors of salvation when listen to chant by saint;
Why not to happen this openly for all people? ||87||

None is to be sorrowful if their determination solves all;
Do they discriminate only for thou? ||88||

Though thou say not in thine fortune, fate becomes prime;
Then, where is the glory of saint's miracle? ||89||

Labouring hard provides saints' happiness to all;
Success in their work multifarious but it not miracle. ||90||

Experience speech emerged out of pure heart of saint;
But, never they conceived it by miraculous means. ||91||

Lord of an elephant to an ant, wondrous it seems;
But, happens it by progress of power as saint's work to people. ||92||

Deeming it miracle, forget people the base of work;
Inactively with blindness, they run after it. ||93||

No importance to miracle, search to be for the tradition of right work;
Spring of knowledge and work to seek from saint's life. ||94||

At core, guidance, the work of saint, not to give offspring, money;
To cure disease, the work of doctor completely. ||95||

Saint, the doctor of ignorance, expert of life progress;
Honourable by pure work in three worlds. ||96||

Their miracle one only, less knowledgeable being moulded cosmic;
Perceived God in all beings, everywhere by these eyes. ||97||

To know their deed, dwarf the sky before these miracles;
Who does ask for *tuntune* of base miraculous power though sounds? ||98||

Saint, incarnation of service, lenient, true transactions for all;
Treats God them great; what for other miracle? ||99||

Simple, loving nature of *sadhu*, deems it miracle in the world;
What miracle when he trusts another self as his? ||100||

Readers! The massive miracle, believes he "the world as his abode";
Labours hard day and night whole heartedly with enthusiasm. ||101||

Fulfils whatever deficient, controls the balance of world by advice;
But, not touch inside of performance, miraculous saint as this. ||102||

But, saint performs everything and no duty for man;
Greatness such one sided sings, not apt it is. ||103||

Not to happen this in village, real knowledge to realise to masses;
Knowledge of real saints to be for duty. ||104||

Saints' strange action, their miracles likewise;
Substracting this unfold true essence to rural people. ||105||

We to elevate ourselves by seeking support of saints and gods;
All to retain in heart, the content of saints' books. ||106||

Village welfare in it, weakness will be eliminated;
About their duties, people will be conscious, perform this, Tukadya says. ||107||

Such *Sri Gramgeeta* book, *Guru*-discipline-self experience-accepted;
Narrated saint's strength here; the Thirty-first Canto completed. ||108||

Notes

1. *Tuntune*—String instrument.
2. Jayatpal—The King Jayatpal challenged Swami Mukundraj while putting his foot to mount his horse and asked him to show the power of Supreme Truth. Mukundraj accepted the challenge and his advise resulted into massive volume of book.

Canto XXXII

Saint's Nature

An audience with the right intent asks, miracle, not sign of saint;
Then in which way do recognise saint? ||1||

Sadhu in sight, here there, how can know right-wrong?
Which are their philosophical forms? Tell us. ||2||

Listening to an audience's question, saluting to all;
Narrate recognition of saints for village welfare. ||3||

When said, no *sadhu* in audiences, it like black-smeared face;
As thus, salutation of me for rural audiences. ||4||

Sadhu everywhere, what can be in equilibrium without sainthood?
Whatever prevails, ceases without sainthood. ||5||

Sati and attitude of *sadhu*, this mega treasure of village;
By which mode of life, will survive without sainthood? ||6||

All tend to devour each other, control it by sainthood;
Who can give peace to people bearing shocks? ||7||

Pity, forgiveness, peace, conscience, the focus of this saint is;
In every work, a person like this indispensable for all welfare. ||8||

But, who can recognise them on the basis of outer?
Sage to recognise by attitude or looking into virtues. ||9||

Otherwise difficult to recognise, many sectarian saints visible;
Outside, some saints embedded with various colours. ||10||

Wear some saffron clothes, some prefer black colour;
Some the pure white raiment on body. ||11||

Some smear forehead, encircle garland, place mark;
Some wear strip of clothes made of coconut's leaf. ||12||

Some smear body with ash, some chant name, near fire;
Some perform *panchyagni karma*[1] by outer mode. ||13||

Some wear rags, some carry a gourd, coarse woolen cloth;
Some drink water through the fold of palms all time. ||14||

Some stand relentlessly, some stand at the door of temple;
Some roam in disguise among crowd. ||15||

Attains someone *samadhi*, some one immerses neck in deep hole;
Takes out after twenty-four hours, at the end, demands for recommendation. ||16||

Calls some poor serviceman, some one incarnation transcendental;
Blows trumpet treating one's king of *yogi*, true, false such many. ||17||

Many saints of many views, many sects of many saints;
Not comprehensible to select the best due to raiment. ||18||

As thus, sign of saint, not recognisable on outer reality;
Requires it association or identification on work. ||19||

Works sometime deceptive too, not knowable internal soon;
Speak words, knowledge, meditation, not recognisable easily. ||20||

Cause for it our nature too, different emotion of different nature;
But, not beneficial to honour saint, no saint on outer raiment. ||21||

Outer righteous work, right conduct, knowledge, place of trust;
Pertaining to our righteous intent, no degradation due to it. ||22||

The best quality, right conduct, no discrimination, vast knowledge;
Virtue of *Guru* there when visible, no one entraps. ||23||

The best ideal of humanism, no sorrow, no joy;
Single conscience, contentment of right work to see in saints. ||24||

Whose narrowness has gone, whose heart has become vast;
Whose conduct ideal, one to be lenient for him. ||25||

To fold hands when uttered saint, to observe nearing;
Never to succumb to falsehood by doing this. ||26||

Not to be greedy by attachment, retain analytical sense;
As thus, not possible for any fake *guru* to caste spell. ||27||

One who is the best disciple, encounter with *guru*, right;
But, with determination, one to respect purity. ||28||

Sadhu, right who has virtues, never without work;
Truth is to be judged on his work. ||29||

Suppose, he where stands, remembers to work with delight;
Sits he there where other people to be sat. ||30||

Where he goes to meeting place, keeps footwear in row;
Or, arranges people to realise beauty of society. ||31||

Where he goes for meal, no deficiency there;
When sees deficiency, involves oneself in arrangement. ||32||

Wherever he works, makes the village paradise;
Service his much revolutionary to elevate village. ||33||

Behaves as one speaks, his love in people's mind;
Performs one's work well not being bridegroom. ||34||

Live without labour, this not sign of saint;
Without desire, people's welfare labouring hard. ||35||

Detached to one's body, but devotee of poor, miserable;
Service oriented day and night, lenient saint he. ||36||

People, God to him, no deception in service;
As power provides treasure of advise to all people. ||37||

To make wiser to an idiot, his observation for ever;
To enlighten material, ignorance, the work of saint. ||38||

This natural tendency of saint, not to discriminate;
Message to be given for ever for the righteous work for all. ||39||

In speech, luminance is, attracts when speaks naturally;
Lenient becomes beings after listening the words of saint. ||40||

Lovable words always of saint, message of sentence vast;
Readiness to work strong with all saints. ||41||

Mega-valour of saint's verdict, when listened, experience of remorse;
Ceases evil tendency naturally with the righteous contact. ||42||

Saint's eye with grace, pilgrimage in his place;
The lesson of freshness gives saint time to time. ||43||

Saint, more kind than mother, detached though wealthy;
Shows one's bankruptcy though rules. ||44||

Rules saint without power, treasure without money;
Though not having wife, family holder worldwide. ||45||

Saint, pious than Ganges, cold, pure, the Sun and the Moon;
Saint, greater than the tree of wish fulfillment, freedom giver. ||46||

Saint's heart, tender, moves his heart with kindness;
Remedies of human welfare with saint. ||47||

Saint's heart though kind, harsher than hard time;
Fearless tendency more, pure with justice, moral. ||48||

One religion with all saints, welfare work of all beings;
Humanism, core religion for all time. ||49||

No caste bar for saint, world family his ancestor;
Whoever will meet, close to him, kind-hearted. ||50||

None to be unhappy, all to be contented;
Though rich or poor, equal to them. ||51||

With happiness of world saint contented, unhappy with sorrow of people;
Oriented always with enthusiasm, saint to the righteous work. ||52||

It, core nature of saint to cultivate love in all;
To honour good people with appreciation. ||53||

Somewhere distress with good people, somewhere tilt to bad people;
But, object single in society to nourish the best. ||54||

Evil people to love, evil to be expelled out;
Good to make, all with power of love. ||55||

Sacrificing all, lacuna to be filled in masses;
Provide peace like sandalwood, saint he is. ||56||

Eradication of superstitious rituals, establishment of human religion;
For this, life will dedicate when demands saint. ||57||

External such beautiful, greater internal than this;
With the company of saint, clears the debt of life. ||58||

His wretched state over who availed the company of saint;
Realises the duty fruits of life. ||59||

With the easeful company of saint, reap the fruits of right message;
Tendency becomes renunciation inside. ||60||

Inside and outside, will elevate all aspects;
Such, the company of saints, an activator of collective rise. ||61||

Elevated life of saint, with devotion renunciated;
Knowledge of self conscience with saint. ||62||

Self power, work power, knowledge power, love power;
Pious art, core power prevails in saint. ||63||

Sea of psychic power, whatever saint determines;
Completed it will be with determination. ||64||

But, every sage, not total rise, lacuna to some extent;
In it, differentiation of power as per states. ||65||

Beings' world and God's world, transcendental as the Supreme state;
Ascends, develops the world of saint but focal point one. ||66||

One who deems people with equality;
In earthy sense, serves day and night, admire people him. ||67||

But, no sorrow, ego, anger, hate he has for anyone;
Not in mind respect and disgrace, contentment in work. ||68||

This saint of the world of beings, saint of God's world likewise;
Recognise 'god', 'goddess' in people with devotion. ||69||

No consideration of nation, raiment, religion, and sect, no discrimination;
Deems the world as the family of God, his conduct elevated. ||70||

Recognise by single place, no rich or poor to him;
No discrimination among king subjects, saint of God's height. ||71||

Attained unison with divine who experienced the transcendental world;
The speech of I and other vanished, realised unity in all. ||72||

Whatever form visible in the whole world, cosmic it has become;
Bear troubles due to illusion of the world, remove them he. ||73||

Dream unreal but immersed in it, wakes he them;
Likewise, with kindness works in masses for happiness. ||74||

All to turn to equality, oneness to implement practically;
Entire world to harmonise at Supreme, thinks saint. ||75||

The Supreme state, not world, all joy personal infused in it;
His living easeful and divine, simple speech, the best Vedas. ||76||

Such different kinds, the different worlds of sages, saints;
There we, small, frail to know. ||77||

As thus, incomprehensible sign of saint; saint knows saintly people;
But, we to know them as per our consciousness. ||78||

Whatever sainthood we know, sainthood enters inside;
When merges with Ganges, a drainage becomes Ganges. ||79||

Ganges flows gently, but whosoever drinks water;
Water remains with him as his palm-fold. ||80||

How can we take Ganges to home though Ganges great;
Experiences peace who arranges to take home. ||81||

Likewise, saint always blissful, kind, lovable, affectionate;
Caretaker of animals, human beings always with the right determination. ||82||

Unravels the essence of the books, ends illusion with their experience;
Simple road they direct to all, cleaning all obstacles. ||83||

To him to surrender, pay heed to his speech;
Whatever spoken, to practice in life with determination. ||84||

Then, life will elevate this road of elevation;
Shows saint road relentlessly to material people with the right intent. ||85||

Listening his message, material beings elevate;
By this mean, all happiness to be experienced by people. ||86||

Saint merges in people, as thus, devotion of people;
Saint, the living idol of *Bhagwat*[2]. ||87||

Friends! Saint implemented whatever God performed;
Reverberated God's sentence everywhere by propagation. ||88||

Work of God's incarnation, skill it in saint;
Brining melody in all, mould masses. ||89||

Forgetting our greatness, enhances the glory of truth;
Not succumb to dignity, glare, off-way. ||90||

Utilising the old sources enlighten masses;
Envisaging time moulds all, the best customs. ||91||

Let it to be the festival of stones, but infusing divine intent;
By it, *sadhu*, saint elevate human beings. ||92||

Whatever apt in all institutions, parties, sects;
Motivate them with the sense of equality, saints. ||93||

Walk with the speed of masses, speak in the language of masses;
But, operate their objective in it skillfully. ||94||

All feel intimacy, no one alien to them;
With appreciation, love they attract old people. ||95||

Onward they march, but no one feels far away;
By this, people progress not succumbing to depression. ||96||

Children to be taught, but high intellect to be kept aside;
Behave as it in practice, *sadhu*, saint for masses. ||97||

Becomes an eye for blind, pours spirit everywhere;
Inroads becoming the formula of equality inside contradiction. ||98||

All human beings to elevate, contentment everywhere to reach;
To each other, everyone to be complimentary, advise such. ||99||

Downpour from a cloud, no *guru*-disciple there;
Self spirited see all, saint, righteous one. ||100||

His advise, an ambrosia, experience of peace when received;
Beings tortured by sufferings, become contented in right company. ||101||

As thus, narrated all in books, elevate our family, saint;
Not this, right time of love will be in village. ||102||

Where saint resides in village, good ends an evil;
Elevates area to area, eliminates sorrows. ||103||

Make saints other like theirs, sainthood in their company;
With efforts life elevates, receiving saint's message. ||104||

Such, the glory of saint, liked by the best of man;
Helpful to all beings, saying mother-father. ||105||

Saints active such, they to be active in village;
Then, village will flourish and survive virtues, Tukadya says. ||106||

Such *Sri Gramgeeta* book, *Guru*-discipline-self experience-accepted;
Narrated right company; the Thirty-two Canto completed. ||107||

Notes

1. *Panchangi karma*—An austere devotional practice sitting in the midst of flaming fire on four sides.
2. *Bhagwat*—The ancient religious script.

Canto XXXIII

Incarnation Work

Ask audiences question, in the company of saint attains sainthood;
Interpreted like this, not convinced by it. ||1||

Saint, incarnation of God; we, rustic of village;
How can we be with them? Impossible this is. ||2||

Listen clarification for this, world in existence from God;
Man himself *Narayan*, showed sign by saints. ||3||

One who born, incarnation; incarnation, all beings;
Infinite forms of incarnation, manifests it with right work. ||4||

Fill their belly some, nurture some of family;
Look after some village, on their levels. ||5||

Work some at state level, for state labour, toil;
To ease the road for people, with pleasure. ||6||

Incarnation this simple, signs of incarnation special more;
Honour of nation in corporal frame carries. ||7||

My nation, my home; nation unhappy as if my body;
For it, relentlessly I will toil to control it. ||8||

One who has assumed this or experienced work;
Enlightened his right work by numerous calamities. ||9||

Incarnation he to call, who cares for righteous people ever;
Hate for evil mind, active for this always. ||10||

Truth, motto of the world, the world to orient towards it;
Whosoever's work like this, firmly incarnation he is. ||11||

Six qualities, in proportion of glory, partly, full, kinds in it;
Knowledgeable, valour, unattached, magnanimous, successful. ||12||

Two sects of this incarnation, one, change of heart, another repression;
One brings revolution with weapons, another with devotion. ||13||

Religion-ethic found in service, saint incarnation, term for it;
Revolution by money, punishment, differences, God incarnation it calls. ||14||

God incarnation not always, come forward in mega events;
Saint incarnation continues to enhance good moral in people. ||15||

Glory of some incarnation, cosmic its cause;
To manifest limit of humanity, their propagation. ||16||

As per one's power, transaction operates;
Road, single, but front backward, walk feet with experience. ||17||

Some improve by teaching devotion, salvage people by chanting;
Some empower by telling knowledge, humanity in people. ||18||

At the end to elevate humans, to teach nation religion and self religion;
Caves of beauty this, of saints in totality. ||19||

No determination, worthless; whatever inspired experience it is;
Such person with divine vision, we call incarnation of saint. ||20||

Trouble some to family; some, enemy of village;
Create some nuisance in nation, orthodox minded. ||21||

One who anti-national and anti-religion, not understands with love;
Inconvenience to all animals by his means. ||22||

No improvement by any measures, entered the winds of cruel attitude;
Shudders by his threat, the mind of use righteous man. ||23||

When limit crossed, incarnation of God comes to help;
To send his body to cease when helpless. ||24||

Those, evil, devil incarnation, trouble people more;
To punish them, incarnations of God manifest. ||25||

Happens this always as wheel of birth and death moves;
Likewise, come saints and gods on the earth. ||26||

Evil and divine tendency, operate with transformation;
Intend saints to establish peace by the power of love. ||27||

Here an audience questioned, though devil unkind;
How has he received the blessing of deities? ||28||

Were qualities not known to them? Why blessings of power?
We don't understand this legend? Tell how is it? ||29||

Listen answer of this, this devil, devotee more earlier;
Pleased deity always by his penance. ||30||

Blessing he received of it, couldn't assimilate it latter;
Misuse horrible of it, he has done reinless. ||31||

At first, procured power in hand, then he forgot God;
Ran after experience of pleasure leaving moral aside. ||32||

Respect his words saints, but an arrogant he becomes more;
Though discontent in people, doesn't care with ego. ||33||

To fill the earthen container to brim, motivation he receives;
For final output completely as of an ant with new wings. ||34||

Though conceived by *sadhu*, saint, no change of his mind;
As thus, the work of incarnation in their hands. ||35||

Convince incarnation of God, operate tentative plans;
At the end take weapons in hand for evil minded. ||36||

Relieve people by this salvation, becomes free from sorrow;
As thus, efforts to be for incarnation indispensably. ||37||

Those who have done this, dispelled sorrow of the world;
Incarnation all they proved, legends they became. ||38||

Still someone does it, looking into his qualities;
Incarnation of the great ones earlier, people deem them. ||39||

Tulsidas passionate earlier, became great devotee, renunciated;
Salvaged world by singing *Ramkatha*; as thus, incarnation of Valmiki. ||40||

Incarnation some deem to be different gods, our devotion it is;
In time to come, they will realise the steps of incarnated works. ||41||

Accept some *Mhasoba* and *Khandoba,* worship some incarnation of power;
Say some incarnation of Rama, Krishna, of great Vishnu. ||42||

Trust some in ten incarnations, appreciate some tradition of Guru Nanak;
Deem some Tirthankara as incarnation, count some twenty-four. ||43||

Worship some incarnation of Buddha, pray for incarnation of Dutta;
Suppose some Yeshu as incarnation of God's son, in the world. ||44||

Say some, Muhammad, prophet incarnation; saint part incarnation;
Trust people in infinite kinds, what to tell? ||45||

Single reason of this, those who have elevated;
Incarnation it assumed by righteous people, treating differently. ||46||

Believe some in Brahma,Vishnu, Mahesh as real incarnation;
Say some, God, never manifested on the earth. ||47||

God is self power, wears never corporeal form;
Elevation of man in realisation of Him. ||48||

Opinions different such of different people, deficiency of truth in it;
Forget they, how to co-link them? ||49||

Those who have become great, called they incarnation;
Accepted they, by whose character they convinced. ||50||

'Old is gold' proved special, none is incorrect;
But, those who experienced truth, attained the level of God. ||51||

Say some, deity, not possible from uterus; performs incarnation miracle;
The saying this, honour of faithfulness. ||52||

What importance of embryo, hell and heaven among gods?
Looking this creeps up illusion, how can he be God? ||53||

To God, paradise, embryo same; arrival and departure natural;
For happiness and sorrow, same admiration before them. ||54||

Though born from uterus, no sorrow to his heart;
As thus, deemed him, not born from uterus by knowledge seeker. ||55||

Otherwise, birth and death same to all, tolerance, power differ;
As per birth, honour, his name operates. ||56||

Incarnation, all human forms but work with power;
Supposition their life liberation, remains it for ever. ||57||

Bring with them *sanskar* of many births;
To elevate material beings, incarnation shows road. ||58||

To perform human works, arrival and departure in human modes;
To work with human parameters, function of incarnation. ||59||

To make happy all human beings, to facilitate all work;
To be infinite being one, pleasure it in heart. ||60||

One who behaved understanding this, incarnation he has become;
Has woven relations on the earth coherently. ||61||

Those who have woven entire world, taught righteous road to people;
Great incarnation they became, in future too they will with determination. ||62||

So incarnation is progressivism, manifests as power operates;
Self sufficient with cosmic sense, deem we incarnation. ||63||

Makes one to all, operates in many uniting in one;
Perfection he has experienced of cosmos. ||64||

Whose supposition vast, whose work elaborative;
Differences in the world he can eliminate. ||65||

The last incarnation he is, great man, centre of progress;
We, part, sprout of him, human religion oriented. ||66||

For determination of audiences, deem incarnation as superman;
Say, perfection of man, the work of incarnation. ||67||

Devotion for deities to be, attains devotee incarnation;
Such is tempo of incarnation up to today. ||68||

Conscience to be seen, which happiness of human beings to seek?
Perform same social work good, colouring psyche of people. ||69||

He to be deemed constructive who worked for welfare of people;
Filled the sea of divine power in him. ||70||

Needs strength for incarnation, requires it self power intense;
One who works as speaks, incarnation is he in people. ||71||

Such the fame of peace incarnation, tell saints to man;
Manifest gods incarnations to bring revolt in nation. ||72||

Peace-incarnation, revolt-incarnation, different work they have;
Preaches one only, stresses another determination. ||73||

Necessary both are, so this plan assumed tactfully;
We to be incarnated as them with determination. ||74||

Otherwise not this or that; can say, this strangeness of incarnation;
But, incarnation is to perform the work of incarnation. ||75||

Lighting human religion, wreckage of evil, protection of righteous;
Sign of incarnation, all accepted, service oriented. ||76||

Those who served the world, honour incarnation;
Without it, the speech of incarnation, our trust it is. ||77||

No importance to knowledge, renunciation as service;
Results success in service in all these means. ||78||

God and Goddess in the world, started chanting, penance;
But, perfection not reached till service not there. ||79||

When service manifested, satisfied numerous lives;
As thus, incarnation they deemed on the earth. ||80||

Rama sacrificed kingdom, secured righteous people, destroying Ravana;
As thus, incarnation became on all tongues. ||81||

Shri Krishna killed Kansa[1], destroyed Duryodhana[2];
Providing happiness to poor and downtrodden, incarnation he became. ||82||

He who has rendered such service, mass incarnation he is;
Recalls his work-miracles, entirely from inside. ||83||

Those who remember, become incarnation rendering service like it;
But, dry sympathy, not sounds elevated. ||84||

Those sacrificed their lives, salvaged the world immersing in self-joy;
Became saint, incarnation, dutiful human beings. ||85||

Rendered service by *sadhu* and saint, contented infinite hearts;
Showed by practice of devotion, the ladder of salvation. ||86||

Rendered service by *sadhu* and saint, recognised *brahma* in beings;
Likewise, service to be render by to us. ||87||

A saint is born, encompassed state to state with fame;
But, his coverage proved incomplete for people welfare? ||88||

Reason for it, we people, no listening to message;
Appreciation for us to salute with folded palm. ||89||

Celebrate people their festival, sing in his honour with trust;
But, service orientation not infused in themselves. ||90||

God will incarnate, so to wait to relieve;
Entered this feeble thought more in people's mind. ||91||

Oh! Now, this all to forget, what saint told to be done;
What pious work is then improvement of man by man. ||92||

The work of incarnation this, being oneself fearless;
Why not to perform with step? With determination victory will be. ||93||

Demise someone with disease; tell, who asks for him?
But, any one demises after service, sing people his fame with trust. ||94||

As thus told, be serviceman, realise oneself as man;
Assimilating signs of principles of incarnation, enlighten the world with fame. ||95||

Not to immerse in ignorance, not to weep for wife, children;
Not to hinder for selfishness, march for human service. ||96||

He who left his selfishness, trust in self of the world;
Oriented towards incarnation, assumed we. ||97||

For this, develop oneself rendering service to village;
From village, one has to travel to the world. ||98||

Our understanding to enhance, work possible to perform;
As then our attainment of incarnation subsequently. ||99||

Service and devotion to God, in performing work, power of nation;
Leads to liberation, enters luminance of incarnation inside. ||100||

Not difficult to anyone; how incarnation work massive?
Not impossible, it is to attain big, villagers! ||101||

Fear that to eliminate, so I spoke with simple intent;
With conscience essence to comprehend, Tukadya says. ||102||

Such *Sri Gramgeeta* book, *Guru*-discipline-self experience-accepted;
Narrated the incarnation work; the Thirty-three Canto completed. ||103||

Notes

1. Kansa—In *Mahabharata,* the maternal uncle of Shri Krishna.
2. Duryodhana—Valorous Kaurava, the character in *Mahabharata.*

Canto XXXIV

Fatalism

Being, part of God, whatever progresses one more;
Elevates to incarnation level in this world. ||1||

Doing service efforts more, becomes being incarnated;
Elevates oneself imparting peace to world. ||2||

Leaving feeble pessimism, truth of incarnation message to attain;
As thus, the principle of incarnation entire narrated. ||3||

Right work to perform to prevail glory in the village;
For it, in all people, inner courage to increase. ||4||

But, an audience speaks, our fortune lower;
As thus, right work we can't perform. ||5||

In mind, we intend to do but time doesn't favour;
Tell, what we have to do for this? ||6||

Friends! Whatever one likes, one extracts time for it;
No one comes against desire while continuing efforts. ||7||

Originates tact due to necessity, increases strength on occasion;
As per like fruits emerge, sowing efforts. ||8||

Say audiences, whether had all became kings after efforts?
We feel fortune to smile for this. ||9||

No thought of kingdom in mind, hinders routine work;
What happens though planned largely in mind? ||10||

Happens as desire but, can one feel to become a beggar?
Aren't many people roam on road useless though desire. ||11||

While walking with ease, container with wealth finds;
See, how do they receive wealth without desire? ||12||

Some born in poor family, started grazing sheep and lamb;
All of sudden fortune smiles, adopted in royal family. ||13||

How can this happen? This intend to ask;
Efforts lead to fruit, doesn't suit here. ||14||

In village, a righteous man, skilful, effort oriented;
Expert in many arts but, no filling of belly. ||15||

Tell what to do more? How can be fruit with desire?
In which way our work is to plan? ||16||

Friends! Your entire saying I listen carefully;
As thus, I answer it in my mode. ||17||

Fatalism of destiny opposes progress;
Obstacle to life in village to village by this. ||18||

Keeping aside feeble despair, efforts to perform;
Then only, our fortune will rise up. ||19||

Otherwise, no one will assign fortune, no return without efforts;
For it, effort only to be deemed as core. ||20||

Some *sanskar* of time before, some efforts in this birth;
Collectively rises in people fruit of fortune. ||21||

Saint Gulab Baba blind from childhood; discipline, *Veda* on his tongue;
This, practical accumulation of birth earlier, not fortune. ||22||

Some *sanskar* before, some work, some company;
Some determination, some power of desire, fruit of fortune in time. ||23||

All of sudden one sees, says fortune smiles;
Decide, people fortunate when attainment of wealth, glory. ||24||

Question creeps up here, who is fortunate?
Listen, I answer now that question. ||25||

One may be wealthy, but may not be fortunate;
Fortune is in happiness; contentment, not in superfluous. ||26||

Fortunate he to be called, who devotes to God;
In other modes, one to surrender to God. ||27||

And ready to do right work, leaving evil work;
Food for belly for ease, happiness to retain. ||28||

Happiness to we only and others to forget;
Not to trust in this ever, he to deem fortunate. ||29||

Becomes fortunate some by theft, laugh people with contempt;
Say progress of fortunate will be seen immediately. ||30||

Then sin will bring calamity, wealth and fortune cease in different way;
But, bankrupt again, how to call fortunate? ||31||

Someone's fortune at night, sometime gains money in gambling;
Next day poverty reverts again in the same way. ||32||

This, manifestation of sin; no, no, this fortune great;
Fortune, it perpetual, sings people fame at back. ||33||

Fortunate, not by money or fortune, not by power;
Fortune one attains by righteous work in life. ||34||

Fortunate, not rich, this not my verdict;
But, rich through best transaction, real fortunate he too. ||35||

One's richness honours others, someone's richness sucks blood;
How can the degree of fortunate to ascribe him? ||36||

Picking up soil, gold becomes, fortune it in fruitful time;
But, ego and addiction miss service, at the end desolation. ||37||

As thus, do efforts, improve our life;
Leave back entire event of saying fortuneless. ||38||

For fortune to determine, firm determination to increase;
As thus, efforts are to be continued keeping aside laziness. ||39||

Whatever high thought to be, high practical conduct to be;
Fortune great it attains, completing entire plan. ||40||

Fortune fruitful by work, heavenly happiness by work;
Everything happens of human being by work. ||41||

Fortune sleeps when man inactive, walks ahead when active;
With determination, efforts turn into fortune. ||42||

Spoke this sages, saint, poet, incarnated great;
Religion books, evidences, spoke people. ||43||

Whose fortune smiles all of sudden, his right deeds accumulate;
As thus, attainment of honour all of sudden. ||44||

Though he would haven't performed, how could he have availed?
There dual approach of God, these words, not suitable. ||45||

Where, which will find, thinking all of sudden fortune smiles?
Even so, humanness in hand ceases. ||46||

You will ask, "what to do?" We have to be effort oriented;
With strong desire, righteous fortune to blossom. ||47||

When time unfavourable, move steps slowly;
But, the righteous work not futile, whatever done. ||48||

Work done with intense desire, though not fructified today;
All of sudden fortune smiles when fruit ripes. ||49||

Turned audiences suspicious in heart, efforts provide desired fruit;
Whatever narrated such, not to convince yet. ||50||

Though determination to search remedies with efforts;
Why do one experience reversibly? ||51||

All attempt to live; who expects to die?
Who has practiced the mean of death before? ||52||

Attempt people to live; call ayurvedic, allopathic doctors;
But, what is their situation? Many lose their lives. ||53||

Prone to illness for many years, state troublesome his;
Company of non-helpful, pathetic scenario at the end. ||54||

Has God done it as he desired to be ill?
Are not efforts directed for his recovery? ||55||

No death for years together though one desires it;
Tell, to which extent, is human desire acceptable? ||56||

We say, Controller, Hari, string of fate in His hand;
Man being puppets, desire, effort futile his. ||57||

Friends! Fine your questions, no strangeness in them;
Innocence this with ease germinated in people. ||58||

Strive for happiness and for sorrows, blame God;
No search for root, speak heavy, theoretical sentence. ||59||

Threw we stone above, fell it on forehead by mistake;
How does gravitation operate from our side? ||60||

Sowed chilly, sugarcane in farm; fruits pungent, sweet in hands;
What is role of water here? Fruits form as sow. ||61||

Such devotion of God everywhere, but doesn't operate on its own;
Fructifies action pious, non-pious, relying on one's deed. ||62||

Why are men created pathetically if this deed of God?
Why have human beings to die prematurely? ||63||

Confine this to us, to take birth and die;
No ground here at all to raise suspiciousness. ||64||

We desire and, as thus, we take birth;
In the world, who has sent and what for? ||65||

Death as it is, cause we for disorder;
When unbearable becomes pain, utterance of words 'save'. ||66||

Thief went for theft, not thought before;
When entrapped in calamity, say, "see, what has God done?" ||67||

How many people to hurt, to whisk away money;
Why God to blame when pain relates to fortune. ||68||

Intends man not to die but brings death evil;
With attachment says, "Oh! God! massive calamity". ||69||

Conduct for death, keeping aside conscience;
How can anyone accept 'no death' when painful experience? ||70||

Saying this, not desire, avenue out there for desire;
Not facilitates at an eleventh hour, needs it reflection. ||71||

Birth due to desire, but requires it fertilization;
To manifest inside, time it consumes likewise. ||72||

Iron to heat by fire and cool immediately;
How can this happen consequently all of sudden? ||73||

Action freely by an individual, experience of its return other;
Fruit of action performed, output of desire only. ||74||

All intend not to die, all intend to be a king;
But, action doesn't follow desire, precisely, intensely. ||75||

Leads it to pain, action performed in past;
Tuberculosis, addiction to desire, impossible to live. ||76||

As thus, tell, power of desire responsible for whatever happens;
Action requires as per desire, then work possible onward. ||77||

Desire, unstable, frequently it changes;
Desire, unflickered, manifests it through action only. ||78||

Never desire expresses desire, visible it through action;
Why happens though say, no? Practically feasible through action. ||79||

People recognise though an emperor uttered, "I, poor";
Doesn't hide though hidden as the Sun behind clouds. ||80||

Likewise desire materialised; now, attitude scared of fruit;
Then another desire expressed, no escape from fruit of death. ||81||

Provide many evidence, unravel they death;
Day, moment, time they tell of ensuing time. ||82||

State such manifested as escaped their attachment from body;
Narrated many fruits mature of others. ||83||

Thoughtful person, conscious, ready to experience fruit;
Don't permit attitude to move on thoughtless tract before. ||84||

Culminates thoughtless one to evil, restless when experienced fruit;
When in excess, neurotic they become like lunatic. ||85||

An attachment increases neurosis, physical drive confused;
Not enduring sorrow, desire his towards death. ||86||

Evil work unbearable in past, as thus instigated to die;
Now, relief it is to them if death arrives. ||87||

Really, death, a dream; place for rest of body change;
But, not solution of sin, good performed. ||88||

As change of cloth to pull new over body;
Being to deem in death, changes body by desire. ||89||

Sometime desire expressed, not comprehensible, not to fructify it quickly;
Here thoughtful one confuses for remedial measure. ||90||

Wears desired transparent cloth, say to retain it for many years;
Such desires to mix but whatever in past to experience. ||91||

Hobby fulfilled when horse of desire whipped;
Then, with fear says, God! Control instantly now. ||92||

Once arrow shot from hand, then no return though desired;
First action of desire in motion to experience. ||93||

Mere desire not useful, becoming *sanskar* it activates;
New desire in this sequence in fruitful form. ||94||

Mind, intellect, consciousness, ego, fifth inner voice supportive;
In these, *sanskar* of desire confirm to facilitate conduct. ||95||

If *sanskar* changes, conduct will be with happiness;
Otherwise, desire momentary, not of any use immediately. ||96||

Sanskar of desire, *sanskar* of duty, storage from time before;
Its accumulation, conspicuous in the forms of sin and good. ||97||

Out of it whatever a man experienced, destiny it speaks;
Experience it to accept, not excusable easily. ||98||

Experience it new craving, desire, and efforts massive;
Action couples with accumulated to taste fruit onward. ||99||

Moves wheel like this, its name, course of life;
Birth and death, pleasure and pain, transaction, the play of desire and efforts. ||100||

Realising this, focus on efforts, otherwise fortune virtual;
Advise saints to the world to improve action. ||101||

No avenue without action; to God, duty elevates man;
Be firm minded, effort oriented, Tukadya says. ||102||

Such *Sri Gramgeeta* book, *Guru*-discipline-self experience-accepted;
Fate-thought narrated here; the Thirty-fourth Canto completed. ||103||

Canto XXXV

Effort's Influence

Explanation in the last Canto, life interwoven by will and effort;
Loss, benefit, birth-death, not without it. ||1||

Today's or tomorrow's our will good-evil;
Without doubt, provides it happiness or trouble. ||2||

Whatever happened, gone; now in future, it to improve;
Fruits, all, we taste of will duty. ||3||

Here, an audience asks, rendered your honour to will and duty;
Tell, which will it is when death impends accidentally? ||4||

Demise some all of sudden though not ill for long time;
Feel of pain in chest, then immediately succumbs to death. ||5||

Fell in well suddenly or victimised by tiger in forests;
Whether was he willing to that situation before? ||6||

Some are killed on the road, some die due to jolt;
Where was it, their will or duty? ||7||

Oh! this miracle of God-fortune, though known to us;
Bind us to work, telling differently. ||8||

Friend! Not to be illusioned, narrated essence of truth;
Fruits receive from God-time-action by will, effort. ||9||

Already, I told, not visible work accidental;
But, in the past, work might have been done by accident. ||10||

Not realised when happened, conscious when situation prevailed;
But, freed him poor transferring burden on fortune. ||11||

Why a thief will kill if one doesn't accumulate wealth;
Why does one dash if one walks cautiously. ||12||

Selecting the best in advance, body, place, company;
How can one be unhappy if diet, walking, with understanding? ||13||

Non-conscience, cruelty, pride, intoxication, lead to death;
Tiger and others, merely chance but efforts our only. ||14||

But, suddenly happens, that too to body only;
How can calamity be if no birth? ||15||

Birth, the play of will, in the world assembly of wills;
Struggle indispensable there; pleasure, pain, fruits of action. ||16||

Here we ask, whether does fate kill, God kill?
Do we eat of anyone? Tell me. ||17||

Rely we on fate, God; even so, blame God;
His work, not to make man unhappy. ||18||

We miss road, misdirect by desire, company;
Then say, how does this happen when result suddenly? ||19||

There deem fate responsible or say an illusion of God;
Otherwise, impact of stars, assume as good or bad. ||20||

Some perform peace ritual for planet, some read script and tie thread;
But, no elimination of wrong insistence on illusion. ||21||

Effects of planets on the world, but they all occasionally;
The store of our good, evil work, fructify time to time. ||22||

Whatever we sow, sprout in respective seasons;
What time has done? Helped to initiate. ||23||

But, no *rui* fruit to coconut tree, reap as we sow;
Water assists it only, as God helpful. ||24||

He doesn't perform, only give to determinant;
Happens when right time comes, facilitating as a chance. ||25||

Time moves with speed; God, inclusive, unison;
With regulation of nature, our works fructify. ||26||

Freedom to act, mega power this in man's hand;
Architect of our fortune, we are. ||27||

For no reverse impact of planets, searched remedies;
In this, action spirited man ready to act. ||28||

By penance, with increase of psychic power, happiness in sorrow too;
In human limit, this God's grace is. ||29||

Friend! Not to forget, we all activators, destroyer;
In it, the role of God, fate, we created. ||30||

Adhering this in life, pure work to perform;
Then only, right track in time to come. ||31||

Though nature or chance, though effect of destiny;
With the best efforts, its flow can be turned. ||32||

If this no possibility, dependent a being would have been;
But, what disciplines give telling many remedies? ||33||

'Behave religiously, speak truth', why does *Veda* speak?
Then, all ritual practices will be unnecessary. ||34||

A being drowns in deep river succumbing to fatalism;
No way out then, when happens this. ||35||

But, this false notion, freedom of action an individual has;
Elevates with efforts, one's foe, a friend one is. ||36||

Happens evil when thinks badly, attains whatever one desires;
Then, why not to grasp greatness, learning all virtues? ||37||

An audience asks, listen I have doubt still;
In the world, all strive for happiness but no one gets. ||38||

Reverse return when did good, experience many;
Though play on an instrument throughout life, no harmony. ||39||

What is reason? What efforts had not been done?
On contrary, many people are happy, though committed sin. ||40||

Listen clarification of this, seem people vary vary;
But, its reason, their efforts myriad. ||41||

Infused different *sanskar* in people, so no unity;
Some with quality, beautiful by birth, others discordant. ||42||

Sanskar, different, some of singing, some intellectual;
Some painting, courage, skills, many. ||43||

Some of wealth and honour, some of spiritual and devotion;
Some of work power, variants. ||44||

Attains *sanskar* whatever one attempts;
As thus, all don't achieve everything. ||45||

One gets wealth, but has no intellect sufficient;
One has intellect more, but no food to eat. ||46||

One seems courageous but seems intellectually bankrupt;
As thus, lunatic or dacoit he proves in life. ||47||

One create the world of words, one regales with singing;
One plays instrument marvellously in childhood. ||48||

One expert in meditation, one conscious in devotion;
One has cosmic knowledge, self knowledge in childhood. ||49||

Single reason for this, one who has done duty consciously;
Sanskar earlier, one fulfilled completely. ||50||

Transformation this desire-*sanskar*, duty-*sanskar;*
What transaction one did, resulted it with efforts. ||51||

Effort oriented he who reflects what one desires;
That work to happen all time with will, pleasure. ||52||

Reflects what in mind, sees what one reflects;
Likewise, let duty to perform with desire, joy. ||53||

If these harmonies, fruitful efforts are;
Otherwise discordance, no resonance with other. ||54||

The sequence of this as the first, firm determination;
When determination firm, turns into the righteous work. ||55||

Determination of some, no delay, their nature likewise;
Sanskar of some in past, some of parents. ||56||

Accumulate these, onward they progress;
Likewise, the consequence of good, evil, fruits. ||57||

The best deeds in past, so an emerald in hand;
Cultivates into downfall subsequently due to evil conduct. ||58||

Enjoyed the wealth of past; in future, no right work;
Experienced he the pain of hell at the end of rule. ||59||

In past, pious work performed, as thus, experience of happiness;
But, crisis when sin committed, surely in time to come. ||60||

Right seeker has trouble, the reason for it clear;
Right oriented pertaining one *sanskar* but other flourish in pain. ||61||

Efforts complete, ideal, flourishment of all *sanskar;*
Strange fruit a man experiences as this doesn't happen. ||62||

Tukaram and Eknath, saints both of equal power;
But, one has trouble, other rich; fruits of different *sanskar.* ||63||

Fruit of waking in morning different, fruit of study varies;
Fruit of the best living differs, never hide. ||64||

Fruit of mind purification varies, fruit of donation entirely different;
Fruit clear of knowledge seeking, not same. ||65||

The best fruit of the best action, but other of evil work;
As such, fruit grows lower in the course of time. ||66||

Whatever welfare work did, sometime it will fructify;
Theory this, not futile anytime. ||67||

So, benefit not fructified, harm when performed right work;
Words these not applicable to wise men. ||68||

Fruit different today seems but, when searched its source;
Easily will realise, efforts were behind it. ||69||

Operates benefit in right effect, harm due to sin in past;
Such mixed transaction function, not recognisable. ||70||

Doesn't know it immediately? What fruit of which religion?
Creates confusion it; increases doubts. ||71||

Different fruit of each action, but evaluates expert entirely;
Nuances of effort, fruits don't unfold with ease. ||72||

Food, not fruit of melodious singing but more happiness in it;
How can it be known until no taste of singing? ||73||

In service of help, self contentment, fruit this great;
There, why to expect gift different by righteous person. ||74||

Our efforts to make better, though did, efforts to continue;
Not small deficiency to be in efforts. ||75||

Not moment to skip, efforts to nourish with foresight;
Efforts complete to be to experience all happiness. ||76||

No one is without efforts; efforts are all pervasive;
But, some efforts give sorrow to beings, people. ||77||

Lead some efforts to fame, some efforts to trap;
Some efforts to end life of self and others. ||78||

As thus, efforts to be good; active, righteous person to ask;
Real effort oriented who don't succumb to greed, status. ||79||

Some efforts revert, their fruits death some;
Some efforts, honest, their return the best birth. ||80||

Efforts cause for death, efforts evidence for birth;
Diagnosis for experience, pleasure pain efforts only. ||81||

Some efforts with plan, bear fruit of fame;
Some efforts to extreme extent, freedom with realisation. ||82||

Some efforts, accumulation in past, manifest experiencing fate;
Efforts superior, where no tendency to pleasure. ||83||

Became their efforts good fate, godliness infusing them;
We merged in us, realising self. ||84||

Friends! Effort oriented to be, not to accept mightiness of fate;
With enthusiasm, one to glitter by work on the earth. ||85||

Made destiny someone rich, engulfed fate some though did good work;
Someone sailed smoothly, uttering 'God, God' without efforts. ||86||

Saying this, ignorant, not to utter it again;
Fruit of contentment for good efforts, surely. ||87||

Our past deed not right, so to curse one;
This not to happen at any time. ||88||

Longing for fruit of other, not to do anything by one;
The sign this real for our downfall. ||89||

To earn what is not, to increase whatever is;
Desire to fructify, this determination to be. ||90||

With determination this *Valya*[1], fisherman, became on the earth;
Saint, *yogi*, hero, turned outstanding in human history. ||91||

Addicted to harlot but, became Surdas[2] pure by efforts;
With him, made the earth pious by *bhajan*. ||92||

This to be learnt with good company, wise man became by this;
Fate will shine like the Sun when industrious. ||93||

Fruit of every effort, with a farmer to converse;
With effort a seed to sow, then fruit of an ear of corn. ||94||

Without effort cooking, without effort food in month;
With fate only transaction, who can tell this? ||95||

To substantiate fatalism, needs it efforts supportive;
Did fate invent aeroplane, telephone etc.? ||96||

The greatness of efforts open, fate efforts outshines;
Saying this incomplete entirely when viewed with foresight. ||97||

The core is effort only, fate too fruit of efforts;
Who can say, fruit and root are without tree? ||98||

Leaving efforts adhere to fate, but beings escaped from both;
Not efforts done fully, fate ran far away. ||99||

Planted someone plant, but sapless turned day to day;
Neglected it by someone, no effort. ||100||

Someone says, life over; someone says, infected by insects;
Someone says, destiny drove it to death. ||101||

Some say, here tree doesn't survive; some say, let pain be escaped;
Some say, what is in our hand? ||102||

Oh! this, all true, but let efforts be done;
Whether tree survives or not, by efforts? ||103||

As thus, manure given, nourished with conscience;
Saved with water, roots, branches. ||104||

Days after a tree blossomed, bloomed with flowers, fruits;
Happened it with efforts, is not this practical? ||105||

Grafting differently, flowers blossom variedly;
Can this happen ever with inactiveness? ||106||

As it, human life, efforts need to be elevated;
Untimely death, grim danger, avert by research. ||107||

Man, greater than nature, the part of divine presence;
Targeted efforts, weapon divine, can create alternative world. ||108||

As thus, tell, do effort, infuse thought power in effort;
Learn, teach, propagate all efforts village to village. ||109||

Nations who practiced this, their glory reached to pinnacle;
Life span increased as they desired. ||110||

Turned fatalist feeble, pragmatic more spirited;
Travelled ahead searching into space. ||111||

Flew to the Mars, climbed Himalaya's peak completely;
Search fire rockets, nuclear rockets, massive hydrogen too. ||112||

Listen from crore miles away, singing, lecture of each other;
Bringing within reach the world, made home to inhabit. ||113||

Efforts performed to full extent, still some space;
Action, not ceased, of those who effort oriented. ||114||

With efforts devotee attained godhood, *yogi* from life;
With efforts immersed one became unattached from sensuous. ||115||

Become village ideal by efforts, happy native nation by efforts;
Become the motto of world peace successful by efforts. ||116||

For this efforts to perform to know God's greatness;
God to bring in between to subdue ego. ||117||

With efforts kingdom to make rich, with efforts to enrich the earth;
With efforts service to adore by an impact of work. ||118||

With efforts elevation of man, not only of village but of all directions;
This, victory of experience, Tukadya says. ||119||

Such *Sri Gramgeeta* book, *Guru*-discipline-self experience-accepted;
Narrated effort orientation; the Thirty-fifth Canto completed. ||120||

Notes

1. Valya—A fisherman who changed into Valmiki, sage, who wrote *Ramayana*.
2. Surdas—Devotee and poet who wrote verses.

Ideal Life Quinate

Canto XXXVI

Art of Life

All beings, parts of God, deems effort as God;
Speak this, saint, book, man, all for ever. ||1||

But, glance at the world, visible, the ballads of nature different;
Nature varies as men step to step. ||2||

Seem it the structure of nature, no place to efforts;
Assumption this in the minds of audiences. ||3||

As thus, comment, listen audiences;
Nature seems different, but not independent it. ||4||

Nature in man's control, works it as he signals;
Determination to vary completely, different nature it is. ||5||

Supreme man, God, no bound to His power;
Man, his image, partially surely. ||6||

As thus, strength infinite in being, manifests silently with study;
No end to self power for anyone. ||7||

All happen when performed, all achieved when attempted;
With study, divine power, attains *yogi*. ||8||

And with power of study, being grows differently;
Fruit as one's trust, so trustful man. ||9||

Determination as trust, good and sin as one's effort;
Likewise, being moulds subsequently with study. ||10||

Nature variation naturally, outcome of study earlier;
One at core, but varied beings pertaining to arts. ||11||

Art of study in life earlier as effort our in this life;
Variation in life brought in beings differently. ||12||

Our art fructified for us, so nature varied;
Here, a blame is not to be on Nature. ||13||

God created the earth in whose uterus beings vary;
No to calculate it by mathematical means. ||14||

Naturally, all life same but due to nature differs;
Resonance of one quality with other seldom. ||15||

Infused one force in the world but seems different due to nature;
Structure and language vary, arts in beings. ||16||

Manifests each being, but variation everywhere;
One present, another absent, such features all over. ||17||

Every being plays artistically on the earth, individually;
Trait, characteristic of one, not seen in others. ||18||

See the fantastic role of beings playing in the world;
Corporeal frames new, varied their styles. ||19||

Many arts, many colours, many natures, many works;
Many garments, ornaments, pleasures, created. ||20||

Differently adored nature, dispersed it in myriad beings;
Assisted nature as arts in beings. ||21||

Art infused totally in being, assembly of merit, demerit;
Experience senses pleasure in varied modes. ||22||

Determines being, imagining blame on others;
In practice, being one with, sees anger, hate. ||23||

One world, God created, but view differs of viewer;
Becomes one happy and unhappy, individually or collectively. ||24||

Woman power, God created, mother, sister, she is;
Experiences being pleasure or pain, pertaining to one's nature. ||25||

In the world of nature, creates a being one's world;
As such experiences pleasure or pain myriadly. ||26||

Vices of anger, hate, deep, listened, experienced their *sanskar;*
Carrying *sanskar* along with takes birth again with art. ||27||

Earlier study, effort, determination, their benefit different;
Necklace of infinite arts in beings, this world. ||28||

To be multiple, God's determination takes forms in beings;
As thus, pull towards others in beings naturally. ||29||

One's determination separate, other's area varies;
But, work with potential attracts others. ||30||

One more artistic than others, influences society more;
Melodious makes creation playing on *Veena* of words. ||31||

Some imagined singing, music, painting, string art;
Verbal art, dance, beautification to attract others. ||32||

Arts of living, of viewing, of speaking, of smiling;
In everything, beauty of art pervades. ||33||

Melodious voice, tender of some and roaring of some;
Harshness in life, stigma decorates some. ||34||

Feel attraction seeing some, reluctant when sees some;
When views mask of some, trembles one's courage. ||35||

Some face serene, manifests renunciation there;
When look at some, titillates senses. ||36||

Anger when sees some, close bond not to break with some;
Feels being to surrender at their feets. ||37||

This, not miracle of nature, but potential of every art;
Remains man effort-oriented, but calls him God. ||38||

Krishna's uncle, Kansa, but one God, another demon;
Single race at core, but art differentiates. ||39||

Makes art God to man, but desolation not to be there;
Brings art totality when experienced self-consciousness ||40||

Unreal art degrades, real art elevates to divine;
Whatever efforts one performs, fruit grows likewise. ||41||

Vishvamitra with art, became *Brahmarshi* from *Rajshri;*
Turned Ravana from race of *brahma* into demon, killed due to his act. ||42||

Acquired Ravana art, pleased God and Goddess;
Increased strength his by artistic skills. ||43||

But, he couldn't assimilate, inclined to experience pleasure;
As thus, art turned desolate with ego. ||44||

Sought Kumbhakarna[1] pleasure, increased art of diet and sleep;
It, the play of cruelty, ended with all. ||45||

Learnt Bibhishan[2] art, immersed in the name of Rama;
Rama supported him, provided happiness completely. ||46||

Gave the kingdom of Lanka, but no attachment to pleasure;
As thus, fame of the righteous person immortal. ||47||

Three kinds of art, *rajas*[3], *tamas*[4], *satvik*[5] beautiful;
Quality one's to be identified on seeking of kind. ||48||

In all art of life, current of *satvik* infused;
Casts spell of love, directs to fame on the earth. ||49||

Art's presence in all, one eats other with trick;
Big one eats small, regulation this life. ||50||

But, this regulation, not humane, decorates it to beasts and birds;
Oviparous, viviparous, microbes, plants, on this way. ||51||

Proceeded human being on that way, caused chaos in the world;
'Might is right', this verdict, not to call art of life. ||52||

Which animals did survive in the world without collective tendency?
Live and let live beings, people, this real art of life. ||53||

This speciality of human being, prevalence of happiness in the world;
Without it, temple of progress dwindles to dust. ||54||

As thus, art different of all beings, live killing others;
But, human art varies, elevates weak one too. ||55||

Dance and singing of beasts and birds, expert man is in all;
But, his humanness different than all. ||56||

Like spider he webs, sings as a cuckoo;
As fish swims, soars high like birds. ||57||

Accumulates as honeybee, builds forts like ants;
Change colours as salamander, dances as a peacock. ||58||

Wear clothes as butterflies, longing for the nests of sparrows;
Such arts all learn, but human art different. ||59||

Lives with neatness, don't waste money;
Coordinates with all as himself. ||60||

Man's nature different, adjusts with all;
Behaves within the contour of the right religion. ||61||

Proceeds with conscience, lifts who is fallen;
Becomes victim for the welfare of others. ||62||

Gives his share to all, not to cause desolation;
Deems he village as his family often. ||63||

Whatever one performs not to cause sorrow to others;
Everyday to behave this way, likes he. ||64||

Thinks with foresight, logic knows he;
To make the world happy as an individual, labours more. ||65||

Those who failed to do so, were not human beings;
Though born in human forms, remained as beasts. ||66||

Whatever is in my home, all happiness to be for others too;
One who always worry for, real man is. ||67||

Skill his, strives he to transfer to others;
Exploitation, downfall, not of anyone by his art. ||68||

No 'art for art sake', adores life as art;
Realising one, shows to others, humanity with sweet words. ||69||

One who adopts art to speak sweetly for greed;
But, it is sorrowful though seems to be lovely. ||70||

Though one dresses well and walks with painted face;
But, his darkness of heart people see. ||71||

Someone learnt tact, literature, acting to lure;
But, society deteriorated due to his selfishness. ||72||

Someone inclined to dance, song, others to painting;
Viewed they, arts elevated human life. ||73||

Experience is that mean tendencies encircled man;
Commercial has become art due to selfishness. ||74||

Behind every artistic skill, some virtues are;
But, ignoring them, picks up evil. ||75||

Reason is, conscious one succumbs to fascination;
Remedy turns to be infectious though painted. ||76||

It isn't but narrowness, no romance but death;
Sweet turns into poison when core surfaces. ||77||

Whatever is inside, surges up time to time;
What is output if one speaks deceptively. ||78||

One who learns to keep aside ego;
People treat him with good intention. ||79||

His every art is sacred, poison turns to ambrosia;
Increases it human power, great art it is. ||80||

To elevate art, conscience is to be;
One is to be alert for upliftment of all. ||81||

Responds to art, comes to know what is unknown;
Art of life flourishes for complete development. ||82||

If fraction, it to weld, quarrel to patch;
Planning for someone to search right track. ||83||

Real art is to learn, directs people in world;
Fame will last after the demise of an artist. ||84||

For fourteen disciplines of knowledge, sixty four arts, selective to be;
One dies with ego if he does not help others. ||85||

Who has less needs and worked for others;
Becomes one with society, is an artist indeed. ||86||

Who has understood this art of life, enhanced humanity;
Treated by others such artist as human god. ||87||

Who has forgotten this, misdirected he is to live;
Torn all family without assistance of pathetic one. ||88||

So spoke I of prime art to colour world with humanity;
All have to live together to make heaven. ||89||

We have to live for ourselves but others too;
Source of our happiness lies in others. ||90||

Great art of all finds unity in all living beings;
When one sees him, provides joy to viewers. ||91||

Mind is not to be aloof, whatever sees is beautiful;
To know it, art to instruct realising self. ||92||

Artist familiar with self power, searching harmony;
Bears the test of time to achieve perfection. ||93||

In perfection, no sorrows, weaknesses, but rarely art aims at;
Who searches remedial measures, is an artist at core. ||94||

Shoulders he responsibility who is conscious of world;
To him, remedial means to know by his art. ||95||

So, to act with joy to make happy human beings;
Whenever lacuna is, one has to cooperate. ||96||

Cooperation to each other is the avenue great;
Brings it heavenly joy to village by this art, surely. ||97||

Art of life this to teach to everyone in village;
Nothing will be deficient to anyone at any time. ||98||

Yogi's art of life celebrates ambrosial festival;
Likewise, happy will be human life by this art. ||99||

Village will be healthy, knowledgeable, blessed one;
Cooperation will make it alive when thought. ||100||

It, of seminal importance, useful for thousand means;
Let, that creeper be grown by various efforts. ||101||

By this, manifest human power in bright luminance;
Nature will serve to all to grow and develop. ||102||

Human being, part of He, why village to be satanic?
Happiness and contentment will be by these efforts. ||103||

So, turn to the art of life for self elevation;
Dispel now chaos caused by fatalism. ||104||

Experience I tell, attain whatever you desire;
Practice self elevation, Tukadya says. ||105||

Such *Sri Gramgeeta* book, *Guru*-discipline-self experience-accepted.
Narrated elevated art of life; the Thirty-sixth Canto completed. ||106||

Notes

1. Kumbhakarna—The pleasure seeking character in *Ramayana*.
2. Bibhisan—The brother of Ravana in *Ramayana*.
3. *Satvik*—One of three aspects of *prakruti, guna,* without which no action possible. *Satva* symbolises the search for wisdom.
4. *Rajas*—Symbolises the life of passion.
5. *Tamas*—Stands for darkness or destructive.

Canto XXXVII
Self Experience

Heard such word, 'experience', an audience asks the question;
We require to tell the road of self-experience. ||1||

Who are you who did efforts? How have you spent your life?
Which is the sign of real self experience? ||2||

Friends! Listen patiently, every being, part of God;
Achieves he whatever duty he performs. ||3||

With conscience if one works, human becomes God;
Awareness of destiny and circumstance paves road for him. ||4||

Nature becomes book to him who likes to elevate;
Tendencies one by one turns into mode to one who knows. ||5||

Needs first right *sanskar*, determination to go ahead;
Not only saints, books, entire world assist him. ||6||

Drowned world awakes him, calamity inspires newly;
The seeker he who dreams for welfare from blow. ||7||

Inside craving for self elevation, all open road to him;
Requires we strength first in us. ||8||

Directs life aptly with firm, real determination;
When walks as dauntlessly reaches to destination. ||9||

Light infused in us, a stone becomes a diamond;
Search people it, with efforts from mine. ||10||

Adorns, the musk in the navel of musk deer, the forehead of king;
Reaches to the head of God the lotus flower by qualities, though born in mud. ||11||

Experience this evidence, godhood in efforts only;
The saint, book, narration of truth, to know by audiences. ||12||

Briefly I narrate as you ask about my life;
With people we, forms of God, this sign of experience. ||13||

To experience this, one has to do hard efforts;
Experiences this, the seeker at the end. ||14||

Flame of divinity luminant, but layer dirty on it;
Efforts to clean it, means it is called as. ||15||

Means these incidental, nature same everywhere;
Holy tendency to experience it, this formula of progress. ||16||

One who accepts this road of progress, enlights conscience inside;
Uplifts he himself, elevates people too. ||17||

This, the pure glory of efforts, listening I searched means;
To know this, describe I life in brief. ||18||

In village small, the masses backward;
Where daily starvation continues, there I born. ||19||

At home, the boon of poverty, but no want of devotion;
Listening right *sanskar,* grew up bearing troubles. ||20||

Curiosity intense inside, but reckless it becomes;
Innocently enduring troubles moved in all. ||21||

Listened little, *kirtan*, deep yearning in it that time;
Inclined to listen the legends of Dhruva, Pralhad. ||22||

Listened sometime discourse of saint, sometime from ancient script;
By ascetic means, increased the inclination of mind. ||23||

Became circumstance responsible to turn to meditation in solitude;
One year span not sufficient to narrate all this. ||24||

Important to tell, available readily to the seeker;
Thought self-oriented here at core to listen by audiences. ||25||

Availed company's fruits, gained the strength of self reflection;
Developed urge firm to see God in heart. ||26||

Then emerged an idea, why had Dhruva undergone penance?
Why shouldn't it happen to me? ||27||

What to do? How to meditate concentrating eyes?
Whom to ask for the contended attitude of being. ||28||

Then began to go to forest, to meditate under tree;
Sometime to perform idol worship in temple. ||29||

Sometime made idol from sand, worshipped with leaves, flowers;
Performed *bhajan* day and night with unflickered mind. ||30||

Increased such determination of love, domain of psychic conceptions;
Adhered to provision of facial meditation in solitude. ||31||

But, not contented, flickered mind at intervals;
At this juncture, *kirtan* to perform with inner urge. ||33||

One's mind to convince, one to satisfy;
To sing, dance, talk with oneself in solitude. ||34||

As thus, left home with clumsy clothes;
Sometime forgot physical consciousness in the anxiety to see God. ||35||

Lived in dense forest, wild people, rich-houses;
Diverse experiences in life, inspired right intent in mind. ||36||

Some mode of *yoga*, some spiritual readings;
Observation of the world in particular, reflected all time. ||37||

Bhajan, week programme, *yagnya*, celebration, ritual, mega-events;
Many work, means, experiment numerous, performed. ||38||

Travelled extensively, roamed in forest, pilgrimage;
Wandering, observed all areas in life. ||39||

Many temples, shrines, institutions, *ashrams*, libraries;
Saw places becoming dauntless in valleys, caves. ||40||

Visited seniors, observed differences in customs, rituals;
Tasted varieties of food, water in regions different. ||41||

Saw places of sages, *gosavi*, an ascetic;
Renounced one, vast experienced one, with *warkari*[1]. ||42||

Travelled by bullock-cart, horse, carriage, elephant;
Bicycle, motor, aeroplane, by all means. ||43||

Saw sea, spacious places, Satpura, Sahyadri, Vindhyadri, forests;
Besides Himalaya, more elevated sky-kissing. ||44||

Scenario marvelous of nature, miraculous glory by human beings;
Luxurious means, modes of knowledge all, saw in the world. ||45||

Viewing all this completely, silenced not mind;
At end, searched for experience in oneself. ||46||

When saw outwardly, no contentment in hand;
This, alienation from self, painful for all. ||47||

What is the world? Who am I? At core oneness is;
When reflected to know, attitude turns inside. ||48||

One principle, compactness of spirit as fragment of snow;
Variations embedded on it, this sign of experience. ||49||

I, the cause for all, vastness this of my spirit;
When familiar, realised in totality, non-duality, in all. ||50||

Then, silenced the craze to see outer gradually;
Whatever I observe, all it seems own self. ||51||

Which to select differently, when all deem here ours;
Joy unbound, spaciousness of mind side. ||52||

An ant and an elephant, atom, molecule, and mountain;
Realised concretely, all my resolutions. ||53||

Still how vast spirit is? No parameter to scale it;
Accumulated infinite galaxies at cosmic level. ||54||

Illusion, God, Supreme, the world, forms manifestation of self;
At the end, no front, no back, principle that me. ||55||

Says, Supreme in all but the language this seems alien;
No different finding when searched, supremeness inside us. ||56||

Seemed first village, temple great, then pilgrimage;
And further appear the forms of nature bigger, bigger. ||57||

But, which is great? Not realised when experienced at core;
On the level of principle, experienced this manifestation of self. ||58||

Massive, intersecting five elements, smaller than atom and molecule;
Keeping aside viewing, realised He in unison nearer. ||59||

There fulfilled complete means, then visualised oneness;
Pleasure-pain and birth-death, similar. ||60||

Beggar and wealthy, these two narrow approaches;
When progressed, no differentiation, similar they, elevated. ||61||

No differences of castes and cults, no sense of I and other, joy, sorrow;
Manifests *Sacchidananda*[2] bliss, in all, same forms. ||62||

Birth and death, became games; cool, all pleasure and pain turned;
When calamity impends, seems it current of love. ||63||

No sorrow left, thought extensively encompassed;
Whatever nature to perform, feel interest in it. ||64||

Fatalism real, eradication of attachment through it;
Joy without desires, no subject orientation for all. ||65||

No passion of decorum, no excess elaboration of poetry-arts;
Experience inner joy of whatever exists in natural form. ||66||

What has made this possible? Which means are applied?
By which measures has dualism ended in oneself? ||67||

When recalled, conscious one becomes, realises when viewed objectively;
When turned inside, grapples, work, essence, all. ||68||

Rendered freedom to mind, queried whatever saw;
Linked work relations as it, experienced self essence in corporeal frame. ||69||

All people as we are then, why to trust in differences?
When this happened, alertness to all avenues of knowledge. ||70||

Adhered my being to this chant, not known whose benediction;
But, with the right intent, I saluted Adkoji[3] as *Guru*. ||71||

Not understand outerly, with faith I accepted;
Worshipped the king of right *Guru,* not to be egoist. ||72||

But, realised inner essence, appearance of *Guru* disciple;
Exists one, non-comprehensive to both. ||73||

To realise this, coherence requires, awakes emotions with it;
With enlightened emotion inside, true self visible at core. ||74||

Then, whatever viewed earlier, feasible it with ease;
Infused naturalness with experience of self nature. ||75||

Nature means perpetual state, natural motion of self;
No action, no distortion in nature. ||76||

Ceaseless love, profound knowledge, unhindered truth, joy complete;
This, sign of nature, fresh, not differentiated, eternal. ||77||

But, not realised this at beginning, so searched in places;
Wonder it seemed, not knowing nature of spirit. ||78||

As consciousness increased, strength expanded;
Mountain range seemed as cow dung cake in future. ||79||

King seemed as house maid, restless to suggest;
Pertaining to these qualities, the world became companion. ||80||

Joy our became vast, urges to make happy sufferer;
Pity I feel though anyone pains in sleep. ||81||

View of otherness vanished, sensual melted into emotion;
With ease other's pleasure and pain became ours. ||82||

Then, retrieved worship-temple, living bodies in sight;
By this mean, welfare of all to be blessed by God. ||83||

Whenever appears lacuna, there mind tilts with pleasure;
Runs towards it with oneness as ours. ||84||

Viewed cosmos in oneself who realised spirit inner;
As the light of divine vision grappled by Arjuna. ||85||

Then, encompassing all directions with infinite bellies, infinite hands;
The most powerful vast form in sight place to place. ||86||

This sight with all, but looks into who opens with reflection;
Road of experience tells saint, the righteous person. ||87||

As the sky, no fragments but appears due to clouds;
Likewise, being ignorant, not separate when experienced. ||88||

Cease livingness of being, poverty, sorrow, beggar;
Achieves with determination, the peak of joy complete. ||89||

Then, destiny his game, efforts miraculous only;
Experience in unison, the world entire in self form. ||90||

Make happy the entire world as ends being one's sorrow;
Left only to feel obliged with inclusive self consciousness. ||91||

For him, no desire left, work with no attachment, his stance;
Then, how can he be hindrance to anyone in the world? ||92||

Worship of Lord, whatever he performs, words of Vedas his speech;
His words, cause movement of people with the righteous intent. ||93||

Without power his strength, greatness of service than revolt;
Donate people, property for the right work when signaled he. ||94||

Ample love in village, strength of his message;
Happy entire people become in village to village. ||95||

Influenced illiterate by his knowledge, message to knowledgeable;
Combat women, children with time fiercely. ||96||

Strength this of self development, fruit of human efforts;
Becoming God, attempt to make all people gods. ||97||

Friends! Study in this mode to proceed adhering to message inside;
Then, Srihari[4] visible encompassing this corporal frame. ||98||

When attained the sign of experience, people will be Lords;
Conscious single in village will elevate village entire. ||99||

Not succumbs to greed, no dilemma of anger, jealousy;
Taste of ambrosia to rural life in his company. ||100||

Such serviceman, the base of the world; treasure of gems he real;
For this, orient towards active spiritual study. ||101||

With efforts man will be Lord, with efforts village will be as heaven;
Glory of unified devotion of saint, village service with efforts. ||102||

Such people to create, the new world will emerge;
With glory, village, world will exist all time, Tukadya says. ||103||

Such *Sri Gramgeeta* book, *Guru*-discipline-self experience-accepted;
With self experience narrated the spiritual; the Thirty-seventh Canto completed. ||104||

Notes

1. *Warkari*—The devotees who believe in the cult of Vitthal in Maharashtra, Andhra Pradesh, Karnataka, and other places, who perform pilgrimage to Pandharpur in Maharashtra to worship the deity, Vitthal.
2. Sacchidananda—Supreme bliss.
3. Adkoji—Saint born at Warkhed in Vidarbha (Maharashtra) and lived for hundred years. Tukdoji accepted Adkoji as his spiritual mentor.
4. Shrihari—The name of Lord Krishna.

Canto XXXVIII

Village Family

Audiences immerse in self message, insist to narrate this;
Told sages, saints this for all people. ||1||

Blissful, blissful self message, supreme joy when listen;
Why to tell here the problem of village service? ||2||

Preposition such of audiences, listen to clear query;
Oh! people concentrating one's mind. ||3||

Inner reflection mine, I tell now real;
Essence of *Gramgeeta* in it complete. ||4||

Though this not mine, the extract of the books by all saints;
Boundless urge of great persons, narrate I the crux that. ||5||

We read their books, listening self message relentlessly;
But, what is their importance? Neglected it. ||6||

Those who have self experience, realised core principle;
Single essence of it, all to make all people happy. ||7||

Entire world to be happy, sanctity to be on all tongues;
Views of evil, wicked people to be pure fully. ||8||

Friendship to prevail in all people, no lacuna to see anywhere;
Whatever beings desire to be fulfilled with justice. ||9||

No jealously or rivalry to be anywhere, no loud wailing anywhere;
No ego, hatred, outrage, improper conduct to be. ||10||

Differences in the world to be ceased, isms to be complementary;
Joy only to prevail everywhere all time. ||11||

Urge this day and night ceaselessly in their minds;
Whoever became great persons in the world. ||12||

Narrated they self knowledge to make happy all people;
To treat all people as forms of self by everyone. ||13||

Described they *bhajan* of God to purify mind;
So, as to view the offspring of God, equal. ||14||

Narrated sacrifice and renunciation, the world not pleasure abode;
To smile fortune for this with service non-attached. ||15||

Compassion, good for others, donation, *yagnya*, more;
Providing more sufferers to be elevated by these means. ||16||

For equality in society, these means on principle level;
Taught collectivity through pilgrimage by sage saint. ||17||

Prasad to give to others, rice to be eaten with same intent;
Distribution of leaves in *Dashera*[1] to increase love, such customs many. ||18||

Trust one in all, man not to contract;
With collective attitude all world to make happy. ||19||

In unison all to live, all to assist others;
Action for welfare of all beings, such words of *Geeta*. ||20||

Pronouncement this from Vedas to live human race with equal happiness;
Purport this of all religions with inner feel. ||21||

But, this not assimilated, remained man backward;
Became entertainment saints' words imbibed with higher knowledge. ||22||

Performed discussion, debate, selecting words of each one;
Direction, not known how to implement it in life. ||23||

Narrated saint cosmic knowledge to make human mind vast;
All to live equally with cooperating each other. ||24||

But, remained it on tongue, increased selfishness more;
No anxiety to anyone when neighbour dies sorrowfully. ||25||

Philosophy for discussion and life for luxury;
Understood man differentiation this wrongly. ||26||

Eclipsed the purport of saint and sage by the planets, *Rahu*[2], *Ketu*[3];
Constructed Rama the bridge, but stones left now as before. ||27||

The stories of saints to tell them, bones Dadhichi[4] gave;
For service of people, laboured day and night sages. ||28||

Made people happy Damaji[5], contentment to Lord in it;
Saint Dadu[6] carded cotton with the sense of service. ||29||

In hand, container of butter, Namdev[7] ran after dog;
Made happy in world, Lord by stitching clothes. ||30||

Cultivated farm Sawata[8], swept Chokhoba[9] village;
Narrated all saints the significance of people service. ||31||

Weaved Kabir[10] clothes, eliminated differences among castes and religions;
Though all this told, no awakening in him. ||32||

Say they, this for *sadhus*, family holder we are;
Good we avail listening those stories by we, sinful. ||33||

Born we for all, came to live collectively;
We to be complimentary to each other, not known to them. ||34||

As thus, village deteriorated, no pure love for each other;
Selfishness everywhere increased without rein in our persona. ||35||

Making *ladu*[11] one eats, other with hungry belly;
This we see in villages, deemed it they ornament. ||36||

Constructs one palatial house, lives another in tiled house;
Hut with dry branches, leaves for third one not to live. ||37||

No opportunity for one, crave another for luxury;
Enjoys one wealth, painful another though labours. ||38||

Always jealous of another, quarrels with another;
Or, relying on destiny calls for God. ||39||

How can this be merged? How can fructify saint-determination?
How can this all be in cosmic form? ||40||

For this, many souls toiled but sorrows in the world not ceased;
Not practiced their message in people's lives. ||41||

For this, remedy to search to prevail happiness and peace in the world;
To satisfy great persons for whatever asked. ||42||

When this determined, principally initiated to think;
Searched avenue to pure hand for planning of village-family. ||43||

Improves message to some people, but deceives social system;
By it, not possible to bring saint-message in reality. ||44||

As thus, social structure to change, planning to be on saint-message;
Cosmic knowledge to activate bringing equality in life. ||45||

Became God infinite though one, decorated with many forms;
But, one when visualised, it to be happen in people. ||46||

One's happiness-sorrow for all, utility of all for one;
For elements and the world, interlocking to be by all means. ||47||

All world, my home, spoke this saint Jnaneshwar[12];
Its practical, beautiful to make our village. ||48||

Ideal system to be of village, so narrated *Gramgeeta;*
Expanded from village to become cosmic. ||49||

Not understood village religion, what can be for world religion?
To know this simply, the mean is of village. ||50||

Man, protector of village, village complimentary to nation;
Nation, the element of world, this to happen really. ||51||

Village, man's everything, no existence to it without it;
Village to be complete, then the glory of man. ||52||

Constructed a building in village, all other houses fallen;
Incorrect it to understand, this enhances our fame. ||53||

Real selfishness it, transcation which elevates society;
In them, no differentiation in heart. ||54||

Reverse happens even though, continues this ballad;
Figure this of rich and poor to wipe out in time to come. ||55||

Our selfishness in heart, but no care for others;
No peace will be in family for us ever. ||56||

As thus, this speech he to continue, who has foresight;
Crated this world by God for all. ||57||

This, speech of real progress, real knowledgeable who recognises;
Study to be done by all people. ||58||

Study, this not to be verbal, intellectual or mere philosophical;
Oh! Village people, life to be collective. ||59||

Attain it will saint's purport, God's determination will fructify;
In practice, cosmic experience will be for all. ||60||

Ask audiences, suggested you collectiveness;
But, its nature not realised for us. ||61||

Listen, it elaboratively practice this, divine oriented;
Due to it, prevails heavenly bliss easily. ||62||

Those who have strength, intellect, power, wealth;
Rob village by selfishness by their means. ||63||

Thinks for personal gain, expects greed readily;
No care for others though demised. ||64||

Narrowness this harmful to feed our family people;
By many means to instigate others to beg. ||65||

As thus, the form to be collective, all village one family;
Labour, eat all people, scene this to be seen. ||66||

Whatever strength, intellect in village, it all amount of village;
If this practices, ailment will end all. ||67||

No scientific knowledge to our labour, want of labour in scientists;
How can production be increased in our village? ||68||

Arid land will flourish if all labour collectively;
Remedies will be searched by intellectuals by new researches. ||69||

By collective efforts, strength will increase everywhere;
River will flow where water not available to drink. ||70||

Lake and well will fill with clear water, crops green place to place;
All currents of river will be for benefit of farm. ||71||

River to merge in sea, its power immense not to waste;
Such God's desire not, it to be for benefit of all. ||72||

As it, human power, intellect not to waste for selfishness;
Wealth, accomplishment to live in village by various efforts. ||73||

Our village, our home, all transaction for all;
Support of all in everyone to be. ||74||

Intellectual work, physical labour, artistic work, skilled work;
Whatever, everyone's work to be offered for society. ||75||

Someone has to be given one's business, someone all belongings;
Someone has to offer entire salary for this plan. ||76||

In it, cobbler, potter to be; carpenter, stone-digger;
Teacher, tailor, blacksmith, artisan, wet nurse, servicemen. ||77||

Farmers to cultivate best, to plan farming well;
Doctors, weavers of clothes, sarees, carpets. ||78||

Whosoever others are in village more they need;
Strength, tact of all to organise for village service. ||79||

Wealth to be given by rich persons, land to be given by land owners;
Labour to be given by workers, by all means. ||80||

Intellect to be given by intellectual, art to be given by artists;
Doctors, *vaidya* to serve, no one to be lazy. ||81||

All people to contribute, land to be given for village's benefit;
Poor men's houses to be repaired at village expenses. ||82||

Land of temple, barren land to be distributed among poor men;
Arrangement to be best of all lives. ||83||

All to contribute time, houses and roads to decorate;
Village to be made heavenly by collective labour. ||84||

None to sleep with empty belly, to all work to be given;
Practice of begging not to be in our village. |||85||

Though worshipper or intellectual, whosoever will do work apt;
He only will live in village, this to tell by collective verdict. |86||

All to work equally by everyone's art aptly;
No such, someone to nourish without labour. ||87||

Turned old after labour, his work to change;
Or, all to nourish if someone falls ill. ||88||

Though *sadhu*, devotee, intellectual, no one to eat without labour;
On contrary, ideal to be for all people. ||89||

The name *Govinda* to chant, work to be done by self;
Love to maintain ever for Supreme being. ||90||

Our work to perform, honest to be with all people;
Take and give all, to do relying on mind clear. ||91||

As Gora Potter[13] made pottery, uttered 'Hari, Hari' always;
But, dishonesty in making pottery, improbable to be happen in imagination too. ||92||

Saint Janabai[14] became but not forgotten to pick up cow-dung cakes;
Likewise, Chokhya devoted pulling corpses of animals in village. ||93||

Real lord devoted, provides knowledge to backward;
Feeds food of the late parents to labourers, poor people. ||94||

No mistake to happen in account, so alert though not greedy;
Contented Padmanabha[15] drinking water to donkey. ||95||

This, his real devotion, spoke the Lord of Cosmos;
Dances in the farm of Sawata seeing work precise. ||96||

This to happen really working for village;
In it, the heart drenched with devotion to place. ||97||

Whatever various industries in villages, their composition to match;
At specific place, different experiments to be in village. ||98||

Time of our work to decide, with strength all to toil;
Whimsically, not to suffer from anxiety for unnecessary. ||99||

Whatever our business, one has to immerse in work for ever;
On stipulated time, the bondage of profession to leave by all. ||100||

On regular time work to perform, regularly to play;
On regular time prayer by all collectively. ||101||

Otherwise collective life, prayer this only great;
Entire labour to be for village with service-motivation. ||102||

Enquiry is to be made for what is not in village?
Flower-bed if not, to be decorated in village. ||103||

Whatever necessary for village life, for it no begging;
By labour like this, by all village to set in order. ||104||

Stitches someone shoes for village, someone sends clothes;
Provides iron-work better for item store. ||105||

Weaving clothes someone to bring, someone to give strips, rope;
Brings someone wooden work better. ||106||

Farms someone month to month, in seasons brings in market;
In every season, pulses, *bajari*, rice, etc. materials. ||107||

Grains to yield by all means, whatever we need in village, home;
The best this, no begging to be from others. ||108||

Whatever we produce in our village, we to consume them;
Whatever left, to be sold in different villages. ||109||

Single shop for entire village, exhibition of everyone's cooperation;l
Money left of profit, belongs to all. ||110||

Entire wealth belongs to all, these industries of all;
This home of everyone, village is. ||111||

As thus, all to come nearer, work to distribute as requirement;
When deficiency more to demand, more to give for treasury. ||112||

Oh, people! Everything available in our village;
When not available, with efforts our village we will make like it. ||113||

Entire wealth of our village, happy place for villagers;
Collectively we will make our village heaven. ||114||

In spite of this, if lacuna, demand we will to nation—father;
To fulfil deficiencies whatever in our village. ||115||

If additional, left in village, with contentment it to give to other villages;
In it, no trace of difference will be in imagination. ||116||

At first, village to be happy, no one to be alien;
Every work we will perform, better in our village. ||117||

Centring this vision, we to expand the world;
To utilise humanity practically of all. ||118||

By whatever means this happen, religion it, knowledge it real;
Links contentment in all people, Tukadya says. ||119||

Such *Sri Gramgeeta* book, *Guru*-discipline-self experience-accepted;
Narrated the collective life; the Thirty-eighth Canto completed. ||120||

Notes

1. *Dashera—Vijayadashami* known as *Dashera*, a major Hindu festival celebrated at the end of *Navratri* every year.
2. Rahu—In Indian astrology, the planets, Rahu is deemed as bad men.
3. Ketu—In Indian astrology, the planets, Ketu is deemed as bad men.
4. Dadhichi—Ancient sage.
5. Damaji—A person with the sense of charity, who opened his grain storage for people.
6. Dadu—Saint in North India.

7. Namdev—Saint in Maharashtra, who worked in Punjab too; wrote both in Marathi and Hindi, whose verses are included in the *Guru Granth Sahib*; devotee of Vitthal.
8. Sawata—Saint in Aranyapur in Maharashtra, who cultivated farm and experienced Vitthal, deity.
9. Chokhaba—Saint in Mangalweadha, Maharashtra, born in downtrodden family; devotee of Vitthal.
10. Kabir—Saint in North India, who has written *dohas* (couplet form), which hammer on superstition, orthodox practices, discrimination.
11. *Ladu*—Sweet eatable.
12. Jnaneshwar—Saint in Maharashtra in 12th century, who penned *Jnaneshwari*, commentary on *Sri Bhagavadgeeta.*
13. Gora Potter—Saint in Maharashtra, was a potter and devotee of Vitthal.
14. Janabai—The sister of Jnaneshwar and devotee of Vitthal.
15. Padmanabha—The name of Lord Vishnu.

Canto XXXIX

Earth's Paradise

Contentment of all people, no heaven greater than this;
Without hate, jealousy brotherhood prevails there. ||1||

Rich and poor no one, no poverty or sickness;
High-low all works, people perform with love. ||2||

No party, no sect, no caste, discrimination, opposition some;
With joy, our village lives like single family. ||3||

This to happen somewhere, call it we heavenly;
Where no emotion, second of otherness. ||4||

In the book, descriptions of heaven and paradise, immerses mind in it;
In it, narrated these qualities, why not we to accept them? ||5||

To pay heed to truth era, but not to leave our ritual;
How can this alleviate the sorrows of society? ||6||

Joy of love in paradise, equality in truth era;
To implement in our village, this duty of all. ||7||

Why does one feel God to incarnate in the world?
Trouble, injustice, unjust conduct not to be in people. ||8||

Though this we like, we have to initiate this task;
Not practising to blame God, futile it is. ||9||

All dear to God, equal as per God's justice;
Then, why in practical discrimination to be? ||10||

Justice of God to bring in the world, then elimination of sorrow;
How can he be devotee who neglects this. ||11||

To all which is for an individual, secrete this of real life;
Involvement in everyone's joy and sorrow, emotional bond of all. ||12||

No addition and substraction for quality, caste or wealth;
Power equal for all in everyone's life. ||13||

All to work with full strength, activities as per power;
As per indispensable needs, happiness equal to be for all. ||14||

Planning such of all to be, no anxiety for entire yours;
Planning worth, collectively to be of food, cloth, business. ||15||

Annual budget to be decided, planning for every person;
Food, raiment, ornament good, house for all. ||16||

Separate profit, separate wealth, separate glory, separate significance;
Separate preferences for anyone not to be left. ||17||

Single cloth, single ornament, single respect, single beautification;
Single food, single power for everyone's work. ||18||

Festivities same for all, feast same for all;
No other eatables to be available for anyone. ||19||

No sweet to village if anyone demises on festive day;
Planning to be for another day keeping aside that day by all. ||20||

Same timing to wake up, enthusiasm different for home work;
Cleaning, meditation, prayer, all programmes collective. ||21||

All to be maintain same living, food habit, cloth clean;
Apt education for all children, viewing suitability differences. ||22||

Same school for education, same tempo of living;
Attachment of love for all everywhere. ||23||

Same arrangement for health, same elevation of men and women;
Responsibility of an individual, same for entire village. ||24||

When guests arrive, they for an ideal village;
They to be distributed among us, happens this. ||25||

But, it has limit, only that work not to be;
Time of guests, duration all, certain is to be. ||26||

Otherwise, letter correspondence when work not necessary;
Days not to consume in entertaining guest. ||27||

Likewise, for celebrations as wedding, entire village to toil;
But, always running here and there not to be. ||28||

Marriage of boys, girls in village, collective mode feasible;
There no reason at all for date and suitable time. ||29||

Let weddings ten, fifty, hundred too in village in a year;
At a time, they to celebrate peacefully. ||30||

At village, wedding place, utensils, sitting arrangement, complete to be;
By village, they to be collected for all. ||31||

Pious, vast, beautiful place, where mind fresh prevails;
All bridegrooms to favour for single place. ||32||

Fresh time and righteous persons, time apt for celebration;
Considering fresh air, water, work to celebrate. ||33||

Assembling all friends in village, everywhere to cooperate;
Bringing bride and bridegroom together wedding to celebrate. ||34||

For marriage, village's money not to be consumed;
Collectively village upliftment programmes to plan. ||35||

All have to sacrifice, village to be an ideal;
None has to separate, such precaution to take. ||36||

Though all family members, offsprings' planning to operate;
More offsprings than two, this not to be desired. ||37||

When a child grows up, feeds on milk outside;
He or she bounds to separate from mother. ||38||

Village to care for children by old, kind loveable women;
Those who can't do other laborious work. ||39||

Wealth and children, all treasure of village;
Increasing it, progress of village to be achieved by apt way. ||40||

Pleasure or pain of our village, all have to realise;
Listening each other's call, with empathy one has to go. ||41||

Whomsoever requires one, he to call for without fear;
No one to put forth hindrance posing problems. ||42||

Viewing importance of work, one has to pay heed;
Understanding in same spirit, mutual help will be. ||43||

What we do for others, same we share;
Such is the nature of cooperation of human beings. ||44||

As thus, one has to help in calamity, labour to share;
All will experience, my family cosmic. ||45||

Being born in the world to cooperate in this mode;
Ignorent being deprived of service, alert to be. ||46||

If anyone has no work, tilts towards any hobby;
With observation, calamity in village to eliminate. ||47||

Who quarrels with whom? Who exploits to whom?
Who craves for selfishness? Our work to observe. ||48||

Who is addicted? Who does gamble?
Who has anxiety? Why? Our work is to observe. ||49||

Some torture women, some trouble parents;
Some don't send their daughters, some elope with. ||50||

To eliminate all these deficiencies, we responsible;
Being residents of village, we have to look after. ||51||

Our performance, not for ours, it all for entire village;
Considering this all to act in anticipation, negation. ||52||

If we consume liquor, we, liquor addicted;
The village also branded as liquor addicted, this happens. ||53||

Then, tell how can state to rule if all liquor addicted;
As thus, the seed of liquor addiction not to sprout in village. ||54||

Someone performs *tamasha*, propagates poison of an entertainment;
Due to it, children dance as if dancers door to door. ||55||

In the garb of dance art, sensual passion blind spreads;
Such improvement misleading not to be in our village. ||56||

This, not art, mockery, source to engulf money;
Such play, group, singing not to perform. ||57||

Support to give whatever is in welfare of people;
Not to nourish bad sect in any village. ||58||

In the best work, the performance of *Ramdhum, bhajan*, art troop;
Physical exercise, sport, entertainment, all. ||59||

Nowhere deception, baseness of *tamasha, dandhar;*
If leader comes without consultation, experience fear. ||60||

Unfamiliar inroads in programme, acts as key figure;
Never this will happen in our village. ||61||

High level of village's intellect, people to know principles all;
Speeches to conduct time to time for village uplift. ||62||

We, someone different, this not to be in dream;
For this, the lesson of knowledge to alive in village ours. ||63||

In our village, prayer temple, where respect for all religion;
Whatever great in the world, God equivalent to us. ||64||

At that temple, anniversaries of birth and death for great persons, festivals;
Collective attitude to be awaken by intellectual power. ||65|||

How many birth, death anniversaries of *sadhu,* deities?
Whatever intent, the righteous work to be performed in village. ||66||

But, intent of all to be pious, coming together in village;
Festival everywhere collectively to be celebrated. ||67||

Village festival of all, in it joy of more ideal;
There adverse tilt is not to be of everyone's mind. ||68||

Otherwise sectarian attitude, caste affiliation, individual orientation;
No time will take to fragment village. ||69||

As thus, no difference to be, enthusiasm in all to be;
Like one family, our village to be loveable. ||70||

Our love real treasure, our labour great wealth;
Our cooperation real status, to be explained to all. ||71||

In village, it to perform, with fame and inspiration village to inspire;
In house to house, people will experience peace and love. ||72||

If anyone lags behind, he to be cared for;
By such, village becomes enriched with versatility. ||73||

No quarrel, conflict in village, no one speaks adversely;
Simple, straight nature, good, of beings to be seen. ||74||

Though differences of opinions, they to resolve in village;
Besides village, no work of court, litigation elsewhere. ||75||

Quarrel to end in village, in election no false deeds;
No intervention in village, such village beautiful to be. ||76||

To tell this proud to feel, ornament it of village;
In village, all righteous people, attachment with all. ||77||

If anyone seen irresponsible, he to warn;
Outward he becomes if not practised this. ||78||

Harmful to village he is if one creates annoyance;
He to bring on track by peaceful efforts. ||79||

Then, all to decide what to do of him in future;
If efforts futile, he to be sent in another village. ||80||

Then, he won't receive his belongings or his wealth;
He to run helter-skelter wherever he has to go. ||81||

Ideal village, mere fiasco where no such staunch step;
By any mean, no stability will be in it. ||82||

An audience asks, in village different problems are;
To which extent all people will solve problems? ||83||

All look after, then when to perform other work?
Tell, how can village life be balanced? ||84||

Listen to a clarification, committee to be formed;
All to nominate their some representatives. ||85||

Elements of the committee better those who render service fully;
Body, mind, wealth for village to sacrifice by them. ||86||

They to make member, five to select among them;
All to see clear minded, honest, justice oriented. ||87||

All production, money to collect, members to measure;
Then, all lives to change on equal line. ||88||

To all, work to provide, management for production to be;
All transactions to look after by five judges. ||89||

All to perform their work, purchase and sale to be controlled by five judges;
And to industry, materials to be provided by judges. ||90||

To village, road to link, trade to develop for village;
Varied relations to develop to make village happy. ||91||

Whatever money, item, human source, transported from village;
It to check completely for village by five judges. ||92||

All planning with five judges, nothing in other's hands;
Others remain relieved to progress village more. ||93||

Once it settled, relieved they from trade, anxiety;
By doing their work become loveable to God, unselfish. ||94||

Five judges mean the messengers of God, care for all definitely;
For this, no different opinions to be to anyone. ||95||

They to care for all, village people to make happy;
Once decision, people to listen the call of five judges. ||96||

Though in village people more, but less it is before five judges;
All time ready for service, sacrificing oneself. ||97||

Whatever five judges speak, the sign of village religion;
In it, the idealness of village in our eyes. ||98||

Our village one family, the core pillar, a judge;
Pressure of justice on all, this pinnacle of progress. ||99||

With justice people behaved in truth era though no government;
Its conversion *panchayat*, democracy, republic. ||100||

Death to this planning, bring it to thy notice;
If judges selected low, harm it to life. ||101|

Panchayat of service deficient, trouble some to village;
Democracy, intent of people to rule there. ||102||

Democracy, welfare of people by people hand to hand;
Being all owners, responsibility real to know. ||103||

Democracy, it is where no one has excuse for work;
Ready all time, all enthusiastic, justice-oriented people. ||104||

Power holder in democracy, not owner definitely;
Administrator of people service, responsibility his. ||105||

All people prompt to work but one who excels;
Rural officer apt, judge or leader. ||106||

Judge in ours, more energetic, practical;
No surprise anymore for him to clean toilet. ||107||

Here importance to virtue, courage, sacrifice of selfishness;
Leader they became of village who trust in village God. ||108||

One who trusted God in village, chanted magic spell of service work;
Honour his to retain, work his to admire in our village. ||109||

Judge he virtuous more, believes in village as controller of world;
Deems single service, mega worship, no other devotion to him. ||110||

No other religion to him, no other work to him;
Service, his single activity, all time to village world. ||111||

His everything for us, as thus, he, our father;
Where no place to caste, religion, sect. ||112||

Such judge to select to realise by trust, thought;
No fiasco to prevail of party oriented game. ||113||

Welfare of all to be, no subjectivity to be there;
One who thinks for welfare of all, leader ours; ||114||

Committee of five people virtuous to operate village for ever;
They to deem entire village as our family. ||115||

One another to consider, hearts of one another to be one;
If deficient, we to understand whatever deficient. ||116||

No inconvenience to village for our persons and family;
Such vision constructive to be of all workers. ||117||

No pain to anyone due to injustice, no trouble to ant too;
Consciousness of this all, time to be to the chief. ||118||

To utilise public property at home, concession to near one;
Leaving it skillfully, public service to perform. ||119||

Our more insistences to keep aside, opinions of people to consider;
Possibly administration to operate unitedly of village. ||120||

God on the tongues of five judges but no ego of power;
Following rules one to experience happiness. ||121||

All to work for all, in the welfare of all our welfare;
Great one to reveal lesson practicing with determination. ||122||

In it, greatness, village life will be self-reliant;
This only real sign of ideal rural state. ||123||

Village state, *Ramrajya*, self-reliance, this self rule;
Spoke universally honoured great ones, progress fine this. ||124||

Our village, one state, mother home of all indispensable;
Whenever such ideals are, our relations there. ||125||

Another village, no rival but our contacts intact;
Cooperation provides judges determinedly to nourish good. ||126||

Village becomes the earth's paradise where judge committee honest;
With its influence, the earth turns pious consequently. ||127||

Where attainment of this, such village becomes focus in state;
Such state if influential, honourable to nation. ||128||

Nation such prosperous, constituent peaceful it of the world;
Whenever selfishness creeps in, harmful it to the world. ||129||

As thus, pay heed carefully, to create paradise in the world;
Sacrifice family to collective principles. ||130||

Read, be quick, then reflecting on it with interest;
Leap into the ideal planning, sacrificing everything. ||131||

Oh! Audiences, have you listened? Then why to waste time?
Will you not sacrifice body, mind, wealth for this work? ||132||

This desire of great one fulfilled knowledge and devotion for apt purpose;
Cease it will inside-outside restlessness of all, Tukadya says. ||133||

Such *Sri Gramgeeta* book, *Guru*-discipline-self experience-accepted;
Ideal village rule narrated; the Thirty-ninth Canto completed. ||134||

Canto XL

The Study of Book

An audience asks with joy, you told about an ideal life;
But, stories, legends, self knowledge in other books. ||1||

Books in village to village, but your script different;
Which to select? Tell for our upliftment? ||2||

Will other books not helpful to make village paradisal?
By which mode will *sanskar* of village percolate deep? ||3||

Listen the answer to this, *Gramgeeta* not different;
Here, no difference any to other righteous books. ||4||

Milking the cows of Upanishads, made *Geeta* mother;
Likewise, all saints' books, in essence in this book. ||5||

In all beings feel of God, experience of saints great;
Interpretation of the principle this in *Gramgeeta*. ||6||

Universal manifestation of *Geeta*, description of Vedas' vast man;
Here active sign of universal God of saints prevails. ||7||

Narration in many books, visions in many pilgrimages;
Anecdotes in many stories, *kirtana* for this. ||8||

Forgot people to cooperate, life, selfish, blind disorder;
Began to deceive people for self benefit. ||9||

By which means will this be eliminated? Search and remedy of this;
For facilitation of great persons on experience. ||10||

Following their steps, speaking their wards;
With complete determination, life fulfillment will be. ||11||

For this book, script to read, people all to awake;
Villages to infuse with *sanskar* with the mean of cooperation. ||12||

To enlight the teaching of humanity, narration and *kirtan* in village;
Reading of holy book, ancient scripts to teach this to village. ||13||

Many anecdotes, narration infinite to elevate human beings;
For this we sing the song of *Gramgeeta*. ||14||

Unnecessary no decorum, to make our life beautiful;
To sprout the seed of happiness in village, this duty of man. ||15||

Man to be healthy and pure, no trouble of addiction;
His transaction, not troublesome to be for anyone. ||16||

This to learn from scripts, *bhajan, kirtan;*
For this, these means planned by saints. ||17||

The best means, social structure; core vision, national;
By achieving welfare of humanity, people to channelise. ||18||

For it, principles to show, sub aspects to understand;
Means necessarily to implement in our village. ||19||

Books must be in couplets, this stance to leave;
The prose-verse easily comprehensible, the best it is. ||20||

Some books, historical, some biographical, some philosophical;
Some *abhang*, ancient scripts to be kept for reading. ||21||

Mere miracles, pile of orthodox practices;
What application of them, when no essence of life? ||22||

Attended reading of script, time passed listening to miracles;
Our intellect not operable, this not to happen in future. ||23||

Metaphorical, ancient books, succumbed people to it;
Reverse meaning extracted they, not believable easily. ||24||

Example this step to step, misdirects mind reading books;
Devotees become fanatic though no grappling of meaning. ||25||

I heard the book, *Harivijay*[1]; narrated, Narad became female;
Giving sixty sons in one night. ||26||

The book heard *Pandavpratap*[2]; narrated sin of great ones;
Measure of molestation consequently here and there. ||27||

Someone's birth from ear, someone's birth from mouth;
Someone's birth from pot, heard such in books. ||28||

Someone's birth from shell, someone's from hair;
Someone elevated while urinating on the phallus of Shiva. ||29||

Boat immerses in water as someone leaves *prasad;*
After accepting *prasad,* comes up as it was earlier. ||30||

Someone ran away with the earth, some urinated as sea;
Donkey grazed in someone's nose when slept. ||31||

Such miracles in the books, tell with assurance;
But, mind doesn't accept for a while what to do? ||32||

Though this kept like this, requires to decipher learned content;
Danced they to heaven too on two fingers. ||33||

Say, oh people! This is, here not to suspect;
Otherwise all have to suffer from sin. ||34||

To mould man ideal, this extract drawn;
Essence of all miracles, made the king of books. ||35||

One who listens this, attains man heaven, freedom;
Telling this to males, females, made society handicapped. ||36||

With reflection, space for doubt cracked;
No one has explained, interesting, metaphorical speech. ||37||

Priest says, pay heed only, become humble saying 'yes';
Then, beings became elevated, suspected ends. ||38||

Understood by *sadhu* and saint, the books with conscience created;
In them, doubts eradicated of masses. ||39||

To mould devotional people, comprehend complete knowledge;
Blessing, debt of saints and sages on us. ||40||

Extracting crux from Sanskrit, made easy the books in treasure in Prakrit;
To know the mode of elevation to masses. ||41||

Ancient Sanskrit, the speech of sage, many languages born out of it;
Likewise, Marathi enriched by saint poets. ||42||

Saint Jnandev, Mukundraj, Chakradhar, Nath, Hansraj;
Made knowledge, easy, comprehensible in the books of Prakrit. ||43||

Samarth Ramdas born, Mukteshwar, Morapant gifted;
Written song, *abhang*, holy books by the writers in Maharashtra. ||44||

In Maharashtra, saint poets, tradition likewise of biographies;
Penned books by many to mould society entire. ||45||

Saints as Swami Vivekananda to vanish illusion of new and old;
Lamps of knowledge lighted in books in many languages. ||46||

As per the nature of book, the message of principle to be sucked from them;
Not to succumb to orthodoxy or dry intellect. ||47||

Knowing our qualification, noticing level of society;
For easy knowledge of ideal, such books to be read. ||48||

Conscience to maintain while reading; what to take from books?
What to leave; how to behave for our upliftment? ||49||

To tell knowledge superficial, read books time to time;
No realisation and peace, leads it to self-destruction. ||50||

Deep spiritual book, for it requires intellect able;
And like Arjuna, an avenue of duty to comprehend. ||51||

Otherwise, read thousand books, but essence not understood;
Then, reading it futile as lunatic. ||52||

Lunatic spoke at length, but its meaning not understood;
As thus, proved he lunatic among people. ||53||

Whatever spoke with the balance of conscience;
Behaved with all strength, human he is. ||54||

One who spoke more but not firm on anyone;
Lunatic we call him as we think. ||55||

This fanatism entered in people, caused chaos of religion;
Man seemed devotional, wise but in reality lunatic. ||56||

Met I righteous person, said, do thou listen my narration?
Read I books for twelve years, knowledgeable. ||57||

Read *Brahmasutras,* Upanishads, Legend, *Bhagwat, Ramayana;*
But, the flame of Supreme not seen uptill now. ||58||

To which extent to read and re-read to know the taste of Supreme?
Tell elaborately which sign is good? ||59||

I spoke with him humorously, "How can achieve life beyond?"
For it, analysis exhaustive to be of righteous books. ||60||

Pounding them in mortar, consume powder with milk in morning;
Or, drinking of water, not fresh, will suffice. ||61||

That man went home, torn off books;
Pounder in the mortar to powder, superficial intellect it. ||62||

In morning he asked, "How many days it to drink?
Tell how shall I shuffle and shake?" ||63||

I uttered, "What intellect runs after blind adherence?"
How can a reader experience without conscience? ||64||

Oh! Did not understand you? Powered, tearing off books;
"How can knowledge be experienced by this?" ||65||

He said, "What to do? Remedy to implement as thou suggests."
Such re-readings, everyday nourishing habit. ||66||

Not comprehended *Brahmasutras, Upanishads, Pancikarana, Vichar Sagar;*
Read swiftly, orally elaborative critical books. ||67||

Now, to which extent to read? Thought in mind to ask you?
With doubt I came to you to clear. ||68||

Told you to powder, followed it at home;
Came to seek thine guidance for thought. ||69||

"Where does face to direct while drinking?"
I said, "What a faithful person? Blind followers, people there." ||70||

Brother! I really missed, deceived by joking with you;
To know your intellect, I was grappling. ||71||

Reading these kings of books, to which extent conscience we receive?
Came to know I strategy on the basis of thine act. ||72||

Orthodox, blindly adhered intellect, no knowledge of Supreme to him;
Purity, introspectiveness, simple, then no time more. ||73||

As thus, tell, listen, real in the books character right;
Living and enlightening, will realise in day to day conduct. ||74||

When to wake up? When to sleep? How to bath and meditate?
Which action to practice to become pure being? ||75||

With which intent to act? Which message to listen?
To which extent it to accept and leave with strength of thought? ||76||

This to memorise first, then duty bound to be;
In time to come, knowledge of onward road to experience. ||77||

In sequence, books to read to know knowledge;
Otherwise, what happens by readings up to death. ||75||

Discipline realisation, *Guru* realisation, then self realisation;
Confirmation of this, saying at the end of experience. ||79||

Narrated saints, reading of discipline with the target of apt books;
But, reading as per comprehension makes life successful. ||80||

Treasure of books magnificent, multi-views of many intellectuals;
Which to select after understanding from it for us? ||81||

Many books for many rights, accepted as per right;
Which our road in it is to be selected? ||82||

It is upto to us to understand to know full requisite of power;
Unfolded in the books to comprehend knowledge. ||83||

An idiot, an illiterate, balanced, pure, dull, analytical, practitioner, trained;
In book, requisite-differentiation shown with the road of elevation. ||84||

Which inflection of diseases to us? To know it definitely;
Remedy for disease to be searched in advance. ||85||

But, if not diagnosed, assistance to seek;
For it, witness necessary of saint and righteous person. ||86||

Otherwise in books, all areas, some benefactor, some harmful;
This happens due to differentiation of states, constructive or destructive. ||87||

For these needs, right contact, one who hasn't micro mind;
Someone attempts to climb steps for self-activation. ||88||

Someone born with *sanskar*, someone dyed by education;
Someone doesn't comprehend experience right of saint. ||89||

As thus, books to read, to understand meaning with concentration;
Selection of this from experienced one for us. ||90||

Mega treasure of books, selection from it;
Keeps essence before practitioners, saint the righteous person. ||91||

At core essence, speech of saint, showing road to people;
Books, mine of knowledge, word idol of divine saint. ||92||

But, interpreting its meaning, common intellect in illusion;
Error due to the change of time, not knowing conscience. ||93||

For this, as per nation and time, importance of the books to be interpreted;
Such is right of saints in time to come. ||94||

Sadhu and saint, sea of power, realise they transaction;
How can life elevate? What to do for it? ||95||

Mean to give? Realise this to them with nature;
As thus, experience of *Guru*, spoke we. ||96||

Which books to be read by whom? Narrated saint good;
Good conduct, all time to practice, reading in advance. ||97||

Our all work to do, sleep and walking in scheduled time;
None to experience sorrow on the earth for us. ||98||

Ending all our work, for service of others to turn;
Ascends he with strength of work for fame and progress. ||99||

The books with such thought to be read first;
Focusing on core meaning, life to be elevated with justice. ||100||

One who understood conduct full, realised active knowledge of means;
Who is *Brahma*? Who is spirit? In reading of books to understand. ||101||

Panchikaran[3] to understand, soul spirit and non-spirit particulars of *Brahma;*
Then, mind doesn't hope for unreal illusion. ||102||

Then, real hearing and reflection, concentration increases;
Sign there of manifestation will realise in us. ||103||

Manifestation of the flame of *Brahma*, achievement of self-joy;
Merged tendency with the colour of self in Supreme. ||104||

Whose vision moves upward, emerge out of physical senses;
His trance with happiness without breakage. ||105||

Devotee of God, not different, realised easily with experience;
In the world, cosmic to be, such happened there. ||106||

Sentences of books elevate tendency, *Guru* message to experience;
Become one with self taste, as without breakage. ||107||

Then, what reading of books? Contentment of whatever done;
Whatever spoken, on its way, knowledge of book it becomes. ||108||

No joy at the time of birth, no sorrow when demise;
In being, self-firmness and absolute form of it. ||109||

For the happiness of this, reading of books time to time;
Perfectness of life at the end in this only. ||110||

To experience self realisation, this means of practitioner;
Firstly, observation of righteous books to be. ||111||

One who understood this before, no chaos for him;
With contentment, he leads to self-realisation straight. ||112||

Self-realisation means divine vision, individual, collective, and beyond;
Time to time we experience myriad forms, uniformly. ||113||

Let be God, saint, man, sinful, good, all;
Experiencing core form, cloud of spirit, the world. ||114||

One who experience this, he for utility of the world;
His conduct expands for all. ||115||

With this intent, books to be given for reading to masses;
It will lead to road of cosmic vision. ||116||

But, hurry for spiritual practice who has no practical level;
For him, unnecessary, the reading of books, one sided. ||117||

Read pure conduct later, first read *Vedanta;*
Happens this as one uplifts water from roof. ||118||

In words, say, 'all Supreme', work will be done what one thinks;
Mega-illusion in people, then atheism will prevail by words. ||119||

Fire of sorrow in village, he will utter 'blissful word';
All this, painted faces, as lunatic will be felt by people. ||120||

For this, village will be pure, love, knowledge, truth, joy;
Will be for all, such responsible books to be in village. ||122||

To all, duty to be realised, how welfare of all be?
How does the world bloom, blossom with body, mind, money? Realise. ||123||

We, residents, all at core, structure of world, drama ours;
With our potential, we have to perform it. ||124||

Knowing such nature, one who behaves, wins in this sport;
To realise this, narrated *Gramgeeta,* Tukadya says. ||125||

Such *Sri Gramgeeta* book, *Guru*-discipline-self experience-accepted;
Narrated the essence of reading books; the Fortieth Canto completed. ||126||

Notes

1. *Harivijay*—The religious script.
2. *Pandavpratap*—The book relates to the valour of Pandavas; the offshoot of *Mahabharata.*
3. *Panchikaran*—The analysis of five elements, supreme element, liberation, worldly pleasure, yoga, and sensual pleasure. Allusion to *Pancharatra Samhitas.*

Canto XLI

Glory of Books

God infused this world, as thus, the world, God is;
Village, core element of the world, *Gramgeeta* for it. ||1||

In it proclamation of village; village, the mother home of pilgrim place;
Village, beautiful base of the world, flood when no village. ||2||

Village, temple of God, man, God's idol, beautiful;
All service of equal kind, worship it ours. ||3||

Gramgeeta, service of words, but firms it the treasure of *sanskar;*
The kingdom of God in village will prevail for all time. ||4||

Gramgeeta ends sorrow, *Gramgeeta* makes death to laugh;
Gramgeeta enhances cooperative principle to blossom human religion. ||5||

Forty days means bored, such trust clear;
As thus, village all will improve by the *sanskar* of *Gramgeeta.* ||6||

As thus, in *chaturmas*[1], while in the meeting at temple, front-yard;
With happiness, *Gramgeeta* to read with the colours of interest. ||7||

But, such intent not to be for re-reading without meaning;
Though not realised, our pile of good coins will be. ||8||

To my contention, reading to be by keeping aside ignorance;
In the beginning, knowledge of money to learn while reading books. ||9||

Realisation of book reading's knowledge, first this, only important sign;
Understanding our reading, the best comprehension to be. ||10||

Our speech to be understood by friend circle too;
What gain through reading, memorisation but not understood? ||11||

What his knowledge to read? Not complete for readers;
Stand up and run away audiences; what meaning to reading? ||12||

Where to read by readers? Where to read with stress?
Where to explain interestingly? Readers to realise this. ||13||

When this not realised, though re-readings entirely;
No focus on the flow of meaning, futile reading it is. ||14||

Message we get in reading, inspires oneself;
Turns for action as spirit in body. ||15||

Such reading first to learn, then re-readings of book;
Then, to know self as per right of reader. ||16|||

Reader to be practical, then can influence audiences;
Otherwise, fun of him among people. ||17||

Books to be read by tongue, reverse conduct at home;
Likewise, flattery outside by people, sarcastically. ||18||

Reads, "speak truth", but no practice of truth;
Says, "call me truthful", how can say villagers? ||19||

I, serpent on wealth but honour me 'magnanimous donor';
Who will accept in our village? Tell, tell. ||20||

No giving of water to poor; says, "call me brave donor queen";
Who will listen this, though beating of drum extensively. ||21||

Come chewing betel leaf and tobacco, speak in lecture, *kirtan;*
Laugh audiences and students when say "leave addiction". ||22||

Priest sat for meal, initiated reading of *shanti* lesson;
But, he beat woman when delayed for serving. ||23||

Says she what peace this is! Resultant of the best chanting;
Divine speaks husband, practice of cruelty. ||24||

Not to happen this now though reader, speaker, teacher, higher;
Responsibility on all, first of self purification. ||25|||

When preachers, readers, practical, then intent comprehensible;
With speed, change of heart in audiences will be. ||26||

Audiences will be devotees when a speaker straight, pure;
Looking at both, masses will appreciate. ||27||

As thus, this to follow by elders, behaviour as spoken;
Then, welfare of village life will be by their influence. ||28||

Here, an audience asks, to meaning, conduct important thou have given;
But, in many books told, re-readings are fruitful. ||29||

Some say, gain of son and wealth when re-reading of books;
Rise of fortune complete will be re-reading of books. ||30||

Some say utter chanting, make thousand decisions;
Say, this road simple, knowledge will be without reading. ||31||

Some say, do penance, read *Bhagavad Gita, Brahmasutra;*
Salvation you will attain when listen words. ||32||

Some say, time doesn't attack the home where books are;
How can we justify this? Tell me. ||33||

Listen answer the righteous persons, resultant interesting full;
Greediness put forth to propagate book. ||34||

The best practice, keep books in collection;
From it, benefit someone, will incur to some extent. ||35||

Listen single speech, but in it mega good;
Narrated great ones to attract people. ||36||

The importance of re-readings, in it principle this;
Sometime its implementation will be by *sanskar.* ||37||

Advocated the penance of chanting to purify life;
Subsequently require some days to practice pure life. ||38||

As thus, I treat this total, but chanter, one sided to me;
From it, no benefit to many people. ||39||

When said, "Show water to horse," retained it in mind;
Didn't know how to drink water? The scenario of people. ||40||

Many such books to be read but no behaviour as it;
How can we demand fruits from them. ||41||

In some books, unreal, irresistible to tell this;
Fiasco it makes of faith when no fruit in hand. ||42||

In books, narrated fruits but no experience of it;
Thousand people told the story of work. ||43||

In books, fruits of happiness, so read the script of active work;
Lazy and innocent pull towards them more calamity. ||44||

Some tell means to others, "End by giving gold";
In home to home fast, penance follow, lure women. ||45||

Read stories-scripts of penance, direct to donate, concluding rite;
Otherwise degradation will be, warn people. ||46||

For filling belly, read scripts time to time;
Making the books of gold, say to offer to God. ||47||

People, attached and confused, let other people tell anything;
Practice they the means of penance as lunatic. ||48||

Irritate they when no fruit, say, "Whether to lick books?"
No birth of son though read book everyday. ||49||

Husband and wife without health, worship stones many with vow;
What will happen? Tell by such means. ||50||

Move round the fig tree, but no improvement in conduct;
What time does require to infect when enjoyed heavy food? ||51||

Oh God! Take us to Pandhari though boarded train to Calcutta;
How can such prayers be fruitful? ||52||

Theft by one in village, says he suffers from evil eye of planets;
To eradicate it, read the script of Saturn but in vain. ||53||

At end, trapped in the hand of police, witness of crime;
Asks he to his *guru,* "Tell the means to escape". ||54||

Though *guru* corrupted, says, "Read the script of Saturn";
Remember with right intent the Canto of the miracles of Shiva. ||55||

Read the legend of Goddess, perform the worship of *Satyanarayana;*
Donation of gold to us, thou will be free soon. ||56||

He practiced what told, read books as means;
Gave money to *buwa* and *brahmin*, no excuse from punishment. ||57||

At end, in prison, says, "Show *guru* nuisance";
Placed he, me in trap, lost whatever money. ||58||

Read script regularly, but no excuse from jail to me;
What to do of worship? Whether books to burn? ||59||

Poor, he will not leave theft, but demand penance to *guru;*
What will do *guru* or books, when a reader deceptive? ||60||

Practiced this in life, but an idiot remained an idiot;
Degradation of a person who tells, "means not effective". ||61||

What to do this? Practice after searching truth;
One to drown, other to take to hell, this not to happen with selfishness. ||62||

Logically it is to tell, truth to practice;
Then one can experience fruit, this happens. ||63||

Presuming this at core, *Gramgeeta* is written;
This book fulfills all desire, listen how it is. ||64||

This, pointed arrow of words, pierces the heart of readers;
As statue shapes, this happens with import of readers. ||65||

Gramgeeta, not for *parayana*[2], shows avenue to people;
Life changes entirely when its meaning understood. ||66||

This not to offer flowers, magnanimous approach of village;
Life giving medicine of the era, treat we *Gramgeeta*. ||67||

Some burnt with sorrow, some annoyed with troubles;
Some helpless, trapped in calamity, provides courage to *Gramgeeta*. ||68||

Torture of people by injustice, *Gramgeeta* paves road for him;
Awakens godliness in all to make divine entire world. ||69||

This will make *sanskar* best, man will be with character;
Happiness and peace will avail, whatever told in books. ||70||

Less intellect will end, knowledge will be after reading;
Real religion one will experience when life brights. ||71||

Love till today lonely, with reflection of book it will increase;
In all manifestation of kindness, such fruit of books. ||72||

Ignorance of mind, by reading it will vanish;
Mind inclines to the righteous work when trust activated. ||73||

Reflection on reading of *Gramgeeta*, self knowledge he experiences;
Sign of saint's divine, vision realises in practice. ||74||

Read *Gramgeeta*, the book, behaved in village like it;
No enemy left for him in village. ||75||

Increased collective tendency, entire village his wealth;
Gramgeeta moulds an idol such of an ideal man. ||76||

Whosoever will reflect on entrepreneurship in *Gramgeeta;*
Presume, in his home money, grain will be ample. ||77||

Who will be the lesson of hygiene and take broom in hand;
His disease will eliminate at that time. ||78||

When initiation of work at that point, output will begin;
Improves character, listening book and understanding its meaning. ||79||

Read *Geeta* in solitude, reflected understanding and its meaning;
In life, ideal percolates inclusive of homes. ||80||

Such house becomes ideal, glitter village with fame and inspiration;
Then, all people behave like it, visible in people. ||81||

What gain is this? Attainment of heaven for all people;
Our village has become the ideal, reading *Gramgeeta.* ||82||

Fruit of *Gramgeeta* not for one, from one to whole village;
Elevation of villages, conduct after reading *Gramgeeta.* ||83||

Reading of means one by one and then its practice;
What gain we have? Can't be told. ||84||

Sanskar structure of *Gramgeeta*, planning of principle;
Village security, village improvement, village structure ideal. ||85||

Progress of many arts, agriculture reform in farming and labour wealth;
Understanding significance of knowledge, progress will be of life. ||86||

Tradition of collective prayer, *Ramdhun*, saint celebration;
Listening, conduct of treasure of avenue, peace for all. ||87||

Reading service of cattle, make our village like it;
Not to see the drought of curd and milk. ||88||

Sanskar all like wedding, society will be pleasant;
Improvement of backward, elevation of nation. ||89||

Women and children will be ideal, when reading of this;
Village will be paradise with reading and practice of *Gramgeeta.* ||90||

No beggars and unemployment in village, no bondage of power to any one;
All will learn wisdom by reading *Gramgeeta.* ||91||

Healthy will be people, no conflict or quarrel in village;
Injustice, addiction, tactics, jealousy will perish. ||92||

Organisation will increase in village, strength will be in all mind;
Structure of world family will prevail in our village. ||93||

Village will be as heaven, man and woman will be happy;
Waves of joy of life beyond will be at home. ||94||

Whatever desire will be, it will be fulfilled by village deity;
Audiences, speakers! no doubt left in my mind. ||95||

Here no superstition, gain of direct experience all time;
Whatever words come out, Govinda they, dear with determination. ||96||

Not I am intellectual to tell intellect;
Inspiration of God manifested in the books. ||97||

Through my form of child, inspired *Gurudeo*, *Chakrapani*[3];
Speech expressed on the bank of Chandrabhaga, wrote in script. ||98||

As speaking of *Veda* by material thing, crossing of snow mountain;
As narration of *Geeta* by server, narration of *Geeta,* deem I. ||99||

So, pray I again and again, my voice, no truth;
Blows craunch of body, voice it of God. ||100||

Active form of *Bhagavadgeeta*, manifested it naturally;
Mega heroic like Arjuna, saying all rural. ||101||

Addressed *Geeta* to Arjuna, *Gramgeeta* for entire village;
None to be backward, so says my God. ||102||

I, merely like child, blessing of saint on head;
As thus, bold words expressed through flute of body. ||103||

Sri Jnanraj, Guru mother, the shadow of his grace;
Fructified it by tradition in the form of *Gramgeeta.* ||104||

Whatever names, description in *Gramgeeta*, blessing of all those;
With confidence complete I trust, *Gramgeeta* will be fructified. ||105||

Gramgeeta, my heart, in it the righteous *Guru;*
Message its bright, glitter it will to village. ||106||

Rustic words structure, I understand it clearly;
Fault whatever mine all, whatever qualities, they of great ones. ||107||

Water of Ganges in sand pot, destroyer of sin, sweet, pure;
As it let readers and audiences, understand treating it pure. ||108||

Our village, backward, though words with deep import planned;
Villagers will say, "Not understood, tell meaning, intellectual." ||109||

Where are intellectuals in home to home? Degraded they whatever are;
Turned to earn, joined job of rich persons. ||110||

Whoever the best left, illusion of tradition they have;
They will say, "endeavour this, non vedic, non-religious". ||111||

Seldom gems of intellectuals, all are from here;
To them this book dedicated, trust we with core heart. ||112||

Such intellectuals to respect those, who virtuous saint by nature;
Their words hypnotic to listen, improve they to village. ||113||

Not to search intellectual any, reader to search from village;
Behavioural, virtuous, honest, kind activator with clear conscience. ||114||

One who reads book with love, goes to farm to till;
Serves when time demands for villagers whatever need. ||115||

Listen, let be of any caste or religion, sect, native, abroad;
Even though he acceptable, who has mission for village upliftment. ||116||

Intellectuals not to read, this I don't to say;
But, not to obstacle work, no dispute futile. ||117||

Intellectual, priest, learned, wise to read necessarily;
Being responsible of society, apt knowledge to give. ||118||

In village, thoughtful teachers to read *Gramgeeta* complete;
Assembling children and elders, it to interest to all. ||119||

Gathering audiences old-young-children, girls-youth-mothers all;
Habit to cultivate in backward, people slowly of progress. ||110||

Whatever female, male, or literate, my humble request to them;
Read *Gramgeeta*, coherence of meaning to explain to literate. ||121||

Without conscience, who reads this book think for progressive village;
His road is for degradation, no excuse for sin to him. ||122||

Sin means to cause disorder, sin means acceptance of evil deed;
Sin means to be powerful, squeezing of poor animals. ||123||

This not to be with readers, whatever gain of *Gramgeeta's* knowledge;
Practicing it, for casting it, faults burns, those harmful. ||124||

For reading of *Gramgeeta,* none has to accept money;
For importance, complete, to village, speaker has to earn. ||125||

Gramgeeta, the book, beautiful to create the character of village;
Its propagation to become oneself pure. ||126||

Whosoever are my dear, they to popularise book;
In home to home, propagation pure of reading *Gramgeeta.* ||127||

In village, *Gramgeeta* to play, all to memorise its formulae principally;
Evidence to provide it, someone does wrong treating all equal. ||128||

In whosoever hand this book, though opened in middle;
Deem it as message in reading by village deity to me. ||129||

Then, his dishonour not to happen, thought to be with conscience;
If not understood, couplet to understand by one knows. ||130||

Reception of the best message, presumption of emergence of good day;
Like it to behave, speak with understanding *Gramgeeta.* ||131||

First listen this speech of *Geeta,* mind to confirm with conduct;
The means of work to make village heaven. ||132||

First reading with trust, grapple all meanings;
Orientation towards work everytime for village ours. ||133||

My contentment in this, improvement in village life will be;
Superficiality will melt of selfish persons. ||134||

Differentiationism will end, love pure will prevail in village;
Joy will be everywhere in all people with all intent. ||135||

Devil and savage in human beings will cease to light divinity;
Pure principle will vitalise in life, new, in all. ||136||

Help of nature time to time, bloom-blossom trees, creepers;
Rivers and lakes will fill with water, not leaving one's limit. ||137||

Health will be ornament of all; poverty, lacuna, ignorance will end;
No one will be miserable or downtrodden, no wicked or evil elements. ||138||

Social structure for equality, peace for beings, human beings;
New inspiration of progress to elevate home. ||139||

The bondage of exploitation or administration will end;
No aggression of rival, village being self-sufficient. ||140||

Slave will be trifold troubles, enmity, sins will cease;
Village being heavenly, peace will be in the world. ||141||

Immortal in heaven wish this, this in the minds of saint, sages;
When such habitation in village, why to go to forest? ||142||

With self realisation, assemblance of saints and righteous persons;
Glory will be imparted to such village with freedom of life. ||143||

With their message on religion and moral, service and devotion in their company;
With their influence, peace and power will awake all time. ||144||

Such resultant fruitful of *Gramgeeta,* fulfilment of saints' determination;
Spoke God in mind, the blessed speech. ||145||

Stands on the brick of the world, *Sadguru*, Vitthal, All Mighty;
Extension of His grace, Tukadya says, *Gramgeeta*. ||146||

Such *Sri Gramgeeta* book, *Guru*-discipline-self experience-accepted;
Let villagers avail benefit always, as thus, dedicated to cosmic form. ||147||

Notes

1. *Chaturmas*—The four auspicious months.
2. *Parayana*—Reading of religious script and commentary on it before masses on an auspicious occasion.
3. *Chakrapani*—Lord Shri Krishna, holding Sudarshana Chakra to eliminate evil.

Select Bibliography

Primary Sources

मराठी

1. तुकडोजी, (1988), *ग्रामगीता*, अड्याल-टेकडी: आत्मानुसंधान केंद्र।

हिन्दी

2. तुकडोजी, (2002), *मेरी जपान यात्रा*, गुरुकुंज आश्रम: श्री गुरुदेव प्रकाशन संस्कृत।
3. तुकडोजी, (1984), *ग्रामगीतामृतम*, श्रीधर भास्कर वर्णेकर (अनु.), अड्याल: अध्यात्मकेंद्र, भू-वैकुंठ।

Secondary Sources

English

1. After, Emily (2006), *The Translation Zone: New Comparative Literature,* Princeton: Princeton University Press.
2. Baker, Mona, Saldanha, Gabriela (eds) (2008), *Routledge Encyclopaedia of Translation Studies,* London and New York: Routledge.
3. Bhatnagar, Y.C. (1993), *Theory and Practice of Translation*, Delhi: Ajanta Publication.
4. Chitre, Dilip (ed) (1967), *An Anthology of Marathi Poetry,* Bombay: Nirmala Sadanand Publishers.

5. Chitre, Dilip (1991), *Says Tuka,* Trans. New Delhi: Penguin Publication.
6. Das, Bijay Kumar (2005), *A Handbook of Translation Studies,* New Delhi: Atlantic Publishers and Distributors.
7. Davies, Alan (2005), *A Glossary of Applied Linguistics,* Edinburgh: Edinburgh University Press.
8. Ghalib, Mirza, (2008), Kuldip Salil, *Diwan Ghalib*, Delhi: Rajpal & Sons.
9. Gibran, Khalil (1993), *The Prophet,* New Delhi: UBS Publishers and Distributors Ltd.
10. Guenthner, M. (ed.) (1978), *Meaning and Translation: Philosophical and Linguistic Approaches*, London: Duckworth.
11. International Federation of Translation (Dubrounik) (1967), *Ten Years of Translation*, Dix Annecs De Traduction, Oxford: Pergaman Press.
12. Karunakaran, K. and Jay Kumar, M. (1988), *Translation As Synthesis: Search for Gesalt*, New Delhi: Bahari Publication.
13. Katamba, Francis (2005), *English Words: Structure, History, Usage,* Oxon: Routledge.
14. Mukherjee, Sujit (1994), *Translation as Discovery and Other Essays,* Hyderabad: Orient Longman.
15. Nagbhushan, Swami O.L. (ed.) (2007), Translators—Nagabhushan Swami O.L., Laxmi Chandrashekhar, Vijaya Guttal, *The Sign: Vachanas of 12th Century,* Hampi: Karnataka University.
16. Nandakumar (2004), *Poems of Subramania Bharati*, New Delhi: Sahitya Academy.
17. Narasimhah, C.D. and Srinath, C.N. (ed.), *Problem of Translation*, Mysore: Dhvyaleka.
18. Nida, E.A. and Tabler, C.R. (1982), *The Theory and Practice of Translation,* Netherlands: E.J. Brill.
19. Nihalani, Paroo, Tongue, R.K., Hosali, Riya (1979), *Indian and British English*, New Delhi: Oxford University Press.

20. Radhakrishan, Sarvapalli (2007), *The Dhammapada*, Varanasi: Pilgrims Publishing.
21. Schelling, Andrew (ed.) (2011), *The Oxford Anthology of Bhakti Literature*, New Delhi: Oxford University Press.
22. Sharma, Satyendranath (1985), *Madhavadeva*, New Delhi: Sahitya Academy.
23. Srivastava, Vishnulok (2009), *Dictionary of Indology*, Delhi. Hindology Books.
24. Subramanyam, Ka Naa (1987), *Tiruvalluvar and His Tirukkural*, New Delhi: Bharatiya Jnanpith.
25. Tagore, G.V. (1993), *Eknath*, New Delhi: Sahitya Academy.
26. Talger Pramod and Verma, S.B. (ed.) (1987), *Literature in Translation: From Cultural Transference to Metonymic Displacement*, Bombay: Popular *Prakashan*.
27. Talib, Gurbachan Singh (2001), *Guru Nanak*, New Delhi: Sahitya Academy.
28. Taury, Gideon (1987), *Translation Across Culture*, New Delhi: Bahari Publication.
29. *The Quran* (tr.) (2008), New Delhi: Madhur Sandesh Sangam.
30. Tuite, Mick F. and others (ed.) (1988), *Genetics of Translation: New Approaches*, Berlin: Springer Verlag.
31. Upton, Clive and Widdowson, J.D.A. (2006), *An Atlas of English Dialects*, Oxon: Routledge.
32. Usmani, B.D. (ed.) (2008), *Encyclopaedia of Mass Communication* Vol. I, Mumbai: Himalaya Books Pvt. Ltd.
33. Vivekananda Swami (2008), A *Concise Encyclopaedia of Hinduism*, Vol. I, A-G, Vol. II, H-P, Vol. III, R-Z, Banglore: Ramkrishna Math.

मराठी

1. काले, कल्याण, सोमण अंजली (संपा.) (1997), *भाषांतर मीमांसा*, पुणे: प्रतिमा प्रकाशन।
2. तिप्पेरुद्रस्वामी एच. (2003), *बसवेश्वर*, रोहिणी, तुकदेव (अन.), दिल्ली: साहित्य अकादमी।

3. तुलपुले शं.गो., (2009), *रमण महर्षी*, कृ. स्वामिनाथन, (अनु.) दिल्ली: साहित्य अकादमी।

4. मुकर्जी, दिलीपकुमार (2009), *श्री चैतन्य महाप्रभू*, नवी दिल्ली: नेशनल बुक ट्रस्ट।

5. राघवन, ए.श्री. निवास (1986), *नम्मालवार*, नलिनी साधले, (अनु.), नवी दिल्ली: साहित्य अकादमी।

हिन्दी

1. भावनाणी, झपटमल खूबचंद (1998), *स्वामी दादू दयाल, जोतवाणी, मोतीलाल*, (अनु.), नई दिल्ली: नेशनल बुक ट्रस्ट, इंडिया।

2. राठी, गिरधर (संपा.) (1994), *शब्दसेतु: दस भारतीय कवी*, नई दिल्ली: साहित्य अकादमी।

Journals

English

1. *International Journal of Translation*, New Delhi.
2. *Indian Literature*, Sahitya Academy, New Delhi.
3. *Journal of South Asian Studies.*
4. *New Voices in Translation Studies* (Electronic Journal), Cosponsered by International Association of Translation and Intercultural Studies.
5. *Signs.*
6. *Sri Gurudeo*, Gurukunj Mozari.
7. *Translation Review,* Center for Translation Studies, Uni. of Texas, Dallas.
8. *The Translator*, St. Jerome Publishing.
9. *Voice of Saint Tukadoji*, Adyal Tekdi (Quarterly in English).

Index